D1172842

Between ANALYST and PATIENT

Between ANALYST and PATIENT

New Dimensions in Countertransference and Transference

edited by

Helen C. Meyers

The Analytic Press

Distributed solely by

Lawrence Erlbaum Associates, Inc., Publishers
365 Broadway
Hillsdale, New Jersey 07642

Library of Congress Cataloging in Publication Data

Between analyst and patient.

Includes bibliographies and index.
1. Countertransference (Psychology) 2. Transference (Psychology) 3. Psychotherapist and patient.
I. Meyers, Helen. [DNLM: 1. Countertransference (Psychology) 2. Professional-Patient Relations.
3. Transference (Psychology) WM 62 B565]
RC489.C68B48 1986 154.2′4 86-8061
ISBN 0-88163-043-8

Printed in the United States of America
10 9 8 7 6 5 4 3 2 1

Contents

Contributors

Jacob A. Arlow, M.D., Past President, American Psychoanalytic Association; Former Editor-in-Chief, *Psychoanalytic Quarterly.*

Morton J. Aronson, M.D., Training and Supervising Analyst, Columbia University Center for Psychoanalytic Training and Research; Assistant Clinical Professor of Psychiatry, College of Physicians and Surgeons, Columbia University.

Elsa J. Blum, Ph.D., Senior Psychologist, Division of Child Development, Schneider Children's Hospital, Long Island Jewish Medical Center; Adjunct Assistant Professor, Saint John's University.

Harold P. Blum, M.D., Clinical Professor of Psychiatry and Training and Supervising Analyst, New York University; Executive Director, Sigmund Freud Archives.

Allen J. Frances, M.D., Professor of Psychiatry, New York Hospital, Cornell Medical Center; Director of Outpatient Department, Payne-Whitney Clinic.

John E. Gedo, M.D., Training and Supervising Analyst, Chicago Institute for Psychoanalysis.

Otto F. Kernberg, M.D., Professor of Psychiatry, Cornell University Medical College and Associate Chairman and Medical Director, New York Hospital-Cornell Medical Center, Westchester Division; Training and Supervising Analyst, Columbia University Center for Psychoanalytic Training and Research.

Frederick M. Lane, M.D., Assistant Director for Progression, and Training and Supervising Analyst, Columbia University Center for Psychoanalytic Training and Research; Associate Clinical Professor of Psychiatry, College of Physicians and Surgeons, Columbia University.

Robert S. Liebert, M.D., Clinical Professor of Psychiatry, College of Physicians and Surgeons, Columbia University; Training and Supervising Analyst, Columbia University Center for Psychoanalytic Training and Research.

James Mann, M.D., Professor of Psychiatry Emeritus, Boston University School of Medicine; Training and Supervising Analyst, Boston Psychoanalytic Institute.

Joyce McDougall, Ed.D., Training and Supervising Analyst, Paris Psychoanalytic Society.

Helen C. Meyers, M.D., Assistant Director for Curriculum, and Training and Supervising Analyst, Columbia University Center for Psychoanalytic Training and Research; Clinical Professor of Psychiatry, College of Physicians and Surgeons, Columbia University.

Robert Michels, M.D., Barklie McKee Henry Professor and Chairman, Department of Psychiatry, Cornell University Medical College; Training and Supervising Analyst, Columbia University Center for Psychoanalytic Training and Research.

Samuel W. Perry, M.D., Associate Professor of Clinical Psychiatry, Cornell Medical Center; Collaborating Psychoanalyst, Columbia University Center for Psychoanalytic Training and Research.

Ethel S. Person, M.D., Director, and Training and Supervising Analyst, Columbia University Center for Psychoanalytic Training and Research; Professor of Clinical Psychiatry, College of Physicians and Surgeons, Columbia University.

Roy Schafer, Ph.D., Training and Supervising Analyst, Columbia University Center for Psychoanalytic Training and Research; Adjunct Professor of Psychiatry, Cornell University Medical College.

Martin H. Stein, M.D., Training and Supervising Analyst, New York Psychoanalytic Institute; Former Chairman of Board on Professional Standards, American Psychoanalytic Association.

Milton Viederman, M.D., Professor of Clinical Psychiatry, Cornell University Medical College; Training and Supervising Analyst, Columbia University Center for Psychoanalytic Training and Research.

Acknowledgments

This volume arose out of the first Scientific Symposium sponsored by the Association for Psychoanalytic Medicine in collaboration with the Columbia University Center for Psychoanalytic Training and Research in March, 1981.

I want to thank all the panelists of the Symposium whose participation in that program made it the success it was: the authors in this volume, whose major contributions made this book possible, as well as the other participants in the Symposium, Drs. Stanley Coen, Arnold Cooper, and Gertrude Ticho, who because of the nature of their topics had other publication commitments. Special thanks go to Drs. Arnold Rothstein, Don Meyers, and Gerald Fogel for their vision and labor in helping to plan, organize, and execute the Symposium and this volume.

I am further grateful to Dr. Robert Liebert and Lawrence Erlbaum for their advice and encouragement in bringing this volume to life and am greatly indebted to Dr. Paul Stepansky and Eleanor Starke Kobrin for their patience and invaluable editorial help in its creation. Finally, I would like to thank Terry Montgomery, who did all the typing and secretarial work for both the Symposium and this volume and who, with the help of Mary O'Driscoll and Noreen Dalton, officiated at the original Symposium.

CHAPTER ONE

Introduction

Helen Meyers

These are exciting times in psychoanalysis. Psychoanalysis has grown in complexity and richness far beyond its early days. Theoretical advances and divergences and their technical and therapeutic implications have created a new dialogue and invited new self-examination. Different theoretical frames of reference and the widening scope of application of analysis have led to a renewed interest in technique and a reexamination and refinement of some of our basic concepts.

This volume examines transference and countertransference—central concepts in analytic technique—in very specific areas in this widening scope of analysis, where they may have unique importance and special usage and yet where they have not been sufficiently explored. This volume is not intended as a comprehensive treatise on transference and countertransference in general (much has already been written on these important topics by others), although we do include, for background, a review of the concepts (Lane) and of their evolving technical uses (Aronson). What is different, and what we have to offer, is a new look at transference and countertransference—their forms, appearance, and uses in some controversial, though essential, areas.

We have focused on three specific areas—analysis of difficult character disorders, analytic brief psychotherapy, and work with and by women. These areas are of special interest and relevance in the current therapeutic scene. Difficult character disorders, including narcissistic personality disorders, borderline conditions, and acting-out impulse disorders, have been in the forefront of current analytic concern as their diagnosis has become more defined and their analytic treatment has become possible with advances in our theoretical conceptualization and clinical technique. In these conditions, transferences tend to be archaic and have their counterpart in difficult and intense countertransference reactions. Both merit special attention by us.

Brief analytic therapies were selected for consideration as a reflection of the continued search for more efficient and more specific treatment approaches. In the hope that goals similar to those achieved by psychoanalysis might be attained in a shorter time, various models of modern brief psychotherapy have been developed. They have proliferated and gained much favor in today's world of pragmatism and productivity. They open new possibilities and also raise new questions. When we change the conditions of the therapeutic encounter from those of traditional psychoanalysis to those of brief psychotherapy, the experience of both participants is likely to change. Do the characteristics of the treatment, as opposed to those of the patient, affect transferences and countertransferences? And if so, how? In these therapies, where regression is not encouraged and the therapist is more real, what is the role of transference and countertransference? Indeed how much of the transaction can be considered as transference and countertransference and how much is real relationship? On the other hand, how often are transference and countertransference overlooked? Should transference interpretations be used at all? What kind, when, how much?

Concern with work by and with women, of course, arises out of the current reevaluation of the psychology of women, the women's movement, the sexual revolution, and the focus on gender issues in the culture in general and in therapy in particular.

None of these areas is new, of course. Indeed many of Freud's early cases suffered from pathology more severe than simple neuroses, and briefer treatments were the order of the day in the time of our analytic forefathers. And, of course, women were both patients and therapists from the beginning. One might even suggest with a bit of whimsy that some of those early treatments were brief psychoanalytic psychotherapies of difficult character disorders in women. So once again we are following Freud's lead. The subject matter is both old and new. But, by purposely and methodically focusing our explorations specifically on these areas, we hope to add depth and perhaps new directions to our understanding of certain aspects of transference and countertransference in particular and of psychoanalytic technique in general.

The authors in our volume, by design, vary greatly in their theoretical frameworks and technical approaches. They do not necessarily agree with each other. But what they share is intellectual rigor, clinical excellence, concern for furthering analytic knowledge, and curiosity about uncharted territory.

TRANSFERENCE

Transference and countertransference are part of analytic history and centers of current controversy. The transference, which at first appeared to be a major obstacle to the treatment when Anna O fell in love with Breuer and Dora reacted to Freud, was soon recognized by Freud to be the major vehicle of treatment, central to the analytic process, and essential for therapeutic intervention. Indeed, the so-called transference neuroses, that is, those pathologic conditions where the patient is able to establish transferences in treatment, were considered by Freud to be the only conditions treatable by psychoanalysis at the time. Transference, defined as the repetition, or rather new edition, of infantile wishes, defenses, conflicts, and object relations experienced within the analytic or therapeutic relationship, continues to hold center stage in current analytic endeavors. Although such transferred repetitions are aspects of all relationships, the technical term transference has tended to be confined to reactions in the treatment relationship, where they can be demonstrated and experienced with clarity, intensity and in depth.

Interpretation of the transference, considered by many as the only mutative interpretation, has been a central tool of analytic work. It is the degree of this centrality that is the focus of a current debate regarding transference. The questions are: Must all analytic interpretations be transference interpretations in order to be meaningful and effective, or can valid analytic work be done with nontransference interpretations, for example, working out triangular issues around significant persons outside the transference? Taking it a step further, can or should the analyst rely on transference interpretations in the here and now only, or is genetic reconstruction necessary? Proponents of "transference interpretations only" point to the power of their impact to clarify distortions, their emotional validity at the point of urgency in the here and now in the analytic interaction. Opponents argue the importance of recovery of memories and the uncovering of the past unconscious. This raises the further question: Is it even possible to establish historical truth as differentiated from narrative truth or do we really construct, between patient and analyst, multiple viable life narratives? Then there are others who are concerned about an overemphasis on transference interpretations leading to the exclusion of other interventions, to blurring the transference with the "real" or nontransference relationship, or to the patients' possible defensive use of transference interpretations.

I am convinced that despite possible misuses, all interpretations must indeed be brought into the transference in order to be mutative. But I would also stress that some degree of reconstruction, approximating not "reality" but early intrapsychic experience, is possible and necessary to lend authenticity, reason and cohesion, a sense of conviction to the emotional impact of what is transferentially experienced and to clear a path for internal restructuring. The individual genetic past remains the indispensable explanatory solution of the irrational and inappropriate distortion of the present, but the present is where the experience lies. It is a circular process. The past informs the present; the present opens the past. Transference and its interpretation and reconstruction together become an explanatory experience.

Another question revolves around the timing of transference interpretations. One side argues that too early transference interpretation can lead to inhibition of the development of the transference. Equating transference with content, they present the time-honored dictum that resistance should be interpreted before content. Their view is countered by the argument that defense and what is defended against must be interpreted together and as they appear in the patient's associations. Resistance and transference, this group argues further, are inseparably interwoven. There is resistance against the development and the awareness of transference, and the transference itself, as a kind of repeating, serves as resistance against remembering and uncovering and resists its own resolution. Therefore, since transference reactions, those characterologic repetitions ubiquitous in all human relationships, are present from the start of treatment, so is resistance. Early dynamic transference interpretations, then, will deal with the resistance and can only further the development of transference.

These considerations, applicable to analysis, are, however, different for psychotherapy, where transference interpretations do not have the same central position and in fact are subject for debate. In the section on brief psychotherapy, this issue of transference interpretation is discussed by our authors. While they all agree that brief psychoanalytic psychotherapy is an important treatment, and understanding of transference and countertransference is essential, they differ widely on the use of transference interpretations, in accord with their different purposes and conceptualizations of the process they are proposing. Viederman, whose psychodynamic life narrative approach is designed for the specific clinical situation of medical crisis, is opposed to the interpretation of transference in that setting. For the achievement of his specific therapeutic goals, he counts on the maintenance of his patients' fundamental, primary, positive transference based on infantile trust and continued omnipotent expectation from the therapist. Mann has a specific model of brief psychotherapy in mind: time-limited therapy. In his comments, he focuses on the study and interpretation of specific transference themes in time-limited therapy, namely, issues around separation. He interprets only these, and only toward the end of therapy. Michels and Perry remind us that such leading proponents of focal therapy as Davanloo, Malan, and Sifneos interpret the transference immediately and vigorously, and along oedipal lines. Frances, who centers his discussion on the question of transference interpretations, concludes that the debate is still open, the data still to be scientifically validated. He suggests that the apparent variations and disagreements in approach reflect partially the difference in the specific syndromes approached and the associated specific clinical indications. He offers tentative guidelines in the hope of specifying situations in which one or another approach might be more effective, which could then be clinically tested.

Another issue of great current concern and a subject for contemporary exploration is the question of what kind of transferences are established and recognized once we go beyond the treatment of traditional neuroses, employ modifications other than classic analysis, pay attention to unexplored factors in the therapeutic dyad, such as gender. Are these transferences different, and in what way? What form do they take; how are they recognized; how are they to be understood; how are they to be dealt with? These are some of the major concerns of our authors and are extensively explored, theoretically and clinically, in this volume in terms of difficult character disorders, brief therapy approaches, and work by and with women.

In relation to severe character disorders, the discovery of the kind of transferences and countertransferences established in narcissistic personality disorders and borderline conditions, and the differences between object relation theory and self-psychology concerning their conceptualization and related technical approaches has been of great interest and has had much impact on current thinking. In the section on difficult character disorders, Kernberg discusses transference and countertransference issues, including the analyst's basic personality, in the analysis with these patients. He focuses particularly on a subgroup of patients with narcissistic disorders who do not show transference regression because of their incapacity to depend, based on their fear of internal primitive aggressive objects. Stein discusses transferences and countertransferences with patients who act out. Gedo addresses the phenomenon of delinquent enactments. Clearly one's theoretical frame of reference should inform one's understanding of the process and affect one's technical interventions. For example, in reference to "acting out," each author contributes a special approach. Kernberg, briefly reviewing transference regression in severe character pathology, and informed by his understanding of the role played by early object relations, views these behaviors as manifestations of transferences infiltrated by chronic and intense aggression that have to be vigorously pursued and interpreted as such. Stein and Arlow, informed by a classical approach, view acting out as symptoms of conflict like any other, to be analyzed by means of interpretation like all other compromise formations in analysis.

Gedo, using the guiding concept of the repetition compulsion, views these delinquent enactments occurring in analysis not as conflict symptoms but as a repetition, a special communication of earlier inhibitions of learning that must be listened to and that requires not interpretation but education.

In the section on work by and with women, the authors address the controversial question of the impact of gender, specifically female gender, of patient or therapist on the transference and countertransference. Clearly, the gender in fantasy runs the gamut of transference-countertransference constellations, but does the real gender have an impact? What are the transference expectations in choosing a female therapist or patient? What actually happens in treatment? What are some specific transference and countertransference issues for female therapists only (such as around pregnancy), for female–male therapy dyads, for same-gender pairs? All the authors agree, although they differ in degree, that while conceptually in a complete analysis all transference paradigms are established and worked through, the actual gender of the therapist does seem to have an impact on the transference, though it is probably a minor variant in the large canvas of individual variations in patients and therapists. Certainly therapist gender seems to affect the timing, sequence, intensity, and what I call inescapability of certain gender-related transferences. A difficult maternal transference, for example, which might have been avoided to some extent with a male therapist, may press forward with more urgency with a female therapist. At the same time, we must note that self-conscious awareness of gender can lead to blind spots that may obscure transferences to the opposite gender object hidden behind the obvious—the paternal object behind the maternal image, the woman behind the man.

The authors also suggest that changes in our understanding of female psychology and current changes in the culture, such as the rise in feminism, have had an impact on what we now perceive in the transference in women and how we deal with it. They explore the variety and complexity of transferences and countertransferences in current work by and with women, what form they take, and how they are to be understood and dealt with, offering their own clinical observations and new conceptualizations. Person describes dissembling, fooling, and ingratiation as special transferences observed in women patients; these seem to be in line with female social attitudes. McDougall, in her revision of female psychology, discusses the impact of unmet archaic needs in the early mother–child interaction, illustrated in transference and countertransference manifestations in a case of a woman in treatment with a woman. Liebert, as the male therapist, concentrates on the special complexities of transference and countertransference when women are in treatment with men. Blum and Blum join their expertise and experiences as man and woman to discuss transference and countertransference in all the different male/female combinations. In light of current role confusion and lack of role modeling, they speculate on a special transference they have observed in current women patients who want their therapist to be an alter-parent.

I have so far concentrated on the transference—current controversies and issues addressed in this volume. I now turn to countertransference. I interposed this rather artificial separation of the two concepts for the sake of clarity, but at some cost to the living whole. Transference and countertransference elements often are both involved in a given interaction, combining, complementing, even colluding. For instance, in the choice of a particular treatment modality, as discussed by Michels and Perry in the section on brief psychotherapy, or in the selection of a female therapist, as discussed by the authors in the section on women, both transference and countertransference expectations may play a role. Both patient and therapist have reasons for their choice or acceptance of who or what was chosen, and these reasons may be unconsciously conflictually determined in both. In treatment itself, transference–countertransference fits often have to be recognized if a particular phenomenon is to be understood. Take the commonly cited finding of relatively greater frequency of preoedipal transferences established with female analysts and oedipal transferences with male analysts. If this finding is valid, what part is played by the patient's transference, as related to the therapist's gender? What part might be played by countertransference in a particular woman analyst who might be comfortable with separation-individuation issues but frightened by erotic oedipal urges, or by countertransference issues in a male analyst who steers the patient away from preoedipal transferences arising from his own fear of feminine identification? Or are the findings due to both transference and countertransference? Transference and countertransference often conspire to avoid examination of "dangerous" areas like sexuality or rage, or the man inside the woman, or the woman inside the man.

COUNTERTRANSFERENCE

Countertransference has become a subject for renewed exploration as our analytic neutrality and resources, our second (or work) selves, are more and more strained in the treatment of more severe pathologies on the one hand, and with different treatment modalities that seem to require more personal involvement, on the other. But, also, in the spirit of our times of scientific inquiry and with the advances in understanding and knowledge in our field, we have turned from the examination of the patient only to find new, searching questions about therapeutic action and process and a need for reevaluation of the analyst's contribution. We are taking a good new look at ourselves. The concept of countertransference has undergone change similar to that of transference, moving from the position of a peripheral obstacle to one of central concern. However, it retained its negative valence as an interference in treatment to be eliminated until recently, when its universality has been stressed and its usefulness for treatment has been advocated by some. Controversy, which for some time has centered on the definition of the concept, the conceptualization of what is involved, as discussed by Lane, has more recently focused on its uses, as discussed by Aronson. Clearly, different conceptualizations of the process will have different technical implications.

The concept of countertransference was introduced by Freud later than transference, when he warned the therapist against responding erotically to the patient's transference love. Countertransference later was described as comprising the deleterious effects of the analyst's own unconscious needs and conflicts on his understanding or technique, the patient representing for the analyst an object of the past onto whom past feelings and wishes are projected; this reaction may be provoked by something in the patient's personality, the material, or the analytic situation itself. This is countertransference in the narrow sense, as defined and understood in classical analysis. At times, this has been further subdivided into the "analyst's transference" and the "countertransference proper," the "counter" referring to its being in reaction to (against) or parallel (as in counterpart) with the patient's transference. Countertransference arises out of a revival of infantile conflicts stirred up in the analyst in identification with his patient's unconscious fantasies and wishes, or with his patient's internal self-representation in a concordant counteridentification, or with his patient's internal object representation in a complementary counteridentification. This is to be differentiated from empathy, that special introspective mode of understanding another's inner experience, where temporary trial identification is quickly followed by disidentification and scrutiny by the observing ego of the analyst. In countertransference, identifications are not transient and are not immediately followed by cognitive awareness. Some have even postulated the formation of a countertransference neurosis parallel to the establishment of the transference neurosis, the working through and resolution of both constituting successful analytic work.

The narrow definition of countertransference has been contrasted with an expanded definition which would encompass the total emotional response of the analyst to the patient, unconscious and conflictual as well as conscious and "real." This has been called the totalistic view of countertransference.

There are also those who see no need for a separate term of countertransference. They feel it is ubiquitous and inescapable, being simply the transference of the analyst, a set of compromise formations that makes analyzing possible and worthwhile for the analyst, and that, like all compromise formations, can shift so as either to facilitate or impede analytic work.

My own definition of countertransference is somewhere in the middle. Countertransference refers to any unconscious conflict or fantasy in the analyst that interferes with his analytic function, his neutrality, or his ability to use himself as a resonating analytic instrument. This may be due to infantile material stirred up in response to the patient's specific transference, where greater vulnerability in the analyst requires less provocation, while a heavy assault might create a countertransference feeling or fantasy ordinarily alien to the analyst. Or it may be in response to some other quality in the patient or the analytic situation; or it may be part of the analyst's character pathology irrespective of the particular patient; or it may be stirred up by an extraanalytic intercurrent event unrelated to the analytic situation. It is, however, essential to tease out its source from within the patient, the situation, or the analyst's past or present, because this will determine the technical approach.

This brings us to the second major current controversy surrounding countertransference: how to deal with it, how to use it in treatment. A small minority of analysts has suggested that once the countertransference is recognized, it is helpful to share it openly with the patient as a validating, demystifying, respectful, and human gesture. Few agree with this approach. In general, it is argued that this would constitute an nonanalytic, confessional, perhaps exhibitionistic or sadistic intrusion, a burden on the patient and an interruption to the flow of the process. The majority of analysts roughly falls into two groups. One group is convinced that the countertransference is nothing but a harmful interference resulting from unresolved problems in the analyst and that it must be quickly analyzed and eliminated—by self-analysis or consultation, if possible, or by reanalysis if protracted. The other group feels that while countertransference must be recognized and resolved to eliminate its impact on the treatment and to learn about oneself for the future, awareness and understanding of the countertransference may also be an important source of information about the patient. It will, of course, be more helpful if it remains a transient countertransference thought rather than a countertransference position. However, even a solidified countertransference, once recognized and understood in terms of the analyst's unconscious contribution and then reexamined in terms of what it was about the patient that set it in motion, can be a powerful tool for understanding the patient's transference communication. But it is the recognition and understanding of the countertransference reaction, not the countertransference experience alone, that is of help.

More controversially, some current theorists have gone a step further, suggesting that countertransference, conceptualized as complementary or concordant identification with the patient's inner self and object world, be used predominantly as an indicator of the inner life of the patient. This relates to the concept of projective identification—a primitive defense mechanism by which, it is postulated, the patient projects an unacceptable part of his inner world, an affectively colored self or object representation, or a combination, into the analyst while retaining a connection or identification with the projected part, for purposes of control. The analyst presumably identifies with this invading, split-off representation and experiences himself in this alien way. If he can use this experience to recognize this invader, it will inform him of the patient's internal world of objects. This is, of course, the patient's inner view of self and object and is not the same as the real object of the patient's past. If the analyst, on the other hand, does not recognize this reaction within himself, then, under the sway of what some call projective counteridentification, he will act out the patient's unacceptable self or object representation. This is a radically different view from the other conceptualizations of countertransference, although it addresses a similar clinically observable phenomenon: it makes the patient the agent and the analyst the recipient, rather than seeing the countertransference as arising from within the analyst. It posits the patient, in fantasy, as putting something foreign into the analyst, rather than the analyst reacting to something in the patient from his own armamentarium. This is the rationale for using what is experienced as countertransference as predominantly a clue to the patient's inner world. However, even in this conceptualization, there is room for complementarity between the vulnerability from within the analyst to react countertransferentially and the degree of assault from the patient's projected inner objects.

These considerations have particular pertinence in current discussions of the treatment of patients with severe pathology, in which connection much of the above was conceptualized. It may, of course, not be necessary to involve the concept of projective identification to postulate that primitive countertransference reactions will be stirred up under the pressure of and in reaction to archaic transferences in patients with severe pathology, and therefore to use these intense countertransference reactions as indicators of the patient's pathology, and, more specifically as clues to the patient's inner world of objects.

These issues are discussed in the section on treatment of difficult character disorders, where all the authors, from different points of view, address the severity of countertransference reactions with these patients. Discussing patients with severe regression in the transference and those without regression, because of their incapacity to depend, Kernberg suggests that careful differentiation and understanding of the countertransference are helpful in diagnosing the nature and severity of the patient's transference resistance and transference regression. This understanding should then lead to appropriate vigorous interpretation. Stein also observes severe countertransference difficulties but sees them as the interferences in the analytic posture that temporarily paralyze the analyst and stop him from proceeding with the regular business of analyzing the patient's compromise formations, which include acting out. Gedo also stresses countertransference problems in patients with delinquent enactments, which he formulates as repetitions of early inhibition of learning. However, he feels that these countertransference reactions are related to frustrations with these patients as they are misunderstood, their delinquent enactments misperceived as acting out, and analysis rather than re-education is pressed on with. A more correct understanding of the process, he suggests, with a correspondingly more appropriate technical intervention, would then alleviate the difficulty.

In the section on brief psychotherapy, the authors take up countertransference issues in relation to the choice of the brief treatnent modalities and their limits, as they arise before and during the treatment. Mann addresses specific countertransference issues related to guilt and separation conflicts in the analyst in time-limited therapy. Schafer, in raising questions about resistance to the recognition of countertransference in choosing and doing brief psychotherapy, explores issues of therapeutic zeal, the need to help quickly, guilt and overevaluation of success. Michels and Perry suggest countertransference elements in both choosing and rejecting brief treatment modalities as well as in failures in both brief and long term treatments.

In the section on work by and with women, the handling of countertransference is not at issue. It is assumed, fairly traditionally, by the authors that countertransference is to be recognized, explored, and resolved to further the analytic work. Instead the authors focus, from their own clinical experience, on the fascinating variety of forms that gender-related countertransference can take, their manifestations, and their circumstances. Special transference–countertransference complexes are suggested in particular gender dyads (male–female, same-gender) and their possible meaning explored. Old myths are examined, then validated or exploded. The authors speculate on the relative impact of new understanding of female psychology and bias, of cultural changes, new ego ideals and loss of role models for patient and therapist, of actual versus fantasied gender in patient or therapist, and of the ubiquitous individual gender-related unresolved infantile conflicts. Some common countertransference pitfalls, together with their circumstances, are suggested as they lead to blind spots, paralysis, and misinterpretation. For example, a female therapist's guilt over sexuality may interfere with the recognition and deepening of an erotic transference in her male patients; or, with her female patients, she may miss the oedipal father transference, finding it difficult to see herself as the object of her female patient's positive oedipal desire, the man within the woman. Or she may suffer therapeutic paralysis in identification with her sexually conflicted female adolescent patient. The new and conjectural, the old and familiar are put forward and reexamined.

In this introduction, I have presented some of the reasons why this volume needed to be written at this time and in this form. I have outlined some of the current controversies and urgent issues for exploration and tried to give small tastes of how the different authors have addressed them. Some viewpoints are controversial, some are traditional, all are current.

CHAPTER TWO

Transference and Countertransference in the Treatment of Difficult Character Disorders

Morton J. Aronson

Transference and countertransference are among the most fundamental of psychoanalytic concepts, the understanding of which sheds light on all human relationships and is at the heart of the psychoanalytic treatment process. This paper addresses the issues involved in understanding the role of transference and countertransference in the treatment of patients with severe character pathology. A review of some of the historical highlights in the development of the concepts of transference and countertransference will provide a perspective for the examination of these issues.

From his early observations of the regularity with which his hysterical patients formed intense emotional attachments to him, Freud, unlike Breuer, who fled from Anna O. and her deepening affection, went on with characteristic genius to study those attachments and made one of his greatest discoveries—the transference. In 1895 (Breuer and Freud, 1893–1895) he considered transference to be false connections from early relationships to the person of the analyst. In 1905, Freud wrote about his abortive analytic treatment of Dora. Later, he realized that she had fled the analysis because of his failure to interpret the transference from Herr K. to him. She acted out the transference instead of experiencing it with Freud. She left Freud as Herr K. had left her, thereby wreaking her vengence. When she returned subsequently for further treatment, Freud turned her away, an acting out on his part that we now understand to reflect his unconscious countertransference retaliation. He now saw transference as new impressions of forgotten persons or as revised editions of them "by cleverly taking advantage of some real peculiarity in the physician's person" (p. 116). The patient relived the past experiences instead of remembering them; thus transference functioned as a resistance to the recovery of lost memories, which was the main therapeutic goal of analysis at that time. The vital role of transference in the analytic process could now be understood. Freud said, "Transference which seems to be ordained to be the greatest obstacle of psychoanalysis becomes its most powerful ally" (p. 117). Subsequently, Freud (1912a) differentiated the nonsexual, conscious, positive transference, which he called "rapport," from the erotic transference and from the negative hostile transference, and characterized transference as consistently ambivalent.

In the analysis of the Rat Man (1909) and the Wolf Man (1918), Freud used interpretations of transference to overcome resistances to forgotten memories. He buttressed his interpretations with his charisma and "human influence" to persuade his patients that the interpretations were correct. He had not yet formulated the concept of transference neurosis nor the technical principles of abstinence and neutrality. In addition to interpretation, he liberally exhorted, educated, and gratified these two patients. For example, he praised the Rat Man, fed him a meal (the famous herring parameter), loaned him a book, and sent him a postcard. Similarly, he praised and educated the Wolf Man, gave him a signed copy of his case report, raised money for him, and helped him to become an unofficial ward of psychoanalysts.

By today's standards, both of these patients would be considered borderline personalities (Blum, 1974; Glenn, 1981). Although their symptomatic improvement was partly based on insight, in significant measure it must also have been determined by Freud's "human influence," which might well have contributed to fantasies of merger with Freud, a narcissistic, omniscient self-object. It is doubtful that a purely interpretive approach would have been effective, given the fragile ego structures of these two patients. In the case of the Rat Man, we cannot know the outcome, since he died in World War I. But we know that the Wolf Man became psychotic when Freud developed cancer.

To return to the development of Freud's theory of transference, in 1914 and 1917 he introduced the concept of transference neurosis, an "artificially constructed transference illness" in which the patient's conflicts were shifted from his neurosis into his relationship with the analyst, where they could now be resolved by interpretation. Thus, the transference neurosis becomes the "battlefield" of the analysis, the patient wishing to put his transference impulses into action and the analyst insisting on subjecting them to scrutiny. Technically, Freud (1912a,b, 1914, 1915, 1915–1917, 1918, 1919) advised that transference should not be interpreted until it became a resistance and until a rapport developed between patient and analyst. This is perhaps the first reference to what has since been called the therapeutic, or working, alliance.

In 1915, Freud emphasized the principles of abstinence and neutrality. To gratify transference wishes would make the analysis of these wishes impossible. To facilitate the analysis, the analyst should reveal nothing of his personal life to the patient: "The doctor should be opaque to his patients and, like a mirror, should show them nothing but what is shown to him" (1912–13, p. 118). The principles of abstinence and neutrality have continued as essential elements of psychoanalytic technique, and arguments about deviations from them have dominated the history of psychoanalysis (e.g., Brenner's, 1979, critique of the technical departure from these principles by Zetzel, Stone and Greenson). Freud himself frequently broke his own rules and played the genial host or encouraging teacher.

In 1920 Freud viewed transference reactions as expressions of the death instinct as well as libidinal instincts. Technically, he suggested that the analyst limit the scope of the transference neurosis to force into memory as much as possible and to leave as little as possible to repetition.

In 1925 Freud summarized his concept of transference and its central role in the analytic process:

> In every analytic treatment there arises, without the physician's agency, an intense emotional relationship between the patient and the analyst which is not to be accounted for by the analytic situation. It can be of a positive or of a negative character and can vary between the extreme of a passionate, completely sensual love and the unbridled expression of an embittered defiance and hatred. This "transference"—to give it its shortened name—soon replaces in the patient's mind the desire to be cured, and, so long as it is affectionate and moderate, becomes the agent of the physician's influence and neither more nor less than the mainspring of the joint work of analysis. Later on, when it has become passionate or has been converted into hostility, it becomes the principal tool of the resistance. It may then happen that it will paralyze the patient's powers of associating and endanger the success of the treatment. Yet it would be senseless to try to evade it: for an analysis without transference is an impossibility. It must not be supposed, however, that transference is created by analysis and does not occur apart from it. Transference is merely uncovered and isolated by analysis. It is a universal phenomenon of the human mind, it decides the success of all medical influence, and in fact dominates the whole of each person's relations to his human environment . . . [p. 42].

The early 1920's saw intense debate over the "active technique" of Ferenczi and Rank (1923), which purported to deal with transference resistances, by repetition instead of remembering, by commands and prohibitions. Glover (1924, 1927, 1928) argued effectively against Ferenczi's active technique and, in a series of technical papers, systematically described typical problems in the development and resolution of transference neurosis and resistance. He delineated transference phenomena according to the new structural model in terms of id, ego, and superego. Freud's work on transference had been done during the period when instinctual drive theory and the topographic model were the prevailing psychoanalytic theories. He did not himself revise his theories of transference in accordance with the 1923 structural hypothesis.

Anna Freud (1936) added to Freud's transference concepts the phenomena of transference of defense, acting in the transference, and externalization. By transference of defense, she meant the patient's repetition in analysis of the modes of ego functioning by which he had defended himself in early childhood from his anxiety-provoking sexual and aggressive impulses. Acting in the transference, a form of acting out, refers to the displacement of feelings and wishes towards the analyst onto other people in the patient's daily life. Externalization, a subspecies of transference and separate from transference proper, refers to the projection onto the analyst of a part of the patient's formed personality structure, such as a superego function, an ego functon, or an id product. Anna Freud, for example, considers narcissistic transferences to be externalizations rather than the repetition of specific childhood relationships.

Strachey (1934) expanded the transference concept with particular emphasis on its superego aspects and declared that the therapeutic action of psychoanalysis rested entirely on the interpretation of the transference. In the transference, he stated, the patient projects unconscious, archaic images onto the analyst. Later, the analyst, a much more benign figure than the early imagos, is introjected into the patient's superego as a result of the analyst's "mutative interpretations." Transference interpretations were regarded as the only therapeutically valid interpretations, and, furthermore, virtually all of the patient's reactions to the analyst were considered to be transference reactions.

Melanie Klein (1932) and her followers considered all behavior to represent repetition of relationships presumed to have existed in the first year of life. Accordingly, every communication brought by the patient to the analyst was thought to represent transference of an early infantile relationship. The Kleinian view has been widely opposed by classical analysts. Loewenstein (1969), for example, said,

> This approach has often led to an unfortunate loss of distinction between past and present, reality and fantasy, between the values of dynamic and genetic interpretations and reconstruction. Such a one-sided understanding of the patient's reactions loses sight, further-

> more, of the difference between transference phenomena and externalization . . . [p. 586].

Fenichel (1941) described the technical aspects in interpretation of the transference as follows:

> The surface first of all, the defense before the instinct—the interpretation must be timely, not too deep and not too superficial; particularly necessary, preceding the interpretation, is isolation from the critical ego. This isolation corresponds to a cleavage of the ego into an experiencing and a judging portion, which with the aid of an identification with the analyst teaches the patient to differentiate present and past. A successful interpretation of the transference must liberate new warded off derivatives and deeper layers, and, as in all interpretations, proves to be a further step in fitting together the separate parts in the mosaic of the entire case [p. 45].

In the late forties and early fifties, Alexander and French (1946) and their followers created a storm of controversy by challenging the basic attitude in transference analysis. The transference relationship, replacing the transference neurosis as the "axis of therapy," was consistently manipulated as a medium of corrective emotional experience rather than merely a repetitive experience. Techniques adapted to a particular case were utilized, such as the timing and frequency of sessions, guidance in everyday life, the choice and timing of interpretations, the assumption by the analyst of attitudes unlike those anticipated or demanded by the patient in the transference, and the use of "extraanalytic transference relationships."

One consequence of the controversy over the Alexander group's approach was a series of contributions by Rangell (1954), Bibring (1954), and Gill (1954) that identified and clarified the similarities and differences between psychoanalysis and the dynamic psychotherapies. In the same 1954 panel, Greenacre, after emphasizing the importance of safeguarding the transference by the avoidance of contamination, examined the nature of the psychoanalytic situation and commented on its "tilted" quality, that is, the unevenness between the role of the patient and that of the analyst. She theorized that the analytic process develops within the matrix of a basic or primary transference originating from a primary need for sensory contact, for the warmth of contact with another body.

Spitz (1956) saw the analytic setting as reviving some of the earliest aspects of the mother-child relationship, and Winnicott (1956) suggested that modifications of technique were required by patients who lacked adequate mothering in their early development. He felt that only when a patient has been able to develop a transference neurosis can the analyst rely essentially on interpretive work. Stone (1961, 1967) expanded on Greenacre's (1954) matrix transference concept, seeing the "primorial transference" as related to efforts to master a series of crucial separations from the mother and with efforts to re-establish union with her expressed in derivative forms at every psychosexual level. Gitelson (1962) also emphasized the parallel between the analytic relationship and the early mother-child relationship. He stressed the anaclitic aspects of the patient's relatedness to which the analyst responds with a diatrophic stance comparable to the support the mother gives the child in the symbiotic phase. In opposition to this trend, Arlow and Brenner (1966) saw the stress on symbiosis as an oversimplification, a genetic fallacy. They emphasized that the analytic situation represents a complex object relationship for the patient that draws upon many phases of psychic development and upon many different kinds of object ties. They objected to the assumption that the psychoanalytic situation regularly recreates the relationship between mother and infant to some significant degree.

Increasing attention to the nature of the psychoanalytic situation has led to a widening of the concept of transference, bracketing the transference neurosis on the one side with its primordial origins and on the other side with its mature, autonomous, nonneurotic aspects. The therapeutic alliance of Zetzel (1956), the rational transference of Fenichel (1941), the mature transference of Stone (1961), and the working alliance of Greenson (1965) all refer to the relatively nonneurotic, reasonable rapport the patient has with the analyst. This rapport reflects an alliance between the patient's reasonable ego and the analyst's analyzing ego. These authors believe that the readiness to cooperate with the analyst is not transference in the strict sense of the term and should be clearly distinguished from it. Sandler, Holder, Kawenoka, Kennedy, and Neuroth (1969) and Sandler, Dare and Holder (1973), although subscribing to the usefulness of the alliance concept, believe that a form of transference itself appears to be an essential ingredient of the treatment alliance.

In recent years, the transferencc concept has been the subject of psychoanalytic debate in two principal areas. The first involves theoretical and technical issues connected with the transference reactions of narcissistic and borderline patients. These are discussed later in this paper. The second involves the role of transference interpretation in the here and now of the psychoanalytic situation. Gill (1976, 1979) is the current advocate of Strachey's view that only transference interpretations are therapeutic.

Gill rejects Freud's dictum that transference should not be interpreted until it becomes resistance. He argues for expansion of the transference early in analysis. The technique for accomplishing this is to interpret the patient's disguised allusions to the analyst, making explicit the implicit transference. The transference reaction is then connected to actual events in the current analytic situation. The major work in resolving the transference takes place in the here and now, and the importance of genetic interpretations and reconstructions are minimized.

Rangell (1979), in agreement with the position taken by most classical analysts (Anna Freud, Stone, Greenacre, Loewenstein), is sharply critical of the "transference interpretations only" approach (Leites, 1977), which obscures "all other important and necessary elements of the analytic process." Rangell believes that overemphasis of transference not only blocks other necessary analytic work (for example, on defenses, extra-analytic relationships, and the infantile neurosis), but can actually prove harmful to the patient by fostering an undue dependence on the analyst that may be impossible to resolve.

Let us turn our attention now to the development of the countertransference concept. Freud's first reference to countertransference was in 1910. He said:

> We have become aware of the counter-transference, which arises in him (the analyst) as a result of the patient's influence on his unconscious feelings, and we are almost inclined to insist that he shall recognize this counter-transference in himself and overcome it—no psychoanalyst goes further than his own complexes and internal resistances permit! [pp. 144–145]

Thus, Freud viewed countertransference as an obstacle to the analyst's understanding of his patient. Although he regarded transference as a valuable ally in the analytic work, he failed to take this step regarding countertransference. He wrote little about the subject directly, perhaps out of reticence to reveal himself further publicly. In a letter to Jung in 1911, criticizing Jung's overinvolvement with a patient, he wrote, "It is best to remain reserved and purely receptive. We must not let our poor neurotics drive us crazy. I believe an article on counter-transference is sorely needed; of course, we could not publish it; we would have to circulate copies among ourselves" (McGuire, 1974, p. 476).

Freud considered countertransference to be pathological—the analyst's inappropriate reactions to the patient based on his own unresolved neurotic conflicts (1912b, 1915, 1931, 1937). He included in the concept more than the analyst's transference to his patient in the sense that the patient might represent someone in the analyst's past. Countertransference also meant that the patient's conflicts and wishes would impinge on the unresolved problems in the analyst, leading to blind spots or inappropriate responses to the patient's transference love or aggression. Thus, for example, if the analyst is threatened by his own unconscious aggression, it might be difficult for him to detect similar impulses in his patient or to placate him when his resentment is directed at the analyst. To overcome these problems, Freud (1910) initially urged that the analyst conduct a continual self-analysis. Then, in 1912, considering this insufficient, he advised that the analyst have a personal analysis of his own, and added in 1937 the recommendation that the analyst be re-analyzed every five years.

Although he did not write about this, it is clear that Freud had profound countertransference problems in his clinical work with his patients. These problems have been the object of recent study in a number of papers and in a recent book, *Freud and His Patients* (Kanzer and Glenn, 1980). Analysts who have followed Freud have learned to use countertransference reactions to advantage in their clinical work. That Freud was able to do this in spite of his claim that countertransference was an obstacle can be seen in a story that Grinker (1973) tells about his analysis with Freud in 1933. Freud at that time was in the habit of keeping his dog in the office with him during the analysis. When the dog would get up and go to the door, Freud would say, "Jophie is bored with you. You aren't producing anything, and he wants to get out of here." When the dog scratched to come back in, Freud would say, "I see Jophie wants to give you another chance."

Early psychoanalytic authors after Freud focused on the basis for the analyst's countertransference and on differing definitions of countertransference. A. Stern (1924) saw the analyst's narcissism, guilt, feelings of inferiority, and homosexual conflicts as the basis for countertransference problems. Ferenczi (1928) also focused on the role of pathological narcissism and emphasized the analyst's need to watch himself for unusual emotional reactions he would have to control. Sharpe (1930) emphasized the need for the analyst to understand his motivations for doing analysis and how they might be involved in countertransference reactions. She stressed the importance of resolving fantasies of omnipotence because such fantasies are frequently projected onto the analyst by the patient. Fenichel (1940) observed that narcissistic needs and defenses against anxiety pose a greater problem for the analyst than his libidinal needs. He felt it was inevitable that the analyst would be angered by the patient's resistance and gratified by his advances in the treatment, but added that this should not impede him in observing and understanding the patient's resistances.

The question of how to define countertransference has been the subject of considerable disagreement in the psychoanalytic literature. The classical position is a continuation of Freud's view of countertransferences as "blind spots," or resistances in the analyst—that is, unresolved conflicts and problems aroused in the analyst that hinder his effectiveness in the course of his work with the patient. The origin of these countertransferences lies predominantly in the analyst's transference towards the patient (A. Reich, 1951; Fliess, 1953; Glover, 1955). For example, A. Reich said, "Countertransference thus comprises the effects of the analyst's own unconscious needs and conflicts on his understanding or technique. In such cases the patient represents for the analyst an object of the past on to whom past feelings and wishes are projected . . . this is countertransference in the proper sense" (p. 26).

In contrast to the classical position is a broadened, or totalistic, approach, which views countertransference as the total emotional reaction of the analyst to the patient in the treatment situation. This point of view, first introduced by Balint and Balint (1939, 1949), has been expanded in the work of Cohen (1952), Fromm-Reichmann (1950), Heimann (1950), Racker (1957) and Winnicott (1949, 1960). Heimann was the first to recognize the positive value of countertransference, a phenomenon that could be utilized by the analyst to extend his understanding of the patient. She said that the distinguishing feature of the analytic relationship is not the presence of feelings in the patient and their absence in the analyst, but the degree to which feelings are experienced and the use made of them. It is the analyst's task to sustain rather than discharge feelings and to subordinate them to the analytic task, in which he functions as the patient's "mirror reflection." The psychoanalytic literature on countertransference is divided between those who regard it as an obstacle to analytic work and those who regard it as a valuable tool.

Kernberg (1965), in a review of the analytic literature on countertransference, states that the classical approach's main criticism of the totalistic approach is that broadening the term countertransference to include all emotional phenomena in the therapist is confusing and makes the term countertransference lose all specific meaning. The classical approach implies that broadening the concept of countertransference tends to exaggerate the importance of the analyst's emotional reaction, with a detrimental shift away from the position of neutrality in which the analyst should ideally remain. Adherents to the classical approach also point out the danger of an excessive intervention of the analyst's personality when his emotional reaction is so heavily emphasized. Kernberg also cites the totalistic orientation's criticisms of the classical approach as obscuring the importance of countertransference by implying that countertransference is something basically "wrong." This may encourage in the analyst a phobic attitude towards his own emotional reactions and, thus, limit his understanding of the patient. Kernberg points out that the full use of the analyst's emotional response can be considered to be of particular importance in the treatment of patients with profound personality disorders and other very disturbed or psychotic patients. With such patients, the countertransference may be helpful in evaluating the degree of regression and in clarifying the transference paradigms during severe regression.

Sandler, Dare, and Holder (1973), finding the classical view of countertransference too narrow and the totalist view so broad as to render the term countertransference practically meaningless, suggested that the most useful view of countertransference might be to take it as referring to the specific emotional responses aroused in the analyst by the specific qualities of his patient. This would exclude *general* features of the analyst's personality and internal psychological structure (which would color or affect his work with all his patients) and would imply: (a) that there are countertransference responses in the analyst, and that these exist throughout the analysis; (b) that countertransference can lead to difficulties in, or inappropriate handling of, the analysis—this will occur if and when the analyst fails to become aware of aspects of his countertransference reactions to the patient, or fails to cope with them even if he is aware of them; (c) that the analyst's constant scrutiny of variations in his feelings and attitudes towards the patient can lead to increased insight into processes occurring in the patient.

Let us turn our attention now to the issues involved in understanding the role of transference and countertransference in the treatment of difficult character disorders.

Difficult character disorder is not a diagnosis we expect to find in the DSM-III. Rather the term refers to those patients whose personality structure produces special and difficult obstacles to treatment beyond those usually encountered in the neurotic patient. Psychoanalysis was developed as a method of treatment for the transference neuroses and, with the advent of ego psychology, for the treatment of neurotic characters. In contrast to patients suffering from what Freud called narcissistic neuroses, these neurotic patients are capable of establishing with the analyst a relationship distorted by past unconscious object relations that constitute the transference. Part of this relationship involves the capacity to develop a therapeutic alliance, which requires stable, mature ego functions of reality testing, object constancy, impulse control, and tension tolerance. The neurotic problems of these patients are disguised expressions of unconscious intrapsychic conflicts, primarily from the oedipal phase of development.

The difficult character disorder is to be found largely in those diagnostic groups between the neurotic and psychotic, such as impulse-ridden, acting-out characters, narcissistic personalities, and borderline personalities. Although they may display neurotic symptoms and behavior, they differ from neurotic patients in a number of essential respects: the origins of their pathology, the nature of ego and superego structure, and the forms of transference displayed in analytic treatment. Many analysts believe that the pathology of these patients is rooted in developmental failure to achieve adequate self-object differentiation and consolidation of part-self and part-object images because of disturbances in the preverbal mother–child dyad. Although oedipal phase conflicts occur, they are shaped and deformed by the intense pregenital disturbances and are characterized by primitive, unneutralized aggression. Structural ego and superego impairments range from the milder (in those patients closer to the neurotic end of the continuum) to the more severe (in those closer to the psychotic). Ego impairment includes poor impulse control, poor anxiety tolerance, utilization of primitive defense mechanisms, poor ability to delay gratification, poor reality testing, and poor and unstable object relations. Superego identifications tend to be primitive and poorly integrated. As a result of these structural impairments, these patients have a limited capacity to form a therapeutic alliance. They cannot sustain the desired cleavage between the observing ego and the experiencing ego so necessary to analytic work. They develop primitive, galloping transferences that are instinctualized and lack the "as if" quality which permits distance and analytic scrutiny. Similarly, these intense transference reactions evoke, in the analyst, intense countertransference reactions beyond those experienced with the neurotic patient. These countertransference reactions tend to interfere with the analyst's neutrality and may lead to overactivity or to defensive withdrawal into silence.

In consideration of these difficulties, traditionally these patients were considered to be unanalyzable but treatable by an amalgam of supportive and dynamic psychotherapy based on psychoanalytic knowledge. However, since the advent of ego psychology, there has been a steady widening of the scope of psychoanalysis to include virtually all diagnostic groups. As Stone (1954) said, "While the difficulties increase and the expectations of success diminish in a general way as the nosological periphery is approached, there is no absolute barrier—psychoanalysis remains the most powerful of all psychotherapeutic instruments" (p. 593).

The issues that have arisen out of the attempt to widen the scope are among the major controversies in current psychoanalysis. Psychoanalysis as a treatment relies on interpretation as its major technique. Interpretation of unconscious intrapsychic conflict and reconstruction of its genetic antecedents as revived in the transference neurosis are the means to provide the insight that leads to therapeutic change. It is generally recognized that psychopathology, to a lesser extent in neurotic patients and a greater extent in nonneurotic patients, is not only the result of intrapsychic conflict but is also related to structural impairments, developmental arrests, and malformed self and object representations. Interpretation and working through of conflict often results in improvement in these ego and superego deficits. It is also understood that, aside from interpretation, developmental advance occurs as a result of the new remarkable experience of the analytic process, the new and unique object relationship, and selective ego and superego identifications with the analyst. Although these changes are part of the therapeutic action of psychoanalysis, they are not produced by educative or manipulative techniques; they are the result of the psychoanalytic process, which relies primarily on interpretation.

A major and controversial trend in the treatment of non-neurotic patients has been the shift of focus away from intrapsychic conflict and towards noninterpretive measures aimed at restoring deformities and deficits of ego organization. Kohut (1971, 1977) is currently the major proponent of this approach. He believes that careful study of the transference reactions these patients manifest enables the analyst to adopt a therapeutic stance that encourages a resumption of the development of arrested, precarious self and object representations. Technically, the analyst conveys his empathic understanding of the primitive states that the patient needs to maintain or achieve. Examples of such states include the restoration of symbiotic-like merger with an idealized object that has been phase-inappropriately disrupted and the reliance on archaic self-object configurations to sustain a vulnerable self-representation. Although the claim is that the activity of the analyst is interpretation, it has become increasingly clear that Kohut (1977) considers empathy to be the instrument of therapeutic change. He says, "It is not the interpretation that cures the patient" (p. 31). The psychology of the self is clearly intended to displace the classical theory of drive and ego development and structural conflict in the understanding and treatment of patients who suffer from developmental impairment. Kohut refers to these patients as "Tragic Man." He acknowledges that classical theory explains the problems of the patients who suffer from oedipal conflicts. These patients he refers to as "Guilty Man."

Gedo (1980) reviewed the presumably narcissistic patients described in *The Psychology of the Self: A Casebook* (Goldberg, 1978) and compared them with the patients described by Firestein (1978) in his book on termination. He found the presumably neurotic patients analyzed at the New York Psychoanalytic Treatment Center scarcely distinguishable as a group from those described in the Goldberg *Casebook*. Despite Kohut's view to the contrary, it appears that Guilty Man and Tragic Man are present in varying combinations in the psychopathology of every patient.

Another major trend in the psychoanalytic understanding and treatment of non-neurotic patients is to be found in the remarkably prolific work of Kernberg (1975, 1976). Utilizing some of the concepts developed by Melanie Klein and the British Object Relations School and relying heavily on the developmental contributions of Jacobson and Mahler, he has fashioned a comprehensive object relations theory within the confines of classic psychoanalytic ego psychology. He organizes character pathology along a continuum from higher range (i.e., neurotic characters) to middle range and lower range characters (i.e., primarily borderlines) according to their ego pathology and particular pathology of internalized object relations. At the neurotic end, repressive mechanisms predominate; and at the borderline end, splitting mechanisms predominate. He rejects the view that the deformed self and object representations seen in non-neurotic patients are manifestations of developmental arrest. He sees them instead as pathological structures serving the purpose of defense. Object images and/or self images with opposing affective linkages are forcibly dissociated in order to alleviate intense ambivalent conflicts. The primitive transference reactions of borderline patients are thus understood to represent reactivation in the transference of part-self and part-object images—all good or all bad. In treatment, the aim of working through the transference is to resolve the dissociations and to transform primitive transferences into higher level, more integrated transference reactions, which are more realistic and more related to childhood experiences. Consonant with the modern view, Kernberg views countertransference reactions not as obstacles to be overcome by the self–analysis of the analyst, but as invaluable tools to guide his understanding of what is happening in the patient and in their interaction.

Unlike Kohut, Kernberg retains the conflict model, the technical neutrality of the analyst, and the analyst's reliance on interpretation as the primary instrument for achieving therapeutic change. Both Kohut and Kernberg[1] locate the origins of pathology in non-neurotic patients in the first two years of life before the development of object constancy, in the preverbal "ice age." Progressive distortions in psychic development are emphasized, but the role of regressive intensification of earlier difficulty in defensive flight from conflict in later stages of development, particularly the oedipal phase, is minimized. The usual balanced considerations of how much fixation of drive and ego development and how much regression are operative in a given case is disrupted in Kohut's and Kernberg's formulations to a more or less exclusive focus on fixation: for Kohut, in arrest of the development of the self; for Kernberg, in consolidation of self and object representations.

Studies of early development have provided valuable additions to psychoanalytic theory, but many analysts are skeptical of the ease and certitude with which adult object relations and transference reactions are so readily connected to such primitive preverbal origins. Clinically, in the analytic situation, it is necessary to be cautious in making such connections. Understanding comes slowly. The analyst immerses himself in the process and only gradually, over a long period of time, does he grasp the various meanings of his patient's conflicts, the nature and quality of the patient's resistances, and the meaning of the patient's transference to him and his reciprocal transferences to his patient. The totally self-involved patient, who fails to show even the slightest interest in the analyst and evokes the analyst's boredom and resentment, may indeed be demonstrating a narcissistic mirror transference reflecting his inability to relate to others, or he may be defensively distancing himself from the analyst out of fear of his libidinal and aggressive wishes towards him. An idealizing transference, eliciting the analyst's discomfiture and guilt, may represent the projection onto the analyst of the primitive, grandiose self of a narcissistic personality. Or it may have a variety of other meanings, including revival in the transference of a relationship with an idealized person in adolescence or a defense against unconscious, hostile, competitive oedipal fantasies involving the ana-

[1]Kernberg (1975) places the essential pathology in borderline patients as originating during the rapprochement phase in Mahler's formulation.

lyst. Hostile, depreciating attitudes about the analyst may represent a primitive, "all bad" part-object transference or an ambivalent conflict or negative transference from a later stage in development.

Psychoanalytic technique and transference are inseparable concepts. It is the neutral, abstinent, largely silent, analyzing stance of the analyst that makes possible the clear recognition of those distortions in the patient's perception of him which comprise the transference. An analytic result, structural change, and the resolution of the patient's neurosis, are achieved by means of analysis of the transference neurosis. The possibility of an analytic result is compromised to the extent that the analyst departs from neutrality, gratifies transference wishes, acts the role of a real parent or teacher. Although therapeutic change may occur, it is likely to be based on transference manipulation, a "transference cure."

The issue of how much human responsiveness the analyst can employ to temper his neutral stance and enhance the therapeutic alliance without compromising the analytic situation is a frequent subject of psychoanalytic debates. Nowhere is the issue more apt than in the treatment of difficult characters. Is the standard psychoanalytic method usable for those of this group considered analyzable, or are technical modifications necessary? Kohut's technique certainly involves considerable transference gratification and manipulation, with the analyst providing empathic solace and supporting the patient's view of himself as having been an innocent child-victim of depriving parents. Kernberg maintains technical neutrality but, in the opinion of this author, his active and early interpretations—dazzling, brilliant, and lengthy—although conveying insight, do, in significant measure, provide gratification of transference longings for an omniscient parent and provide a cognitive verbal holding environment.

This chapter has attempted to provide historical background and current focus on the issues involved in determining just what constitutes difficult character disorders and what considerations arise regarding their psychoanalytic treatment, their transference, and countertransference features.

REFERENCES

Alexander, F., & French, T. (1946). *Psychoanalytic Therapy.* New York: Ronald Press.

Arlow, J. A., & Brenner, C. (1966). Discussion of Elizabeth R. Zetzel: The

psychoanalytic situation. In: *Psychoanalysis in the Americas,* ed. R. E. Litman. New York: International Universities Press, pp. 133–138.
Balint, M., & Balint, A. (1939). On transference and counter-transference. *Internat. J. Psycho-Anal.,* 20:223–230.
______ (1949). *Primary love and psycho-analytic technique.* London: Tavistock, 1965.
Bibring, E. (1954). Psychoanalysis and the dynamic psychotherapies. *J. Amer. Psychoanal. Assn.,* 2:745–768.
Blum, H. P. (1974). The borderline childhood of the Wolf Man. *J. Amer. Psychoanal. Assn.,* 22:721–742.
Brenner, C. (1979). Working alliance, therapeutic alliance, and transference. *J. Amer. Psychoanal. Assn.,* 27:137–157.
Breuer, J., & Freud, S. (1893–1895). Studies on Hysteria. *Standard Edition,* 2. London: Hogarth Press, 1955.
Cohen, M. (1952). Counter-transference and anxiety. *Psychiat.,* 15:231–243.
Fenichel, O. (1941). *Problems of Psychoanalytic Technique.* Albany, NY: The Psychoanalytic Quarterly.
Ferenezi, S. (1928). *Final Contributions to the Problems and Methods of Psychoanalysis.* New York: Basic Books, 1955.
______ & Rank, O. (1923). *The Development of Psychoanalysis.* New York: Nervous and Mental Disease, 1925.
Firestein, S. (1978). *Termination in Psychoanalysis.* New York: International Universities Press.
Fliess, R. (1953). Counter-transference and counter-identification. *J. Amer. Psychoanal. Assn.,* 1:268–284.
Freud, A. (1936). The ego and the mechanisms of defense. *The Writings of Anna Freud,* 2. New York: International Universities Press.
Freud, S. (1905). Fragment of an analysis of a case of hysteria. *Standard Edition,* 7:1–122. London: Hogarth Press, 1953.
______ (1909). Notes upon a case of obsessional neurosis. *Standard Edition,* 10:153–318. London: Hogarth Press, 1955.
______ (1910). The future prospects of psychoanalytic therapy. *Standard Edition,* 11:139–151. London: Hogarth Press, 1957.
______ (1912a). The dynamics of transference. *Standard Edition,* 12:97–108. London: Hogarth Press, 1958.
______ (1912b). Recommendations to physicians practising psychoanalysis. *Standard Edition,* 12:109–120. London: Hogarth Press, 1958.
______ (1914). Remembering, repeating and working-through (further recommendations on the technique of psycho-analysis II). *Standard Edition,* 12:145–156. London: Hogarth Press, 1958.
______ (1915). Observations on transference love (further recommendations on the technique of psycho-analysis III). *Standard Edition,* 12:157–171. London: Hogarth Press, 1958.
______ (1916–1917). Introductory lectures on psycho-analysis. *Standard Edition,* 15 & 16. London: Hogarth Press, 1963.

——— (1918). From the history of an infantile neurosis. *Standard Edition,* 17:1–123. London: Hogarth Press, 1955.
——— (1919). Lines of advance in psycho-analytic therapy. *Standard Edition,* 17:159–168. London: Hogarth Press, 1955.
——— (1920). Beyond the pleasure principle. *Standard Edition,* 18:1–64. London: Hogarth Press, 1955.
——— (1925). An autobiographical study. *Standard Edition,* 20:1–74. London: Hogarth Press, 1959.
——— (1931). Female sexuality. *Standard Edition,* 21:221–243. London: Hogarth Press, 1961.
——— (1937). Analysis terminable and interminable. *Standard Edition,* 23:209–253. London: Hogarth Press, 1964.
Fromm-Reichmann, F. (1950). *Principles of Intensive Psychotherapy.* Chicago: University of Chicago Press.
Gedo, J. (1980). Reflections on some current controversies in psychoanalysis. *J. Amer. Psychoanal. Assn.,* 28:363–383.
Gill, M. (1954). Psychoanalysis and exploratory psychotherapy. *J. Amer. Psychoanal. Assn.,* 2:771–796.
——— & Muslin, H. (1976). Early interpretation of transference. *J. Amer. Psychoanal. Assn.,* 24:779–794.
——— (1979). The analysis of the transference. *J. Amer. Psychoanal. Assn.,* 27:263–287.
Gitelson, M. (1962). The curative factor in psycho-analysis. *Internat. J. Psycho-Anal.,* 43:194–205.
Glenn, J. (1981, January). The Rat-Man: Historical and Contemporary Views of Freud's Psycho-therapeutic Approaches. Presented at a joint meeting of the Long Island Psychoanalytic Association and the Nassau Psychiatric Association.
Glover, E. (1924). Active therapy and psychoanalysis. *Internat. J. Psycho-Anal.,* 5:269–311.
——— (1927). Lectures on technique in psychoanalysis. *Internat. J. Psycho-Anal.,* 8:311–338.
——— (1928). Lectures on technique in psychoanalysis. *Internat. J. Psycho-Anal.,* 9:7–46, 181–218.
——— (1955). *The technique of psychoanalysis.* New York: International Universities Press.
Goldberg, A., ed. (1978). *The Psychology of the Self: A Casebook.* New York: International Universities Press.
Greenacre, P. (1954). The role of transference: practical considerations in relation to psycho-analytic therapy. *J. Amer. Psychoanal. Assn.,* 2:671–684.
Greenson, R. (1965). The working alliance and the transference neurosis. *Psychoanal. Quart.,* 34:155–181.
Grinker, R. (1973). Medicine's living history. *Med. World News,* 14:14.
Heimann, P. (1950). On counter-transference. *Internat. J. Psycho-Anal.,* 31:81–84.

Kanzer, M., & Glenn, J. (1980). *Freud and His Patients.* New York: Aronson.
Kernberg, O. (1965). Notes on counter-transference. *J. Amer. Psycho-Anal. Assn.,* 13:38–56.
______ (1975). *Borderline Conditions and Pathological Narcissism.* New York: Aronson.
______ (1976). *Object Relations Theory and Clinical Psychoanalysis.* New York: Aronson.
Klein, M. (1932). *The Psycho-Analysis of Children.* London: Hogarth Press.
Kohut, H. (1971). *The Analysis of the Self.* New York: International Universities Press.
______ (1977). *The Restoration of the Self.* New York: International Universities Press.
Leites, N. (1977). Transference interpretations only? *Internat. J. Psycho-Anal.,* 58:275–287.
Loewenstein, R. M. (1969). Developments in the theory of transference in the last fifty years. *Internat. J. Psycho-Anal.,* 50:583–588.
McGuire, W., ed. (1974). *The Freud/Jung Letters: The Correspondence Between Sigmund Freud and C. G. Jung.* Princeton: Princeton University Press.
Racker, H. (1957). The meaning and uses of counter-transference. *Psychoanal. Quart.,* 26:303–357.
Rangell, L. (1954). Similarities and differences between psychoanalysis and dynamic psychotherapy. *J. Amer. Psychoanal. Assn.,* 2:734–744.
______ (1979). Contemporary issues in the theory of therapy. *J. Amer. Psychoanal. Assn.,* 27:81–112.
Reich, A. (1951). On counter-transference. *Internat. J. Psycho-Anal.,* 32:25–31.
Sandler, J., Holder, A., Kawenoka, M., Kennedy, H. & Neuroth, L. (1969). Notes on some theoretical and clinical aspects of transference. *Internat. J. Psycho-Anal.,* 50:633–645.
______, Dare, C., & Holder, A. (1973). *The Patient and the Analyst.* New York: International Universities Press.
Sharpe, E. (1930). The technique of psycho-analysis. *Internat. J. Psycho-Anal.,* 11:251–277.
Spitz, R. (1956). Symposium: Transference: The analytic setting and its prototype. *Internat. J. Psycho-Anal.,* 37:386–388.
Stern, A. (1924). On the counter-transference in psychoanalysis. *Psychoanal. Rev.,* 11:166–174.
Stone, L. (1954). The widening scope of indications for psychoanalysis. *J. Amer. Psychoanal. Assn.,* 2:567–594.
______ (1961). *The Psychoanalytic Situation.* New York: International Universities Press.
______ (1967). The psychoanalytic situation and transference: postscript to an earlier communication. *J. Amer. Psychoanal. Assn.,* 15:3–58.

Strachey, J. (1934). The nature of the therapeutic action of psychoanalysis. *Internat. J. Psycho-Anal.,* 15:127–159.
Winnicott, D. W. (1949). Hate in the counter-transference. *Internat. J. Psycho-Anal.,* 30:69–74.
——— (1956). Symposium. On Transference. *Internat. J. Psycho-Anal.,* 37:386–388.
——— (1960). Counter-transference. *Brit. J. Med. Psychol.,* 33:17–21.
Zetzel, E. (1956). Current concepts of transference. *Internat. J. Psycho-Anal.,* 37:369–376.

CHAPTER THREE

On the Therapeutic Limits of Psychoanalysis: Delinquent Enactments*

John E. Gedo

One chapter of my book, *Advances in Clinical Psychoanalysis* (1981b), was devoted to "the current limits of psychoanalysis as therapy." I focused there on two sets of constraints that may defeat psychoanalytic efforts, however far we may go in adapting treatment technique to the individual requirements of given patients (cf. Gedo, 1979). The first boundary of our therapeutic effectiveness is the occurrence of regressive episodes in the course of which the analysand loses the capacity to cope with the exigencies of everyday life, thus necessitating placement in a sheltered environment. The second boundary is the covert presence of delusional convictions, particularly when these unalterable beliefs concern the acquisition of valid knowledge. Patients afflicted with this variant of omniscience mistrust whatever new information they encounter in their analysis, even though their unwillingness or inability to change false beliefs may often hide behind a screen of verbal assent.

The focus of this chapter is on other aspects of these boundaries of the therapeutic scope of psychoanalysis. I should state at the outset, however, that I am by no means certain that the psychopathology I delineate here actually differs from the adaptive deficits described in my previous work on this topic. I wish merely to shift the point of view from which we approach this subject, concentrating now on the unfavorable significance of delinquent enactments within the analytic setting for the final outcome of treatment.[1]

---

*An earlier version of this chapter appeared in Gedo, J. *Psychoanalysis and Its Discontents.* Copyright 1984 by Guilford Press. Adapted by permission.

[1]Individuals whose behavior betrays gross defects in integrity—criminals and psychopathic characters of other types—probably continue to be excluded from the practice of most psychoanalysts. Still, the steadily widening scope of the personality disturbances treated by means of the analytic method has inevitably confronted practitioners

As I have previously tried to show via clinical examples (Gedo, 1979, 1981b), it is feasible to establish an effective analytic process with delinquent individuals, at least with those who do not exceed the analyst's anxiety tolerance through criminal or other dangerous activities. In my experience, most patients of this kind are well able to tolerate forthright statements about the nature of their behavior, including, if necessary, candid avowals by the analyst of the manner in which such activities conflict with his personal system of values (see Gedo, 1984, chap. 6). Generally, it turns out that at bottom the patient has been in conflict about his delinquent propensities, and that the analyst's implicit or explicit endorsement of codes of conduct based on responsible mutuality often opens the way to some form of idealizing transference (Gedo, 1975).

It is precisely the exceptions to this generalization that constitute one of the subgroups of patients for whom psychoanalysis has little to offer. I suspect that in my own practice I screen out most prospective patients thoroughly committed to corrupt values through early and explicit insistence on their acceptance of precise business arrangements, especially with respect to schedule and fees. I can recall several instances of patients with delinquent propensities who decided against working with me, following extended exploratory consultations that seemed promising, after I made it clear that I would not look on unilateral interference with my procedures merely as analytic material to be processed with detachment. Perhaps the clearest negative response to my policy occurred with a professor of law (!), who reported a first dream in which he was participating in a hockey game against the local Chicago team. At the decisive moment, he picked up the puck and carried it to the opposing team's goal, like a runner scoring a touchdown in football. When I commented on his wish to be exempted from the ground rules of analysis, he replied angrily, that I might be correct, but that he could not collaborate with such a stickler for rules. He walked out of the session on the spot, never to return. My intervention may have been ill timed technically, but the patient's transparent reaction revealed his imperative insistence on being allowed to alter the rules to his own

---

with an increasing number of patients whose delinquent propensities do not become apparent until the therapeutic regression induced by the psychoanalytic process has been set in motion. Many of these contingencies simply follow from the misleading information such individuals are likely to provide in the course of initial consultations. There are other instances, however, in which the delinquent behavior is in fact without precedent in the patient's adult life—it represents a return to modes of organization that were more or less successfully warded off in adulthood and are reactivated only within the analytic setting during treatment.

advantage; hence, his decision to discontinue treatment was probably sound.

Another patient started treatment by proposing to defraud his insurance company to our mutual profit. He responded to my statement that I could not be of benefit to him if I condoned his delinquencies by confessing (*sic*!) his lifelong wish to become an honest person. An idealizing transference subsequently emerged, based on the precedent of one of his important relationships of early childhood. In this case, however, as in so many others (see case #3 in Gedo, 1979), the principal intrapsychic conflict turned out to involve the clash of competing value systems acquired in differing childhood contexts. Although the outcome of this conflict was in doubt for about two years, the patient was ultimately unable to reject and condemn the behavior of his father, a man who had never bothered to hide his criminal activities from his son.

It is of great interest that the childhood conflict between the world of this man's charismatic and delinquent father and that of his loving, self-sacrificing, and humble maternal grandparents was recreated in the course of the analysis via the formation of a complex constellation of *transferences*. If the analytic relationship revived, for the most part, the exploitative but lifesaving bond to his Sicilian grandmother, the patient also managed to repeat the circumstances of his childhood attachment to his father by submitting—with exceptions of Machiavellian subtlety and provocativeness!—to a tyrannical and unscrupulous mistress. He was quite able to despise his father for "not living like a white man," as he delicately put it, but was unable to oppose or even criticize his paramour's cruelty toward his children in the present.

In the end, the analysis suffered the same fate the grandparents' moral code had undergone in later childhood—it was dismissed as both impractical and excessively puritanical. No doubt the patient would have preferred to enjoy his power and pleasures without having to sacrifice his integrity, but his dreams repeatedly portrayed this bigoted person scoring the winning touchdown in the Superbowl and then performing a savage victory dance as a black man—that is, a criminal.

I have organized this case vignette around the issue of the analysand's inability to repudiate his own corruption; it would be just as cogent, for other purposes, to formulate the material in terms of very different facets of his psychopathology. The patient's decision to sacrifice the analysis in order to appease his mistress, for example, could only have been based on the assumption that their relationship would preserve the relative peace that had supervened in his life as a result of the analytic work. Such a view constituted a repudiation of the cumulative evidence we had collected in the course of our collaboration, not to mention the interpretations I had offered during the same period. This man's pathology, in other words, included some defect in the capacity to process information. Although the treatment did not unequivocally reveal the presence of delusional thinking, the case does not constitute an exception to my previous categorizations of analytic failures caused by subtle thought disorders. In this instance, I did indeed witness several transient episodes of pseudologia fantastica, that is, periods during which the patient actually believed his own lies.

Another way to put this same point is to recall that the relatively primitive mode of organization characteristic of delinquent individuals implies a whole array of adaptive deficits, involving multiple lines of development (cf. Gedo & Goldberg, 1973). If we choose to pay closer attention to the issue of object relations, for example, we could approach the same patient's psychopathology from the vantage point of his simultaneous symbiotic enmeshment with a number of individuals and with the periods of acute stress that ensued when certain of these indispensable people pulled him in varying directions. From this perspective, we might describe the limits of effective psychoanalytic treatment in terms of the extent to which the analysand's symbiotic needs become focused within the analytic relationship. If a significant propensity to form symbiotic attachments continues to find outlets in extra-analytic contexts, we probably face a poor prognosis.

Let us pursue a bit further the object relations perspective on delinquent behavior. For the past generation, it has been a commonplace of the child analytic literature that the treatment of delinquent youngsters is unlikely to be successful unless one or both parents, whose attitudes codetermine the nature of the child's behavior, participate in the therapeutic process. General consensus about such findings probably led to the emergence of family therapy as a rational treatment modality for individuals whose personality organization is characterized by those symbiotic attachments we might term "syncytial"—these attachments call to mind a mass of cytoplasm that has discernible nuclei, but has not undergone actual division into separate cells. We may recall, in this connection, that Aichhorn's (1925) successes with delinquent adolescents were achieved in a residential setting where he had plenipotentiary powers—where the patients did not have to contend with the undertow of symbiotic ties to family members who had a vested interest in perpetuating their maladaptive behaviors. I believe that the applicability of the same principles to certain adult patients has not been sufficiently emphasized.

This symbiotic constellation is often more blatant than in the case of the Pinocchio-like character I have just described. One instance of the more obvious kind concerns a young woman who was able to profit from almost two years of steady and accurate analytic feedback about the nature of her delinquent performances to reassess the actualities of her desperate situation. She was at first maximally uncooperative as an analytic patient, but the history of her exploitative and fraudulent behavior toward most persons gradually emerged nonetheless. The exception to this pattern was her relationship to her mother, a narcissistic woman who had been unable to cope with a child (i.e., the patient) whose infancy had been a nightmare of feeding problems. This apparent paradox in the patient's behavior was all the more puzzling because she was filled with hatred for a father who had always been kind and solicitous toward his beautiful little girl.

I encountered very little difficulty in reaching consensus with this woman about her vanity and selfishness, her ruthless sadism, and her hypocrisy and fraudulence—the analyst's reality-tested valuation of the patient's delinquent enactments is integral to the process of dealing with persistent childhood illusions; it imparts credibility to his role as the patient's optimal disillusioner. In this particular case, the cogency of the portrait that confronted this patient in my analytic looking glass quite rapidly addicted her to the treatment, so that the worsening bulimia that initially prompted her to seek assistance disappeared in about a year. She was pleased and relieved to be able to confide in someone who recognized that, but for her father's practically limitless subsidies, she would have tried to manipulate and defraud men by becoming a high-class hooker. In fact, her propensities in this direction occasionally spilled over into the enactment of a sadistic perversion.

As it was, the patient tried to guarantee her welcome in my office by taking steady, albeit menial employment for the first time. With this development, her father began a barrage of so-called encouragement to induce her to undertake training for one of the major professions. It was at this point that her genuine humiliation at her lack of skills and accomplishments came into focus. It emerged that one source of her hatred for her father was his blind disregard of her lack of interest in, or suitability for, the type of difficult endeavors he wanted her to tackle. Clearly, he wanted to exploit her to satisfy his own narcissistic needs. The patient's initial inability to cooperate with the requirements of analysis echoed her despairing sense that she could never succeed in ways that would impress her father. Yet, she was simultaneously unable to trust my assessment that, far from being an underachiever, she had done well to graduate from college. The issue was finally settled when, on her own initiative, she underwent psychological testing which confirmed that her intelligence was barely above average.

Although the patient was more severely mortified at her competitive disadvantages than she had been at being identified as a psychopathic character, none of her encounters with unpalatable truths about herself caused her to regress in any way. Above all, she needed not to be confused by the unrealistic fantasies that other people were prone to spin around her, largely because she could act to perfection the part of the well-bred lady. As part of arriving at a reliable self-assessment, it was essential that she prove to herself that she could be self-supporting, despite the fact that she had to borrow to pay the fee for her continuing analysis. At my insistence, she formalized the latter arrangement through a written contract whereby the money for analysis was advanced to her out of her share of her parents' estate.

Even this concrete reminder of her autonomy proved to be insufficient, however, when further developments alerted her parents to the possibility that the patient might proceed to structure her future in a way that would make her independent of their influence. At first she was interested in the compromise solution of making a marriage acceptable to the family. But she soon came to terms with the fact that her characterological hatred of men made the prospect of any marriage—much less one meeting her parents' social requirements!—exceedingly implausible. Convinced she would have to forge a different type of future through her own exertions, she arranged to return to school to acquire skills commensurate with her aptitudes. This decision, of course, made her dependent once more on family assistance.

It came as a complete surprise that it was the patient's *mother,* until then the sole family member to have disapproved of her irresponsibility and lack of "realism," who now began to question the necessity of this difficult new enterprise, rapidly undermining the patient's tenuous resolution to persevere in a program to achieve self-sufficiency—including her commitment to the analysis. The mother strongly recommended switching to some form of once-a-week group therapy. Too late, I realized that this girl's persistent fantasies that she would not only inherit much of her father's wealth, but also his prerogatives as the mother's primary companion, were not merely reflections of an unresolved negative oedipal constellation. They also constituted responses to her mother's unspoken promises and expectations! Faced, after decades of frustrated longings, with the imminent consummation of this quasi-incestuous pact, the patient inevitably came to see the analysis as an obstacle and an inconvenience, soon discarded, albeit with some shame.

I suspect that covert symbiotic attachments in adult life are more frequently formed in relation to a spouse (as in the case of the man who sacrificed his analysis to appease his mistress) and less often persist in their original version vis-à-vis one or both parents (as in the last example I offered). The outcome of analytic efforts seems to depend not on the mere presence of symbiotic needs—many patients with such requirements rapidly form stable, if archaic, transference bonds to the analyst that gradually supplant their primitive attachments to others, and, in fact, give the analyst added therapeutic leverage. This circumstance has accounted for many transient "transference cures" in psychotherapy or in analyses that fail to heed adequately these archaic aspects of the treatment relationship. Thus, the destructive persistence of archaic transferences that are extraanalytic and thereby threaten to overwhelm the influence of the working relationship with the analyst must be accounted for on some other grounds.

One possible reason for the occurrence of such a split transference may be historical—this condition may constitute a repetition of the very circumstances in childhood that led to the structuring of this form of psychopathology in the first place. The delinquent girl whose mother seduced her to abandon the analysis was probably prevented in childhood, in much the same way, from making full use of the relationship her father offered her. I have already alluded to the childhood precedents for the moral conflict of the male patient who yielded to the pressure of his mistress to give up the quest to become "an honest man." In other instances, however, this explanation does not seem applicable; in fact, the siren call of delinquency frequently does not seem to emanate from a symbiotic matrix per se.

I may be able to illustrate such a circumstance through the example of a man who entered analysis because of stormy marital conflicts that turned out to be caused, for the most part, by his delinquent behavior. During several years of this lengthy but ultimately unproductive treatment, the patient used the influence of his wife as a resistance in the analysis in a way that suggested the persistence of a split transference of the kind found in the two cases I have just discussed. As a consequence of her own treatment, however, the patient's wife gradually learned to extricate herself from this symbiotic enmeshment, so that her behavior and expectations could no longer be blamed for his. Probably as a result of his wife's progressive refusal to preserve the status quo ante, the patient lost interest in the marriage and eventually initiated divorce proceedings, albeit with obsessional indecisiveness. This sequence of events finally clarified the fact that the analytic transference had been characterized for some time by the same negativism that formerly caused his marital problems. Now that his "resistance" could no longer be attributed to the influence of his spouse (with whom he had less and less contact now that she was liberated), we were able to discern its actual *raison d'être*: negativism protected him from a loss of the sense of selfhood. This regressive collapse now began to be enacted within the analysis in the form of various failures to live up to the expectable performance of patients seeking psychological assistance.

These disruptive episodes, or (from another vantage point) these unexpected bouts of irresponsibility, always presented difficult technical problems; the specific variant I found most trying was the patient's tendency to lapse into a noncommunicative use of speech. Most often, this activity led to the production of associative chains that did not seem to have any consensual meaning. Lest I be misunderstood in turn, let me stress that these utterances were not merely difficult to understand from a psychoanalytic viewpoint; they made no coherent sense of any kind, even though the patient remained unaware of the fact that he had failed to communicate any meaning. To me, it seemed that on these occasions he was vomiting words. At the same time, the vomitus obviously consisted of phrases or even sentences that sounded like everyday speech. If I asked him to explain what he meant by such an utterance, the patient was often bewildered, but the question generally restored his capacity to communicate with me in an appropriate manner. Without prodding of this kind, he could not consistently stay in touch with his own thoughts, occasionally covering his confusion by parroting the statements of others (or things he had formerly thought) as if they were his current associations.

Needless to say, these brief confusional states were highly disturbing to the patient; and his delinquency, negativism, argumentativeness, and provocative behavior were unconsciously designed to protect him from regressing into them. If I temporarily succeeded in overcoming all such obstacles and a brief period of untroubled collaboration ensued, he was generally overtaken by panicky paranoid fantasies about me. Such fantasies probably served to rationalize his sense of impending loss of self-cohesion in terms of an external threat from my direction. Nor did I ever succeed in altering this vicious circle through my attempts to put the sequence into words, for his capacity to grasp the intended meaning of my explanatory efforts would also be lost at crucial junctures. In this archaic maternal transference, he was unable to learn from me, but felt utterly bewildered without external assistance. He eventually extricated himself from our therapeutic impasse by withdrawing in an angry huff.

This material suggests that delinquent enactments in the analytic setting are just as likely to signify the analysand's inability to tolerate a symbiotic bond as the analysand's propensity to develop extra-analytic transference attachments of an archaic nature. It further shows that, in these primitive syndromes, we are usually confronted with a sea of troubles, including the thought disorders and threats of adaptive disorganization I previously designated as the practical boundaries of the scope of psychoanalysis as therapy.

Am I conceding, after all, that the traditional policy of viewing delinquent enactments as contraindications for psychoanalytic treatment continues to be justified?[2] It is certainly clear that we can only undertake analyses with such patients if we are prepared to tolerate complications and disappointments of the kind I have described in this chapter. Nonetheless, I do not believe that we should follow Shakespeare's injunction to leave these troublesome people to Heaven. In an encouraging number of cases, the kinds of problems that defeated my efforts in the foregoing examples proved to be analytically manageable through the special techniques I have advocated in my recent work (Gedo, 1979, 1981a, 1981b). Here, I wish to consider some of the technical lessons to be derived from the case material I have already presented.

First, I must emphasize that from an adaptive viewpoint, these treatments were extremely beneficial for all three patients. Their interrupted analyses failed to resolve their archaic needs to live in a symbiotic union, but they did succeed in bringing these needs to the patients' attention so that they could rearrange their lives to compensate better for these personality deficits. I suspect that these outcomes were similar to those which Kohut (1977) claimed as the expectable results obtained through *his* methods with patients suffering from "narcissistic personality disturbances"; in his view—which

---

[2]This policy is aptly encapsulated in an anecdote concerning Sigmund Freud's response to the potential referral of a patient with perverse and delinquent propensities. He wrote one of his students: "[A.] will always strive to mislead the analyst, to trick him and push him aside . . . nothing would be gained by having him come into treatment with me or anyone else . . . In the most unfavorable cases one ships such people . . . across the ocean, with some money, let's say to South America, and lets them there seek and find their destiny" (Weiss, 1970, pp. 27–28).

The therapist's expectable response to the task of undertaking a psychoanalysis with a person organized in archaic modes could not be articulated more clearly or forthrightly. Of course, Freud's statement must be understood in its historical context as well. It was written in 1920 as a concession to the powerlessness of psychological methods when confronted with the effects of the repetition compulsion, as opposed to the efficacy of such methods in the treatment of transference neuroses, that is, conditions under the sway of the pleasure principle.

I do not share—the acquisition of "compensatory structures" signals the readiness to terminate such analyses.

In my sample, a variety of dangerous behaviors (such as the woman patient's bulimia and forced vomiting and her incitement of strange men to sadomasochistic enactments; the fraudulent character's resort to dangerous driving, financial extravagance, and alcohol abuse; the third patient's actionable professional malfeasances) was replaced by the frankly symbiotic transference bonds established in the analytic setting. I have no information about the subsequent fate of two of these individuals, but I believe that all three learned enough in the course of our work to enable them to seek further assistance should they fail to extract the necessary symbiotic sustenance from their human milieu.[3]

Second, I should call attention to the extraordinary importance of the analyst's continuous monitoring of his own affectivity in response to the *actualities* of the patient's enactments in these cases. I suspect that my inability to overcome the technical difficulties in these specific instances may have been related to insufficient appreciation of the true extent of my aversion for the conduct of these individuals at the climactic phase of each of the analyses. I do not mean that my disapproval of certain aspects of their behavior was unknown to me (or to them!), but only that I was still surprised in all three instances by the *relief* I experienced when these clinical responsibilities came to an end.

I had not allowed myself to be drawn into malfeasances of my own, to be sure, but it was still difficult to avoid feeling like an accessory to many of the patients' delinquencies. Thus, the woman patient consciously rejoiced in the thought of wasting her siblings' inheritance by staying in analysis indefinitely (at the highest fee she could encourage me to charge!) by refusing to adhere to any of the ground rules of Freud's procedure. This was not simply a fantasy: weeks and months would go by that could only be characterized as

[3]I do have follow-up information about one patient, the man who left analysis at the insistence of his mistress. More than a year later, he requested my assistance in obtaining optimal psychoanalytic care for one of his children. He expressed gratitude for the satisfactory results of our collaboration. After terminating treatment, he succeeded in concluding an equitable divorce, resumed relations with his children without involving his mistress in this painful enterprise, and brought his other affairs into reasonable order. He was making excellent professional progress, and even life with his mistress had become more peaceful. He emphasized that he was trying hard to live up to the ideals he had begun to profess in the analysis, however difficult he found it to adhere to them all the time. We agreed that he could resume work with me if he ran into major problems in this effort.

the enactment in the analysis of this scheme of malice and destructiveness—and my failure to put a stop to this "crime" was always construed by the patient as complicity in her designs, motivated by my wish for financial gain. The fraudulent man's virtual abandonment of his brood of young children—while he externalized responsibility for all moral judgments onto me in the grandmother transference—also put me in a position I found extremely distasteful. (My reactions were fortified by accusatory letters from the children's mother, calling on me to do something about the outrage!) Perhaps in an effort to curb my disapproval, I probably adhered too scrupulously to a position rationalized as one of analytic neutrality with respect to these enactments, thereby leaving others to fill the patients' symbiotic needs. I suspect this circumstance may have formed the main reason behind my lack of therapeutic leverage when the patients' other symbiotic partners went into opposition about the analyses.

In contrast, I may have swung too far in the opposite direction vis-à-vis the third patient's abuse of his naive and somewhat pathetic spouse. Specifically, I ended his previously interminable obsessions about the desirability of dissolving their failed marriage by stressing that his sole remaining motive for maintaining the status quo was an angry wish to exploit and punish her. Although the patient thereupon released his victim (and thus relieved me of the potential burden of sharing in the responsibility for her torture) without disputing my interpretation, he was probably justified in his later reproaches that I had been excessively committed to one particular mode of resolving his conflict—the one that presented no conflict for me! In other words, the wish to abuse his wife may not have been the *only* motive left for staying with her; it was merely the motive I knew about. In retrospect, I should have explored other possibilities: perhaps the availability of a masochistic partner was a prerequisite for maintaining the therapeutic relationship without unmanageable anxiety about loss of his sense of autonomy.

The technical problems that defeated me in these specific analytic efforts may not remain unmanageable in the future if they can serve as object lessons to expand our therapeutic armamentarium. They may help us to stay on the razor's edge that separates the Scylla of leaving regressed patients to wallow in their perplexity from the Charybdis of intruding on their autonomy in decision making. We must be guided by the realization that in these cases the delinquent behaviors represent a primitive channel of communication, the dramatic enactment of crucial archaic transactions for which these patients usually have no other vocabulary. The implications of this conclusion for various aspects of therapeutic communication cannot be considered here. Let me observe, however, that as a consequence of increased clinical experience with acting-out patients who carry out these activities within the treatment setting—patients who have therefore also been referred to as "acting in"—the analyst's attitude toward the basic rule of free association has had to undergo a gradual shift. We no longer expect all our analysands to be able to express their thoughts exclusively through verbal language, and we have more or less abandoned the view that departures from the verbal interaction we command are simply resistances to be overcome. There is much to be learned from these primitive enactments, if only we can successfully decode their meanings in a reliable manner (cf. Segal & Britton, 1981).

In recent years, a consensus has been developing about the significance of the analyst's own affective responses within the analytic transaction as one of the relevant guides to these meanings (see Gedo, 1981b). Traditionally, these reactions on the part of the analyst have been classified under the rubric of "countertransference" (Tower, 1956). The evidential value of continuously monitoring the countertransference, however, has largely removed the onus that was originally attached to this term (see Gardner, 1983). If we have reason to believe that, other things being equal, our ordinary therapeutic stance is benevolently neutral, then subjective propensities to depart from this stance may be pregnant with clinical meaning. When we find ourselves reacting to an analysand as if he or she were a scoundrel who should be exiled to the Amazon, it is probably safe to conclude that this primitive fantasy points to our perception of an archaic transference that involves attitudes of ruthlessness and unconditional entitlement.

Needless to say, as the targets of such impossible expectations, analysts are quite likely to respond in idiosyncratic ways, that is, with countertransference attitudes in the narrower, pejorative sense of that term. The potential variety of such reactions precludes extensive discussion here, but we may briefly consider two patterns I have frequently encountered in case discussions and in the course of my own clinical work. The more commonplace of these inappropriate responses is some type of refusal to acknowledge the reality or, still more commonly, the significance of an analysand's delinquent behavior, generally by invoking a reductionist formulation of the behavior in terms of putative structural conflicts. A somewhat less frequent but more interesting pattern is that of correctly perceiving the analysand's irresponsible enactments, but regarding their perpetrator as a fragile and pitiful being in need of "empathic" support.[4] Both patterns of countertransference proceed from the ana-

---

[4]I encountered an example of the defensive disavowal of an analysand's fraudulent manipulations in the course of supervising the work of a woman colleague whose initial response to her aggressive male patient was fury about his ability to bully her into starting treatment in accord with his preferred conditions. As soon as the analyst had mastered the explicit fantasy of having been raped by her patient, she began to minimize the mounting evidence that his conditions for the analysis included a fee much lower than he could afford; he had concealed his actual resources at the time they had discussed these matters. Instead of addressing herself to this issue with consistency, as a matter *actually* to be remedied, the analyst insisted on attempting to decipher it as if it were a neurotic symptom. This sadomasochistic impasse was eventually brought to its natural conclusion when the patient casually left town, allegedly to pursue a favorable career opportunity. Even then, the analyst denied that this confidence man had ever hurt anyone, presumably because her own pain did not find a place in her emotional accounts. He came, he saw, he conquered, and he departed for the Amazon! To put the matter differently, the analyst's failure to own up to her value judgments about the patient's behavior did not constitute empathic acceptance of him; on the contrary, her silence only led him into anxiety and confusion.

I can also draw on my supervisory experience to illustrate the second pattern I have chosen to discuss. The patient in question seemed pitiful indeed, a woman past her prime who neglected to inform those who screened her application to the low-fee clinic about her excessive drinking or the major congenital anomaly that deformed her thorax. I can briefly sum up her "acting in" with her female analyst in terms of an erratic refusal to take seriously the agreement to communicate her experience in the treatment setting. The analyst was keenly aware of the manipulative intentions behind these grim games of hide-and-seek, and she tried earnestly to maintain an analytic attitude in what seemed to be a most discouraging clinical dilemma. In the course of several years, it became more and more apparent that a policy of empathic concern and tolerance for the patient's limitations would not suffice to overcome a therapeutic stalemate.

I had, from the beginning, advocated a focus on the predictably dire consequences of the patient's insensate bouts of irresponsibility, but the analyst found herself unable to issue these warnings with firmness or conviction. Although she realized that she was dealing with a trickster, she seemed to be afraid of the disruptive potential of putting a stop to the enactments—and even of labeling them with the designations they are generally given in the adult world.

In this instance, the impasse was broken after the analyst convinced herself that a change of tack was imperative. She was able to modify her approach, I believe, because she came to realize that she had projected an aspect of her own childhood self onto the patient. One of the more painful of her early experiences had involved depreciating comparisons of her physical appearance with that of a sibling. But the analyst had erred in assuming that her patient's primary problem involved self-esteem; the latter did not even experience humiliation when she was challenged about her misbehavior. The presenting psychopathology, it turned out, was derived from a more archaic phase of development; this patient was lost in a haze of depersonalization and reacted to any valid statement about herself with the shock of recognition and relief. It followed, then, that the analyst's expression of realistic concern about the disruptive consequences of her irresponsibility about her own treatment reverberated with her mother's efforts in later childhood to make contact despite the patient's aloofness and withdrawal; it did not resonate with the mother's initial disappointment with her defective child. This analysis, it should be noted, was carried to a successful termination.

lyst's failure to acknowledge the need to make value judgments about patients' delinquent behaviors both in and out of the analytic setting.

Far from being fragile beings in danger of disintegration is insufficiently appreciated, many patients organized in archaic modes tend to be tough, resilient, and quite used to hearing unfavorable judgments about their behavior. It is true that they are also likely to be obnoxious and spiteful when they are frustrated, but, in my clinical experience, they seldom if ever experience the truth about themselves as a shattering blow. Kohut (1971) has rightly called attention to the danger of bearing false witness to our patients by depreciating them, and his demonstration of the specific pathogenic effects of overt and covert depreciation in childhood is one of his important clinical contributions. It does not follow from these facts, however, that patients need the corrective experience of being appreciated by their analysts—as some of the more cavalier "self psychologists" would have us believe (cf. Goldberg, 1978). On the contrary, they respond with the same anxiety and confusion to fatuous overestimation that they experience when their actual worth is denied or overlooked.

The *content* of archaic enactments can generally be interpreted in the same way that we deal with structured unconscious fantasies that are communicated verbally. Quite often, these enactments turn out to have perverse sexual connotations, generally connected with the oedipal phase of development. Although the interpretation of the varied meanings of such material is one of the crucial tasks of these analyses, I believe that insight into these meanings will be maximized if the analyst postpones interpretation until these issues emerge in the context of the transference.

In my experience with archaic personalities, it has not been terribly useful to stress the defensive displacement that leads to acting out, instead of reliving, within the analytic situation. I have found it much more productive to delay interpretation of the unconscious meanings of the enactments on behalf of consideration of the form in which these messages are encoded. To be sure, the *liaisons dangereuses* of these patients are generally replete with sadomasochistic and homosexual implications. Nonetheless, the most urgent technical task in such analyses is inquiry into the meaning of the patients' insensate flirtation with danger, not enlightenment as to the obvious implications of such matters as bisexuality, etc. When, as a result of a consistent policy of challenging their disregard of the serious risks incurred through their enactments, these patients come to grips with their magical expectations that analysts can repair or undo whatever damage they might cause, they then begin—often, so it seems, for the first time—to develop conflicts about their impulses. Frequently, such conflicts are first manifested in growing fears that they will be dismissed from treatment if they fail to heed the voice of reason. As usual, Freud had it right: the voice of the intellect does ultimately gain a hearing—provided it is backed by credible sanctions!

Much later in the analysis, the patient's specific oedipal configuration, inevitably impregnated with an archaic sense of entitlement and grandiose illusions of sexual adequacy, usually emerges within the transference. The crux of the therapeutic task at this juncture goes beyond the interpretation of impulses and/or defenses, which often practically speak for themselves. It consists, instead, of lengthy efforts to eliminate the residues of childhood illusions. In the case of the young woman I have discussed in this chapter, for example, the illusory beliefs turned out to include convictions that her parents were literally immortal and that her own pregnancy fantasies had a reality basis through parthenogenesis or immaculate conception.

Let me at this point try to draw the threads of my argument together. Faced with the daunting task of dealing with those phenomena of the repetition compulsion that create irresponsible actions on the part of analysands within the analytic situation, analysts may be tempted to master their own sense of helplessness by responding to these contingencies in a manner that disavows their actual significance as primitive communications. Among the various avenues of denial, two are of special importance: (1) the tactic of regarding the patient's delinquency as a neurotic compromise formation, and (2) that of misidentifying the patient as unable to face the truth about these transactions without being severely traumatized. Yet, the usual response of persons organized in archaic modes to the description of their disruptive activities and to accurate predictions of their consequences, preferably conveyed with appropriate gravity and urgency, is one of gratitude, relief, and increased commitment to the task of self-inquiry.

We see, then, that the management of delinquent enactments clearly depends on the capacity of individual patients to accept the values inherent in psychoanalysis. If analysis is to succeed, patients must, sooner or later, espouse truthfulness, probity, reliability, and fairness to others. In my clinical illustrations, I have tried to demonstrate concretely how values and value judgments enter into the analytic enterprise at various levels. I have argued (1) that the analyst's status as a valuing creature is central to the analytic process with delinquent patients, insofar as the analyst's ability and willingness to communicate his own value judgments in the course of the therapeutic work are essential to his indispensable role as provider of optimal disillusionment; (2) that the concordance between the patient's values and the values intrinsic to psychoanalysis is central to considerations of analyzability; and (3) that the values of a particular analyst are central to the range of patients he or she can effectively attempt to analyze.

REFERENCES

Aichhorn, A. (1925). *Wayward Youth.* New York: Viking, 1963.

Gardner, R. (1983). *Self Inquiry.* Boston: Atlantic-Little Brown.

Gedo, J. (1975). Forms of idealization in the analytic transference. *J. Amer. Psychoanal. Assn.,* 23:485–505.

_____ (1979). *Beyond Interpretation: Toward A Revised Theory for Psychoanalysis.* New York: International Universities Press.

_____ (1981a). Measure for measure: A response. *Psychoanal. Inq.,* 1:289–316.

_____ (1981b). *Advances in Clinical Psychoanalysis.* New York: International Universities Press.

_____ (1984). *Psychoanalysis and Its Discontents.* New York: Guilford.

_____ & Goldberg, A. (1973). *Models of the Mind: A Psychoanalytic Theory.* Chicago: University of Chicago Press.

Goldberg, A., ed. (1978). *The Psychology of the Self: A Casebook.* New York: International Universities Press.

Kohut, H. (1971). *The Analysis of the Self.* New York: International Universities Press.

_____ (1977). *The Restoration of the Self.* New York: International Universities Press.

Segal, H., & Britton, R. (1981). Interpretation and primitive psychic processes: A Kleinian View. *Psychoanal. Inq.,* 1:267–277.

Tower, L. (1956). Countertransference. *J. Amer. Psychoanal. Assn.,* 4:224–265.

Weiss, E. (1970). *Sigmund Freud as a Consultant.* New York: Intercontinental Medical Book Corporation.

CHAPTER FOUR

Countertransference, Transference Regression, and the Incapacity to Depend*

Otto F. Kernberg

DIMENSIONS OF COUNTERTRANSFERENCE

The relationship between countertransference and the psychoanalyst's personality may be considered according to at least three conceptual dimensions. The first is what I would call a spatial, or "field," dimension and has to do with what actually is included under the term *countertransference.* I think of this field as a series of concentric circles, the inner ones representing the narrow concepts of countertransference, the outer ones representing the broader concepts. The temporal dimension differentiates acute from long-term "permanent" countertransference reactions. A third dimension is represented by the severity of the patient's illness.

The Countertransference "Field"

Countertransference, narrowly defined as is it is within ego psychology, is the analyst's unconscious reaction to the patient (Little, 1951; Reich, 1951). One may restrict the term further to the analyst's unconscious reaction to the patient's transference (Kernberg, 1975). This concept is in line with the original meaning of *countertransference* in psychoanalytic literature and adequately allows for "blind spots" in understanding the patient's material derived from the analyst's unresolved neurotic conflicts.

A second, broader circle encompassing the first one extends the concept to the analyst's total conscious and unconscious reactions to the patient. This concept includes the analyst's appropriate emotional responses to the patient's transferences and to the reality of the patient's life and the emotional effects on the treatment situation

*This chapter originally appeared in Kernberg, Otto F., *Severe Personality Disorders.* Copyright 1984 by Yale University Press. Reprinted by permission.

determined by the analyst's own reality as it may become affected by the patient. The justification for this broader concept of countertransference derives from the effects on the treatment of the deeply regressive transferences of borderline patients, the acting out that characterizes severe character pathology in general, and the unconscious (and conscious) destructiveness of some narcissistic borderline and paranoid patients, which may threaten not only the treatment but the patient's—and even the analyst's—life.

A still broader circle includes, in addition to the two just mentioned, the habitual specific reaction of any particular analyst to various types of patients, a reaction that includes countertransference dispositions and manifestations as defined and the analyst's general personality traits. Certain personality traits may become activated in certain treatment situations,with both defensive and adaptive functions in response to transference onslaughts.

Much apparent controversy regarding the management of countertransference derives from the different ways in which countertransference has been defined. A comprehensive definition that includes the entire spatial field of countertransference phenomena while still clearly differentiating the components of this field may resolve the problem.

The Temporal Dimension

Three types of countertransference reactions can be distinguished on the basis of time. First are acute or short-lived reactions, which, according to how countertransference is defined, may be determined solely by the patient's transference or by the total patient/analyst interaction.

Next are long-term countertransference distortions: subtle, gradual, and insidiously expanding distortions of the analyst's attitude toward the patient over an extended period of time. As Tower (1956) has pointed out, these are often recognized only retrospectively. They usually occur in working with a particular transference pattern, especially in the early stages of treatment, when resistance intensifies that pattern. The resolution of that transference pattern by interpretation may illuminate the chronic countertransference distortion, which now disappears, together with the shift in the transference. The analyst can alert himself to such long-term countertransference reactions by comparing the "special" reaction a given patient evokes in him with his reactions to other patients.

Finally, a still more extended countertransference reaction is the "permanent countertransference" described by Reich (1951), which she believes (and I agree) reflects the analyst's character pathology. It hardly needs to be said that the analyst's personality plays a role in any analysis. His position of technical neutrality does not mean that the patient cannot distinguish and recognize many aspects of the analyst's actual appearance, behavior, attitudes, and affective reactions. In fact, one might say that patients hang the fabric of their transference onto the protuberances of the analyst's personality.

Whereas these real aspects of the analyst lend themselves to rationalization of transference developments, they do not deny the origin in the past of the patient's transference, and they do not necessarily correspond to the analyst's character pathology. Patients rapidly become expert in detecting the analyst's personality characteristics, and transference reactions often first emerge in this context. But to conclude that all transference reactions are at bottom, at least in part, unconscious or conscious reactions to the reality of the analyst is to misunderstand the nature of the transference. The transference is the inappropriate aspect of the patient's reaction to the analyst. The analysis of the transference may begin by the analyst's "leaving open" the reality of the patient's observations and exploring why particular observations are important at any particular time.

If the analyst is aware of realistic features of his personality and is able to accept them without narcissistic defensiveness or denial, his emotional attitude will permit him to convey to the patient: "So, if you are responding to something in me, how do we understand the intensity of your reaction?" But the analyst's character pathology may be such that the patient's transference reaction to him results in the erosion of technical neutrality. When the analyst is incapable of discriminating between the patient's realistic and unrealistic perceptions of him, countertransference is operating.

Countertransference and the Severity of the Patient's Pathology

I have described in earlier work (1975) a continuum of countertransference reactions, ranging from responses to the typical analytic patient, who establishes a well-differentiated transference neurosis, to reactions to a psychotic patient with psychotic transference. Countertransference reactions to the borderline conditions and pathological narcissism occupy an intermediate position on this continuum. The more regressed the patient, the more the analyst is forced to reactivate regressive features in himself in order to keep in touch with the patient. This brings the total personality of the analyst into the foreground. The more regressed the patient, the more his characteristic pathogenic conflicts are infiltrated by primitive aggression, expressed in the transference as direct or indirect attacks on the analyst. Such attacks activate an emotional response in the analyst reflecting, as Winnicott (1949) pointed out, his reaction not only to the transference but also to the total patient/analyst relation. Under such circumstances, the broader concept of countertransference becomes operational. The more regressed the patient, the more global will be the analyst's emotional reactions.

The analyst's global reactions, then, include not only countertransference dispositions in a restricted sense but also what Racker (1957) calls "complementary identifications" with the patient's activated and projected object representations. The analyst's understanding of the unconsciously activated internalized object relations in the transference is thus enriched. In contrast to Racker, however, I would stress that in a position of complementary countertransference, the analyst may identify not only with the patient's "internal objects" but with his projected self representations as well, while the patient enacts his identifications with an internalized object representation.

The activation in the psychoanalytic situation of a primitive internalized object relation within which patient and analyst maintain their reciprocity but repeatedly exchange their roles (identifying themselves alternately with self and object representations) has fundamental diagnostic and therapeutic functions. To utilize these developments therapeutically, the analyst must maintain strict analytic boundaries to control acting out and preserve his internal freedom for fantasizing ("reverie") in order to diagnose the projected aspects of the patient's object relations. The analyst must also continually separate out such projected material from his own countertransference dispositions (in a restricted sense) and must transform his introspection into transference interpretations that preserve an atemporal quality until confirmatory material permits genetic placing. In other words, the analyst's tolerance for distortions of his intrapsychic experience under the impact of transference regression in the patient may become empathy with what the patient cannot tolerate within himself. The empathy may eventually generate crucial knowledge for transference interpretations.

Grinberg (1979) has proposed differentiating the analyst's complementary countertransference, derived from the activation in him of past internal object relations under the influence of the patient's transference, from "projective counteridentification," when such activation stems almost entirely from the patient's transference. This proposed distinction enriches the analysis of countertransference reactions. In practice there is always a complementary relationship between the internal world of the patient and that of the analyst activated in countertransference developments.

As the severity of the patient's illness increases, his expression of emotional reality takes nonverbal forms, including behavioral communications that may include subtle or crude efforts to exert control over the analyst. These efforts may be so extreme as to threaten the boundaries of the psychoanalytic situation (a phenomenon examined further in the next section). Such developments, however, should not lead to the frequent mistake of expanding the concept of countertransference to include all the problems the analyst has in handling difficult patients. Errors owing to lack of experience or knowledge are just that, not countertransference.

COUNTERTRANSFERENCE AND TRANSFERENCE REGRESSION

In view of the dimensions along which countertransference can be classified and their connections with the analyst's personality, I think there is an advantage in maintaining a comprehensive concept of countertransference. To link the analyst's unconscious reaction to the transference with his total emotional reaction to the patient makes it possible to diagnose how the patient's transference leads to distortions in the psychoanalytic situation and also to evaluate the analyst's realistic emotional reactions and his countertransference in a more restricted sense.

Under ordinary circumstances the analyst's character pathology or personality restrictions should have little or no effect. But with severely pathological patients whose intense primitive aggression infiltrates the transference, the analyst's personality will be subjected to countertransference reactions in a broad sense, which may result in activating his pathological character traits. Especially when treatment is stalemated and in the presence of severe negative therapeutic reactions, the analyst's broader emotional reactions may depend on his personality characteristics.

Perhaps the most vulnerable aspect of the therapist's personality under such extreme conditions is his creativity as a psychoanalyst. By creativity I mean the capacity to transform the patient's material imaginatively into a comprehensive dynamic formulation or into an organizing central fantasy or into a particular experience that vividly and concretely illuminates the entire material in new ways. Psychoanalytic creativity is intimately related to concern for the patient and to maintaining an awareness of the patient's positive qualities in the face of his unremitting aggression. One of the sources of this creativity is the analyst's ability to sublimate his aggression via the "penetrating," clarifying aspects of analytic technique. Concern, as Winnicott (1963) has pointed out, has deep roots in the wish to undo aggression by providing love to a significant object. Obviously, the analyst's creativity also expresses the sublimatory aspects of his libidinal investment in the patient. It is only natural for the patient's aggression to be directed precisely at this creativity. The narcissistic patient in particular focuses his envy on this analytic creativity, the source of what he is receiving from the analyst.

When the analyst is faced with the patient's effort to denigrate, neutralize, and generally destroy his technical equipment, self-respect, and personal security, his confidence in his ability to counteract these tendencies by tolerance, understanding, and creative interpretive work—without denying the severity of the aggression in the transference—permits him to continue working with the patient and thus to continue to be a good object for the patient in spite of the aggression directed toward him.

But concern for the patient, especially at times of violent acting out of the negative transference, also renders the analyst more vulnerable. His attempt to keep in touch with a patient's "good self" while being berated for his comments and silences and to maintain not only respect for the patient but an awareness of the loving and lovable aspects of his personality requires that he be emotionally open to the patient. This, of course, exposes the analyst even further to the onslaught of the patient's aggression. The defensive withdrawal from attack, the sharpened affirmation of social boundaries that protect us from sadistic assaults under ordinary social circumstances, is deliberately reduced in the analytic situation, a circumstance that may tempt the patient to extreme unreasonableness and demandingness.

By the same token, the threat of unbearable guilt forces the patient to resort increasingly to primitive projective mechanisms to justify his aggression; and primitive projection, particularly projective identification, is a powerful interpersonal weapon that "unloads" aggression onto the analyst. The patient may provoke the analyst into counteraggression and then, triumphantly, utilize this development as a rationalization of his own aggression. In treating borderline patients or patients with severe character pathology, there are times when paranoid fantasies regarding these patients may invade the analyst's free time in almost uncanny ways, illustrating the reversal of persecutory fantasies in the transference. Finally, because the analyst stands for the patient's weak, frail, submerged good self, the patient may project his good or idealized self representations onto the analyst, almost "for safekeeping," and yet need to attack them under the effects of aggression and envy, originally self-directed. Racker (1968) has stressed the high risk, in such circumstances, that the patient will successfully reinforce whatever masochistic traits the analyst may still retain.

In the long run, patients with severe chronic regression and primitive aggression prevalent in the transference, or patients with severe negative therapeutic reactions reflected in their consistent "spoiling" of the analyst's work and his positive disposition toward them, necessarily activate the analyst's normal narcissistic defenses, geared to protect his creativity and self-esteem. This may now complicate his acute countertransference reactions. By the same token, the analyst's ability to sublimate, which protects and preserves his creativity and self-esteem in the face of aggression, may become crucial in delimiting, localizing, and keeping within reasonable bounds whatever countertransference reactions he develops.

COUNTERTRANSFERENCE AND THE INCAPACITY TO DEPEND ON THE ANALYST

Oddly enough, the clinical situations just described can be produced when there is minimal transference regression and almost total absence of manifest aggression in the transference. I am thinking of certain patients who have a chronic incapacity to depend upon the analyst. These patients present subtle, pervasive, and highly effective transference resistances against being dependent on the analyst and against the related regression in the transference in general.

Clinical Characteristics

On the surface, these patients convey the impression that they are incapable of establishing a transference relationship; they seem to be presenting a "resistance against the transference." However, this resistance is part of a complex transference pattern that reflects a particular subtype of narcissistic character pathology. Because the term *dependence* is vague and ambiguous, this pattern requires further clarification.

I am not referring to patients who present actue or chronic resistance against "depending" on the analyst because they are afraid to submit to a feared parental image or are afraid of heterosexual or homosexual longings or have reaction formations against passive oral needs and against intense ambivalence from many sources. I am referring, rather, to patients who, from the beginning of treatment, establish a remarkably stable relation to the analyst characterized by difficulty in really talking *to* him about *themselves.* They talk to the analyst in order to influence him or talk to themselves about themselves, leaving the analyst with the distinct feeling that he has been eliminated from their awareness.

These patients have great difficulty in listening to the analyst as a stimulus for further self-exploration. They have a constant, unwavering, automatic way of listening as if they were searching for hidden meanings, for the analyst's intentions, for the "mechanisms" operating in his mind, his theories and technique. They cannot permit themselves to be surprised by what emerges in their own minds in response to his comments. They conceive of psychoanalysis as a learning process in which knowledge comes from the analyst, to be carefully screened and evaluated by them and then consciously assimilated or rejected.

These patients cannot conceive of any knowledge about themselves that may emerge from their unconscious, surprising them, and that requires truly collaborative work with the analyst in order to be understood and integrated. They usually have great difficulties in experiencing sadness, depression, and guilt, which would reflect deeper concerns for their internal world; they cannot conceive unconsciously of the mutuality of a good mother/child relation and cannot, in an unconscious sense, "care" for themselves. They dramatically illustrate the narcissistic incapacity to love oneself and to trust one's internal world.

Although what I am describing is a typical transference configuration of narcissistic personalities, not all narcissistic personalities present these characteristics. This particular configuration is not linked to the severity of narcissistic pathology, which is generally expressed in extreme pathology of object relations, antisocial features, and paranoid transference regressions (including paranoid micropsychotic episodes). Hence, one may find the incapacity to depend in narcissistic patients with both favorable and very unfavorable prognoses for treatment. Also, although this transference configuration, once detected, is fairly similar from case to case, the underlying conflicts and repressed transference dispositions vary a great deal. For example, in the course of resolving this transference resistance, one may find depressive reactions related to unconscious guilt, severe paranoid trends reflecting condensed oedipal/preoedipal conflicts, or homosexual conflicts. Some patients present a general incapacity to fully experience emotions and to verbalize them in relation to very early traumatic circumstances. McDougall's (1979) description of countertransference developments under such circumstances corresponds to my own experience.

Impact on the Analyst

The transference picture I am describing has a profound effect on the analyst's countertransference and seriously challenges his creativity.

First of all, insofar as these patients never really form a deep emotional relation to the analyst, they convey the impression that no transference is developing. Particularly for the inexperienced analyst or candidate, patients who can associate freely, who appear to have the freedom to submerge themselves into primitive fantasy, childhood memories, and emotional expression, and yet who develop no transference may be puzzling and disquieting. The situation is very different from that created by the obsessive patient, whose intellectualization and rationalization, isolation, reaction formation, and other high-level defenses convey a difficulty in experiencing emotions although the patient is deeply involved in the transference.

Second, these narcissistic patients' constant scrutiny of the analyst's interpretations, their unrelenting "interpretive" scanning of all his comments, may have a paralyzing effect on the analyst's communications over an extended period of time. This is a more effective effort at control than the usual narcissistic attempt to keep the analyst's interpretations within a certain range, to make sure that he does not say anything unexpected (which would evoke the patient's envy) or anything too easily devalued (which would trigger severe disappointment reactions). In contrast to these "range restrictions" in what the patient can accept from the analyst, the patients under review receive everything in ways that tend to neutralize or eliminate the direct emotional impact of the interpretation. They leave the analyst with the impression that he has been talking to himself or that his communications, once expressed, have evaporated before reaching the patient.

In addition, the consistent screening of the analyst inevitably results in the patients' careful mapping of his "real" features, his peculiarities and idiosyncrasies. The analyst may have the uneasy feeling of being exposed to a somewhat benign, perhaps slightly ironical, amused, or obviously suspicious scrutiny, a more pervasive attempt at control than occurs in any other analytic relation.

Furthermore, these patients "learn" the analyst's language, his theory, his preferred expressions so completely that they can combine descriptions with interpretive considerations so skillfully "spliced" that the analyst can no longer differentiate emotion from intellectualization or regressive fantasy from psychoanalytic theories. In fact, the patient himself cannot differentiate what is authentic, what comes from him, and what he has learned from the analyst. It is all assimilated into a psychological structure that prevents either the patient or the analyst from learning about the unconscious aspects of the patient's pathology. In the end, the patient himself is the victim of his incapacity to depend on the analyst.

The effect of these developments on the analyst may be a loss of spontaneity. Rather than work with evenly suspended attention, he may attempt defensively to control his own communications. The apparent lack of transference involvement and development over a long period of time may induce in the analyst a discouraging sense that nothing is really happening, without his being able to pinpoint where the difficulty lies. He may finally come to feel a sense of paralysis and futility. He may even end up in collusion with the patient, splitting off session from session in a repetitive pattern of giving up and starting all over again.

Therapeutic Approach

It is not very difficult to diagnose a stalemate stemming from a chronic defense against dependence. To resolve it, however, taxes the limits of the analyst's capacity to work with countertransference reactions along the entire spectrum of the dimensions outlined earlier, especially his capacity to maintain his creativity. In particular, this stalemate taxes the analayst's evocative fantasy, his capacity to use his emotional knowledge about how a patient and an analyst relate to each other under ordinary circumstances. I refer to what Loewald (1960) described as the underlying relationship between patient and analyst in the psychoanalytic situation: One person dares to depend on another, and the other in turn accepts that dependence while respecting the first person's autonomy.

It is helpful for the analyst to maintain in fantasy a clear image of how a "normal" analysand might respond to his interventions, exploring his own reactions while experiencing himself in an open and safe relationship with the analyst. These conditions are present when the patient's observing ego is working in collaboration with the analyst. The analyst's capacity to experience himself both as an analyst and as a patient in a dependent position may create a highly subjective and experiential, yet realistic, frame against which the patient's incapacity to depend can be diagnosed and gradually interpreted.

Careful attention to the patient's reactions to interpretations is the best guide to exploring and resolving this complicated transference resistance. The patient may, in his effort to diagnose "how the analyst did it," impute to the analyst intellectualization and extraneous theories or "countertransference" reactions. This may open the road to clarifying with the patient how difficult it is for him to conceive of the possibility that the analyst has responded spontaneously and is interested in helping the patient improve his self-understanding rather than in manipulating him or brainwashing him with theories. In this context, the analyst may suggest that the patient is depreciating his own fantasy life and capacity for emotional experience, although he seems to be questioning the analyst's capacity for spontaneous introspection. The typical paradoxical reactions of narcissistic personalities who, after feeling helped or understood by the analyst, develop an increased need to deny such help or understanding may also be used to clarify this pattern by facilitating the interpretation of spoiling operations (Rosenfeld, 1964).

At times, the "meaninglessness" or the lack of emotional contact between patient and analyst may be repeating a specific pathogenic relation with parental objects. The hopeless, angry, stubborn patient challenges the analyst to demonstrate the difference between the present analytic encounter and the past. Unconscious envy of the analyst, perceived as independent and secure in his creativity, and the corresponding need to spoil his work complicate that challenge. The difficulty is that the interpretation of this pattern may itself be prematurely and intellectually captured by the patient and woven into his associations and his denial of psychic reality. Here, consistent working through and attentiveness to the defensive use of intellectualized insight may prove helpful.

Quite frequently, the focus on the patient's unconscious identification with a frustrating, sadistic, persecutory object from his past, which makes him distrust both the analyst and his own internal world (at bottom, an aggressive and rejecting maternal introject who denies the patient's dependent needs together with his emotional life in general), may clarify and resolve this pattern in the context of the analysis of the component identifications of the grandiose self. Here, the self-idealization of the patient who denies his need of others is condensed with identification with an aggressor (who has not yet become unmasked as an aggressor toward the patient's normal, infantile, dependent self).

An interesting development in patients who are beginning to work through this type of transference is the tendency, whenever some new understanding has been achieved, to revert to denial of any emotional relation to the analyst. Thus the pattern, which had originally been consistent and permanent, now begins to oscillate, reappearing when the transference relationship deepens. Repeated interpretation of this pattern when the analyst recognizes its reemergence may facilitate working through, although the repetition may often evoke in the patient the complaint that the analyst is continuing to focus on the same issues and is thus denying the patient's progress.

In these patients, the development of severely regressive transference dispositions and intense emotional reactions—even if they are strongly paranoid—indicates movement in comparison with the previously stable transference resistance. The prognosis for patients who never become able even to understand the nature of this incapacity to depend on the analyst is much poorer. To differentiate these two kinds of patients takes time. Intellectual acceptance of the analyst's interpretation of the patient's incapacity to depend on him has to be differentiated from emotional understanding, which eventually is translated into shifts in the transference.

REFERENCES

Grinberg, L. (1979). Projective counteridentification and countertransference. In: *Countertransference,* ed. L. Epstein & A. Feiner. New York: Aronson, pp. 169–192.

Kernberg, O. (1975). Countertransference. In: *Borderline Conditions and Pathological Narcissism.* New York: Jason Aronson, pp. 49–67.

Little, M. C. (1951). Countertransference and the patient's response to it. *Int. J. Psycho-Anal.,* 32:32–40.

Loewald, H. (1960). On the therapeutic action of psychoanalysis. *Internat. J. Psycho-Anal.,* 41:16–33.

McDougall, J. (1979). Primitive communication in the use of countertransference. In: *Countertransference,* ed. L. Epstein & A. Feiner. New York: Aronson, pp. 267–304.

Racker, H. (1957). The meaning and uses of countertransference. *Psychoanal. Quart.,* 26:303–357.

——— (1968). *Transference and Countertransference.* New York: International Universities Press.

Rosenfeld, H. (1964). On the psychopathology of narcissism: a clinical approach. *Internat. J. Psycho-Anal.,* 45:332–337.

Reich, A. (1951). On countertransference. *Psychoanalytic Contributions.* New York: International Universities Press, 1973, pp. 136–154.

Tower, L. E. (1956). Countertransference. *J. Amer. Psychoanal. Assn.,* 4:224–255.

Winnicott, D. W. (1949). Hate in the counter-transference. In: *Collected Papers.* New York: Basic Books, 1958, pp. 194–203.

——— (1963). The development of the capacity for concern. In: *The Maturational Process and the Facilitating Environment.* New York: International Universities Press, 1965, pp. 73–82.

CHAPTER FIVE

Acting Out—Transference and Countertransference: Technical Considerations

Martin H. Stein

Acting out is often discussed as if it were a symptom pathognomonic of the "difficult" patient, or even confined to that vague and subjectively defined category. Although it is true that persistent acting out makes for a very difficult, if not an impossible analysis, it is a phenomenon that occurs in all analyses, sooner or later. While it does constitute a particularly challenging form of resistance, analyzing it can be one of the most productive tasks undertaken by the participants. It places the analyst himself under the greatest strain because it is likely to arouse troublesome countertransference conflicts. But it need not constitute a serious threat to the analysis if the underlying pathology is not too severe and if the analyst can keep his head when confronted with transferential assaults.

We need not, therefore, confine ourselves to a class of "difficult" patients since we do not always agree on the definition of "difficult,"and the term implies the existence of another class that might be described as "easy." It is true that some patients find it easier to accept and use the analytic process; others cannot do so with the same facility. There are some patients whose sessions one anticipates with a higher degree of pleasure than others', but they are not necessarily "easier." Their analyses too sooner or later will present problems all the more difficult because they may not have been anticipated. The resistances are more subtle and clever, the traps better hidden, the acting out more "reasonable." The process, therefore, is challenging, but by no means easy, although the ultimate result is likely to be favorable (Stein, 1981).

Psychoanalysis depends on listening to and interpreting the patient's associations, including his dreams, fantasies, and behavior, yet it can be argued that its central task is the analysis of resistance, namely, the analytic manifestations of intrapsychic conflict and its effects. Although resistances are defined by their function of impeding the analysis, we have understood for a long time that until they are analyzed, no real analysis has taken place.

Resistances are resolved most tellingly, if not exclusively, in the transference. An analysis that goes swimmingly is easy for a while, putting no great strain on the participants; but aside from increased knowledge on the part of the analyst and a deceptive sense of comfort on the part of the patient, nothing much has happened. lt is only when things get really difficult, often downright unpleasant that the analytic process may be said to have begun in earnest. It is now that the analyst must, on the one hand, exert himself to achieve understanding of his patient's struggles and convey that understanding to him, and, on the other, tolerate the patient's discomfort and his own during what may be a long and sometimes agonizing process. Acting out is almost invariably a feature of these crucial phases of the work.

I discuss acting out in this context as a manifestation of the resistance in neurotic patients, not marked by the kind of gross disorganization seen in psychoses, nor in less flagrant forms, in severe narcissistic pathology. Freud (1914) defined it thus: "We may say that the patient *did not remember* anything of what he has forgotten or repressed, but *acts* it out. He reproduces it not as a memory but as an action; *he repeats it,* without, of course, knowing that he is repeating it" p. 150. All individuals are capable of acting out under some circumstances, but some show a particular tendency to do so with relatively little provocation. This tendency may be considered a character trait, manifested by a history of repetitive, complex patterns of behavior, generally precipitated by one or another kind of frustration. These patterns demonstrate certain features that are distinctly at variance with what appear to be the dominant modes of the personality. Acting out is likely to be more prominent in severe neuroses but is by no means confined to them (Stein, 1973).

Some confusion has resulted from the loose usage of the term. The impulsive behavior of delinquents and criminals, some violent, antisocial and self-destructive activity, much sexual promiscuity, the defiant or merely mischievious actions by which patients attempt to provoke their analysts, may or may not represent acting out. Whether or not the term is applicable depends on the degree to which the phenomenon satisfies a number of criteria. The behavior must be patterned and repetitive, ego syntonic at the time it occurs, marked by some limited and transitory impairment of judgment and reality testing; episodes of acting out might be thought of as periodic, repetitive and "stupid" acts performed by intelligent people. Finally, it should be seen ultimately to conform to the pattern of an unconscious, organized fantasy, generally in the form of a narcissistically dominated dramatic performance.

As an attempt to deal with conflict by action rather than thought, acting out is more subject to the pleasure principle than to the demands of reality; it employs to a greater extent the logic of primary rather than secondary-process thought. It constitutes, therefore, a vivid example of ego regression, in several of its aspects: temporal, in that it reenacts the past in a relatively literal fashion; functional, in its employment of primitive defenses, that is, denial and isolation; in its preference for action over thought, accompanied by a suspension of delaying mechanisms. Finally in its demonstration of topographic regression, for it includes subtle or even obvious interference with conscious awareness, which is replaced in part by modes of thought closer to the dream, a feature that may give some clues to understanding its underlying nature.

When during the course of analysis we become aware of a major episode of potentially disruptive behavior, we are at first at a loss to know what it is. We cannot be sure that we are dealing with a true episode of acting out as an expression of the tranference neurosis until we have taken steps to analyze it, to be sure that it is not simply an impulsive, chaotic action, characteristic of impulse disorders or psychoses; or an isolated symptomatic act, a parapraxis, of far less significance; or a piece of experimental behavior, common in adolescence, as described by Blos (1963).

For example, after some years of analysis, a very intelligent young man engaged in a series of ventures that ultimately were revealed to have been episodes of acting out. He changed his occupation to engage in a potentially profitable but highly speculative series of ventures. Using his family's capital and his own, he invested heavily, hoping to turn a quick profit in a field in which he had relatively little practical experience. Convinced that his essential goodness of character and superior intelligence would ensure his receiving the rewards he deserved, he tried to deny what he knew very well—that without hard work and a certain amount of luck, he might face bankruptcy.

He engaged in a series of cliff-hangers, during which his mood oscillated between desperate anxiety and guilt to varying degrees of elation. His worries were easy enough to understand; on more than one occasion he found himself in serious danger of losing all his own and his family's money. His elation was supported by the fragile conviction that all was for the best, that everything would *have* to come out all right. Not only was he being backed by a generous father (who was understandably apprehensive), but he had the advantage of an all-wise analyst, who would surely help him avoid serious trouble by protecting him from the dangers of the business world. He was sufficiently realistic not to expect me to give him any useful advice about business; his confidence was grounded in archaic, magical expectations.

Behind this touching faith in my powers and his wish to make me proud of him, it was not very difficult to infer a powerful desire to destroy me through behavior that would, at the very least, be a reproach to the analysis, and, at worst, a destruction of it and of me too. At the same time, he would dissipate his father's capital and destroy him as well. It became difficult for me to resist the temptation to blurt out, "Don't be a fool, stop taking those crazy risks!" Fortunately, it was possible to analyze the dynamic constellation, which included the fantasy that his father and I were so powerful that we could protect him from any dangers and at the same time protect ourselves from his destructive fantasies, the latter all the more urgent because of the very power he attributed to us. He was in any case getting a good deal of gratification, if not pleasure, out of making us apprehensive about his apparently self-destructive behavior. It took over a year of this before the suspense ended. I am relieved to report that disaster was avoided after all, brilliantly, but by an uncomfortably narrow margin.

As we approached the end of the analysis, he realized more clearly that he had been reassuring himself for years with a fantasy that analysis would allow him to achieve a kind of idyllic existence, completely happy, entirely carefree, with no conflicts and no anxieties, like life in a beautiful garden surrounded by lovely flowers and limitless love. This, in turn, could be traced to a persisting fantasy of a "golden age" of childhood, in which he and his parents lived in perfect concord—they never had, of course—and beyond this, to fantasies of what it must have been like in his mother's womb, in Eden before the Fall. This goal could be achieved by the complete elimination of conflict and of the countless vicissitudes of life—in other words, only by death. Understandably, he was reluctant to accept such a disagreeable conclusion.

Later it was possible to demonstrate the role of highly charged oedipal conflicts, which took on regressive, narcissistic forms in this neurotic man whose personality was not seriously impaired and whose object relations were basically intact. In these barely sensed dream-like fantasies, he had discovered a means of achieving all his infantile goals, innocently and apparently without risk. During latency, his attempts to deal with his intense oedipal conflicts had resulted in the development of a set of tic-like movements, evidently magical gestures intended to kill and at the same time to ward off danger. In adolescence, although usually a prudent youth and certainly an intelligent one, he had indulged in foolhardy adventures, frightening to him and to his parents (so far as they knew about them). These were a bit more than adolescent high jinks, or even the experimental behavior described by Blos. They might have led to disaster, and only just failed to do so; finally they led him to seek treatment.

In analysis, it was not easy for him to accept what all of this meant; to recognize that his wish for freedom from conflict was based on an illusion; to accept that such a goal could never be achieved short of death; and to resign himself to the fact that I was not God, nor even an all-wise guide for the perplexed. At this point he associated me even more closely with his father, for whom he had a sincere love and admiration, accompanied by the most intense competitive hostility. Faced with these developments, he railed at me for making false promises and letting him down; he went into a period of mourning for his father, who had died a short time before; he regretted his vanished youth and the loss of his beautiful dreams of a lovely garden in which he would find a perpetually young and loving mother.

His pronounced tendency to overidealization could not be readily accounted for by a history of parental neglect, nor by evidences of developmental defect. Rather, it was a manifestation of aggressive defense against the most intense oedipal conflicts, including a Cain-Abel fantasy related to his older brother, the structure itself being a corollary of unresolved oedipal wishes. Characterologically, he combined elements of generous son and brother and hostile competitor.

Although at times his acting out was massive and threatening, it could be dealt with by interpretation, without such departures or "parameters" as prohibition, warning, manipulation, or reality testing. As a dramatic manifestation of the transference neurosis, it could be treated, first by pointing out its repetitive, patterned and dramatic structure and its narcissistic preoccupations; second, by interpretation of the transference in terms of the current situation (as emphasized by Greenacre, 1950, 1963, 1968, and Gill, 1979). Only later could the underlying fantasy be described and traced to its historical sources: variations on oedipal themes; the wish for conquest and reunion with his mother; loving and destructive impulses toward his father and brother, including the wish to castrate them, which was accompanied by the fear of suffering the same fate, in the form of financial ruin.

These conclusions were borne out by the analysis of a dream he reported at the height of the crisis: he was visiting a brothel in the company of an older clergyman. The women were ugly, and their genitals resembled seashells and sharp-edged coral. He awoke in a state of great fear. He associated the razor-sharp coral with some of the messier aspects of his business. The clergyman, representative of the Lord, was I, the guide who would, through analysis, give him the courage to visit a brothel and protect him in this dangerous adventure into the genitalia of the unknown woman, the classical mother-prostitute. Success in business was equated with a forbidden sexual conquest, related to his wish to make a "killing." He was, incidentally, potent and happily married. His belief in his own invulnerability and my magical protection represented not so much a narcissistic character disorder, as described by Kohut (1966, 1971, 1977) and by Kernberg (1975), but rather a narcissistic regression in a neurotic, but well-integrated individual.

During crises of acting out, countertransference forces may be extremely powerful. This creates a temptation to be carried away by rescue fantasies, which play a significant role in the personalities of many, if not all analysts, and to share freely the mature wisdom ascribed to us by our patients, so that we find ourselves advising them how to conduct their lives. It is especially at such times that we are obliged to remind ourselves that whatever special wisdom we have is largely confined to our understanding of mental life, of consciousness, defenses, autonomous and other ego functions and the analytic methods available for helping patients to deal with them. They generally know and understand much more about their affairs than we possibly can, and we are qualified to deal only with those interferences that arise out of the neurotic illness.

To restrain ourselves, to avoid what are called, perhaps too easily, "acceptable parameters," requires a high degree of patience and self-control. To listen and try to understand, perhaps for a long period, is not easy when we are tempted to warn, protect, or prohibit. This is especially true as we react to the transference implications of the patient's behavior, the overwhelming need for affection, the urgent sexuality, the anxiety, contempt, defiance—all of which may be represented in the acting out. (See Bird, 1957, 1972; Greenacre, 1950, 1963, 1968; Stein 1973, 1982.) When a patient we are trying to help places himself, apparently quite arbitrarily, in a situation that threatens disaster to his personal life, his career, his finances, and his analysis, we find ourselves inevitably in the grip of very strong feelings. Such behavior looks like sheer ingratitude, and we experience powerful pressures to react accordingly, thus relinquishing our proper function as analysts.

One of the frequent determinants in acting out is the need to test the analyst, to try his nerve, to seduce him into committing technical errors, to fall into a kind of "counter acting out." In order to propel the analyst into active manipulation, some patients will do everything they can to mobilize his guilt and fears of professional failure, calling into action the rescue fantasies that have been under control all along. For the patient, this represents a victory, although a distinctly pyrrhic one, for the analysis is likely to be destroyed. As a consequence, the strain on the analyst is very great, more intense in some respects than it is on the patient, whose suspension of judgment and reality functions allow him to ignore the signal anxiety that should warn him of danger. It is just as well that the analyst has no access to such relief. His capacity to deal with the danger will depend on control of his own anxiety and the mobilization of his skills in evaluating the phenomenon and analyzing it, if it is in fact analyzable.

Thus, rather narcissistically but not without reason, we are inclined to regard acting out as a trap set specifically for us, to provoke and frighten us, to disappoint our expectations, to put us in the wrong no matter what we do. We are reminded of the ordinary behavior of adolescents in relation to their parents, a point deserving special emphasis in view of pervasive tendencies to look for the roots of acting out exclusively in the preverbal phase of childhood. Certainly that is a crucial phase in the development of such tendencies, ranking in importance with the inborn endowment of the individual. But later phases of development, for example, adolescence, also exert a profound influence, often being decisive in whether acting out will lead to clinical and personal disaster or, on the other hand, will constitute an analyzable and clinically useful phenomenon.

It is also not always easy for us in such situations to avoid indulging in righteous indignation and moral superiority. It is tempting to employ our superior wisdom and moral stature, such as it is, to put things right, before we have studied the situation in depth and achieved some understanding and sympathy. At such times, the demands on the analyst for self-control may appear virtually superhuman.

Admittedly, it is all very well to advise patience and understanding while the analysand's actions seem to threaten the fabric of the analysis itself, if not that of his whole life. The quandary may be stated succinctly: the neurotic patient appears to be doing something that may affect him seriously and adversely; we can help him to deal with it, nor merely for the moment, but effectively over the long run, only by analyzing its unconscious sources. The process takes a long time, during which patient and analyst may be placed in a series of apparently untenable positions. How then to defuse the bomb without having it blow up in our faces? Neither impatience nor an attitude of laissez-faire will do.

Although at such points we may, through informed speculation, work out some of the underlying meanings of the patient's behavior, just as we guess some of the unconscious meanings of a manifest dream, we are limited in our capacity to interpret, especially in conveying a useful understanding of the transference implications. If we do, after all, interpret on the basis of informed speculation, we are likely to be met with an openly disbelieving response, which is dismaying, or worse, an acceptance, which is flattering. The latter, sadly, is likely to be an intellectualized and compliant response, leading most often to further and more complex episodes of acting out. About all that can be done in the beginning, therefore, is to make clear the repetitive nature of the actions, to place them as far as possible in an historical context then later to tease out the narcissistic and regressive elements, for example, lapses in reality testing and ordinary common sense. Ultimately, the relation to the transference and to archaic fantasy can be explored. If, in the first place, no repetitive pattern can be ascertained, it is probably best to reconsider whether one is dealing with acting out as a clinical phenomenon and to reevaluate the suitability of the patient for analysis.

It is sometimes possible to make use of a principle elaborated by Lewin (1955) and discussed later by Stein (1965). Freud evolved his theory of dream interpretation originally not only for its own sake, but perhaps even more with the purpose of understanding neurosis. With the advent of ego psychology, not very much attention was paid to the possibilities of using our understanding of dream psychology in this context. But is is possible to conceive of the acting out patient as a dreamer who needs to be awakened from time to time to remind him where he is and what he is doing. Acting out is, of course, not dreaming in any literal sense, for the inhibition of action characteristic of the dream state is not in effect. But the attempts to gratify a complex of archaic wishes, the profound narcissistic regression, the displacements, the predominance of magical thinking, and the transitory suspension of reality testing, all have their analogues in the dream work. Recognizing this may make it easier for the analyst and ultimately the patient to view the phenomenon with more detachment and less exasperation. The risk that the dreamer may walk in his sleep, so to speak, can be better assessed and often alleviated by waking him in a proper fashion, that is, by interpreting. The analogy is worth considering.

We might think of the patient cited earlier as if he were dreaming much of the time. He was in fact a highly imaginative and creatively endowed man, characteristics not unusual in such patients. In his acting out, he entered a highly narcissistic phase, as we all do in our dreams. Interpretation aroused him from his "dream," if only for a time; and, as he became "awake," his acting out became progressively less urgent and more subject to reality testing. His fantasies were not lost, but they had become, to use Ernst Kris' apt phrase, less "poignant." They were no longer likely to dominate the conduct of his life and influence his major decisions.

Another matter: it is questionable whether our main efforts should be directed toward *preventing* action. We are, after all, not in the business of transforming Macbeth, nor Prince Hal, into Hamlet. Some acting out, especially in adolescents and young adults contains a good deal of truly experimental behavior, learning by trial and error, as unconscious fantasies are employed for the direction of some aspects of life. We need not feel responsible for helping our patients avoid unhappy love affairs, for example. It may be enough to make it possible for them to live through these troubling experiences, if they acquire some understanding in the process. Analysis is not a substitute for life. Timid and overprotective analysts are likely to be no more successful than parents of the same stripe, and they have less excuse for their errors.

Although some analyses of neurotic patients who are prone to acting out go on far too long and may end in futility, the cause for the unsatisfactory result is to be sought not only in intractable pathology, but also, and perhaps first, in departures from the analytic mode, which have been unrecognized or inadequately thought out. The analyst may have fallen into a trap from which he cannot extricate himself either because he denies its existence or is too anxious or inexperienced to deal with it analytically. As a consequence, sometimes he gives up on the analysis without a serious effort to understand and analyze the transference resistance, a decision that has resulted from the reactivation of his own unconscious infantile fantasies and the intolerable anxiety that may accompany such regression. This may take the form of a sense of frustration, which impels him to conclude that the patient was characterologically unanalyzable. In that case, the opportunity to analyze may have been lost for good, and prospects for other treatment are rendered far more difficult.

This is quite different from a reasoned decision that analysis is not possible, for example, when a patient, having made some analytic progress, becomes afflicted with a serious and persistent chronic illness or suffers a loss that changes radically the circumstances of his life. We cannot avoid recognizing the limits of the analytic process, and we should admit that we can analyze only those individuals who have the motivation and the capacity to deal with so demanding a task. We must deal honestly with those whose life situation is too fixed or whose psychological resources are not up to the demands. It is then that we should consider significant changes in procedure. In such situations it is often useful to seek the cooler judgment of a colleague, who may enable us to see things in a different light, to repair what may have looked like a hopeless analysis, to advise the employment of another modality, or perhaps arrange a judicious transfer to another analyst.

Even so, after all the potential pitfalls have been considered, neurotic patients with acting-out tendencies should be offered the option of psychoanalysis as a first choice, If this is not possible, or if the advice is rejected, or if analysis proves after a trial to be inapplicable, we should do something else and by all means call it by another name. Less than this is fair neither to the patient nor to the profession. When analysis is feasible, however, the work done with a piece of acting out can become a breakthrough, a crucial determinant in the resolution of the transference neurosis, the point at which everything seems to come together.

To return to our central issue, we may consider exactly how countertransference *conflicts* affect both the incidence of acting out and how successfully it can be treated. In the course of any analysis, episodes may occur in response to unavoidable frustrations, for example, analyst's holidays and other absences, planning for termination, chance extraanalytic encounters, and the like. In most cases, it is not difficult to bring these circumstances into the analytic situation and resolve them successfully—unless, of course, the analyst himself, out of anxiety and guilt, avoids them and fails to understand their significance. Other intercurrent episodes are less inevitable; analysts are not always at their best. Tempers flare, arguments occur, important facts are forgotten, attention wanders, one has been tactless. It is in these instances that the analyst's "countertransference neurosis" may lead to trouble, especially if he fails to analyze his own errors and repair the damage. To attempt to conceal the error, to react defensively, may effectively disrupt the analysis.

The analyst may also react with excessive anxiety to his patient's characterological hostility or urgent sexuality, leading him to play down these phases of the work and thus encouraging repression at the expense of analytic progress. Such behavior on the part of the analyst may precipitate action by the patient, if only to engage the analyst's attention. Or he may unconsciously identify with his patient's impulsiveness, deriving vicarious satisfaction from the patient's exciting adventures. This is a special risk for a profession that demands such extreme discretion in professional and personal life alike that it may predispose one, absurdly, to moralistic attitudes and stodginess of manner. Such characteristics seldom elude the notice of patients and may, in fact, encourage them to act for the sake of upsetting a person they perceive as rigidly conventional.

Some analysts, without necessarily being moralistic, place an exaggerated value on a "sensible" way of life and consistent reasonableness. It is hard in principle to fault such an attitude, but we should recognize that in practice it may stimulate an opposing reaction in patients, analogous to adolescent behavior, in which transference resistance takes the form of *unreasonable* action. This is understandable; individuals who make a point of being invariably reasonable can make others very uncomfortable and inspire them to all sorts of excesses. It becomes so tempting for patients (and not only patients) to ruffle the feathers of such perfect beings. This is hardly an indication for less reasonableness or more unconventional behavior on the part of analysts, only that its effects on patients should be recognized and brought into the analysis.

In summary, unresolved countertransference conflicts that occur in the course of analyzing patients prone to acting out may lead to a number of difficulties for the analyst, manifested by overidentification with the patient, failure to understand and control his own anxiety, and loss of the analytic attitude, which combines sympathetic understanding and detachment in the necessary proportion. The resultant difficulties are sometimes fatal to the analysis, but need not be. In many cases, they may be corrected by analytic self-scrutiny, often with the aid of advice from a colleague, who can play a role in reaching a decision whether to continue, modify, or transfer. In any event even the "easiest" patient who acts out presents a very complicated problem. If this implies that in order to navigate with any degree of safety the analyst must be a vertible Odysseus, it is no more than a fair statement of the facts.

REFERENCES

Bird, B. (1957). A specific peculiarity of acting out. *J. Amer. Psychoanal. Assn.,* 5:630–647.

——— (1972). Notes on the transference: Universal phenomenon and hardest part of analysis. *J. Amer. Psychoanal. Assn.,* 20:267–301.

Blos, P. (1963). The concept of acting out in relation to the adolescent process. *J. Amer. Acad. Child Psychiat.,* 2:118–143.

Freud, S. (1914). Remembering, repeating and working through. *Standard Edition,* 12:145–156. London: Hogarth Press, 1958.

Gill, M. (1979). The analysis of the transference. *J. Amer. Psychoanal. Assn.,* 27:263–288.

Greenacre, P. (1950). General problems of acting out. *Psychoanal. Quart.,* 19:455–467.

——— (1963). Problems of acting out in the transference relationship.

Emotional Growth. New York: International Universities Press, 1971, pp. 695–712.

______ (1968). The psychoanalytic process, transference, and acting out. *Internat. J. Psychoanal.,* 49:211–218.

Kernberg, O. (1975). *Borderline Conditions.* New York: Aronson.

Kohut, H. (1966). Forms and transformations of narcissism. *J. Amer. Psychoanal. Assn.,* 14:243–272.

______ (1971). *The Analysis of the Self.* New York. International Universities Press.

______ (1977). *The Restoration of the Self.* New York. International Universities Press, 1977.

Lewin, B. (1955). Dream psychology and the analytic situation. *Psychoanal. Quart.,* 24:169–199.

Stein, M. (1965). States of consciousness in the analytic situation, including a note on the traumatic dream. *Drives, Affects, Behavior,* 2, ed. M. Schur. New York. International Universities Press, pp. 60–86.

______ (1973). Acting out as a character trait. *The Psychoanalytic Study of the Child,* 28:347–364. New Haven: Yale University Press.

______ (1981). The unobjectionable part of the transference. *J. Amer. Psychoanal. Assn.,* 29:869–892.

CHAPTER SIX

Discussion of Transference and Countertransference with the Difficult Patient

Jacob A. Arlow

It seems fitting to address the present topic by recalling a statement by Loewenstein (1957). He said that "genuine progress in psychoanalysis depends upon a consistent framework of theory, augmented by clean analytic work." Although he was considering the subject of transference in regard to interpretation, these principles apply even more cogently to problems of countertransference. Sharp delineation of our concepts and a marshalling of appropriate and significant data are fundamental to the examination of the topic of this panel.

Dr. Lane's (this volume) definition of transference implies a concept much broader than one with which I would be comfortable. For me, transference is a technical term that should be limited to manifestations in and growing out of the analytic situation. Phenomena one encounters outside the analytic situation do, indeed, represent repetitions of derivatives of persistent unconscious fantasies, but they do not occur in the uncontaminated setting represented by the analytic situation, the setting that makes precise interpretation of phenomenology possible. Dr. Lane mentions several approaches to the concept of transference. According to one approach, transference phenomena represent residua of attempts to resolve conflicts. This, of course, is essential to our understanding of the nature of the neurotic process, which reflects the dynamic effects of persistent, unconscious fantasies. Transference, however, is not simply a matter of repetition of developmental processes. At a certain point in the individual's development, psychological experience is organized and a large portion of this organization, particularly the part involved in conflict, takes the form of an unconscious fantasy. In discussing acting out, Dr. Stein points out that unconscious fantasy requires a certain degree of development before it is structuralized as a repetitive, dynamic force in the individual's psychology. The events of the analysis, as seen from the examination of the transference, recapitulate some of the methods by which the patient tried to master early conflicts, which originated from wishes represented in persistent, unconscious fantasy. The methodology of psychoanalysis is based on the psychoanalytic situation, which represents a standard, experimental set of conditions, so arranged as to facilitate the emergence into consciousness of derivatives of unconscious conflicts. If it were not so, there would be no serious need to use the technique of free association or to place the patient in a position where he would be unaffected as far as possible by external stimuli.

These last thoughts pertain to Dr. Aronson's (this volume) comments on Kohut's (1971) concepts. If indeed Kohut's approach puts aside the significance of drive theory in favor of developmental defect, we are justified in asking why he and his followers continue to use the analytic situation and the method of free association as a means of gathering data upon which to base their interpretations. This criticism applies as well to their use of dream interpretation. If one dispenses with the importance of drives, what need is there to study the associations attached to specific elements of the dream? Under such circumstances, the temptation to interpret dreams phenomenologically, that is, directly from the manifest content, becomes very strong, and indeed it seems to be characteristic of much of the material presented by Kohut.

Now to approach certain problems of definition. There is considerable confusion as to what is understood by countertransference. Because of this confusion, appropriate use of countertransference as an instrumentality of technique has been obfuscated. In general, I have found the views of Annie Reich (1951) on this subject most substantial. She says:

> Countertransference . . . comprises the effects of the analyst's own unconscious needs and conflicts on his understanding or technique. In such instances the patient represents for the analyst an object of the past onto whom past feelings and wishes are projected, just as in the patient's transference situation with the analyst. The provoking factor for such reactions may be something in the patient's personality or material, or something in the analytic situation as such. [p. 26]

This definition Annie Reich describes as countertransference in the narrow sense. On another occasion (1960), she said,

> One of the prevailing misconceptions is the equation of countertransference with the analyst's total response to the patient, using the term to include all conscious reactions, responses and ways of behavior. This is as incorrect as to call transference everything that emerges in the patient in relation to the analyst during analysis, and not to dis-

> tinguish between the manifestations of unconscious strivings and reality-adapted conscious behavior or observations. The analyst is for the patient and the patient for the analyst also a reality object and not only a transference or countertransference object. There has to be in the analyst some (aim-inhibited) object libidinal interest in the patient which is a prerequisite for empathy. Conscious responses should be regarded as countertransference only if they reach an inordinate intensity or are strongly tainted by inappropriate sexual or aggressive feelings, thus revealing themselves to be determined by unconscious infantile strivings [p. 389–390].

The psychology of analytic empathy is very much to the point. Intuitive understanding is based upon trial identification. Understanding comes about in the following way: (a) the analyst becomes the object of the patient's instinctual strivings; (b) in a special *transient* way the analyst identifies with the patient and in this way participates in the patient's feelings; (c) he can then recognize these feelings and the underlying instinctual strivings as belonging to the patient, that is, he again becomes detached from the patient. Thus, the analyst acquires knowledge about the nature of the patient through an awareness of something going on in him. The capacity for empathy is based on the fact that in the unconscious we are all endowed with similar strivings. In trial identification, primitive ego mechanisms of introjection and projection are regressively revived temporarily for the specific ego purpose of understanding the patient. The analyst should not lose sight of the patient as a separate being. But this delicate process of trial identification is fraught with many hazards, and its failure may show itself as countertransference. For instance: (a) the analyst may react to the impact of his patient's instinctual strivings with a direct response. Such responses arise from the analyst's own infantile motivations. (b) The analyst may be stuck in some of these trial identifications because they please him too much, and he may become unwilling or unable to relinquish them. Instead of going through a transient identification for the purpose of understanding, he remains identified with the patient or the patient's object. He behaves or feels like the patient, which may tend to motivate him to overlook the patient's defenses; or contrariwise he may feel guilty, the guilt stemming from the wishes connected with the unconscious fantasy he shares with the patient.

Heimann (1950) proposed to use the analyst's emotional responses, his countertransference manifestations, as a substitute for empathy. This is not desirable, because when the analyst becomes involved, there is always the danger that he will lose his objectivity, especially in regard to transference phenomena. This may lead the analyst to introduce something that is not inherent in the patient, but only in the analyst's psychology. When the analyst becomes aware of an unduly strong response to the patient's material, he should regard this as a warning of some obstacle interfering with appropriate functioning. Countertransference as such, therefore, is not helpful, but readiness to acknowledge its existence and the ability to overcome it is.

There are some authors who have a different understanding of the analyst's overly intense responses to the patient. They do not regard such phenomena as interferences with appropriate comprehension of the patient's material. On the contrary, they claim that the nature of such countertransference manifestations corresponds to the impulses and defenses being experienced by the patient at the same time. For them, the experience of countertransference is said to open a direct pathway into the patient's unconscious (Heimann, 1950). Such concepts confuse the transient form of identification followed by redetachment, as occurs in empathy, with identification and projection.

Some analysts of the British (Kleinian) school, because of the emphasis they place on pregenital, aggressive conflicts and on the mechanisms of introjection and projection, tend to see the analytic process almost completely from this angle. According to them, the analytic process consists of a mutual identification and a set of projections between analyst and patient (or parts of their respective personalities). To introject or to take over the analyst's healthy personality is thought to form the important part of the process of cure (Strachey, 1934). To Kleinians, the analyst has become identical with the patient's infantile objects via "complementary identification" and, accordingly, the analysis of any countertransference reaction inevitably reveals a portion of the forgotten infantile history. In this spirit, if the analyst feels anger towards the patient, it is taken to indicate that the infantile object was angry with the patient. The analysis of the countertransference thus supposedly brings to light the development of the transference. Because it is assumed that the analyst's emotional experience and his responses to the patient are identical with those of the original models, the interplay of transference and countertransference in the analysis is taken to replace recall of the past and its reconstruction. This constitutes a fundamental difference in methodology.

Another misconception about countertransference should be noted, because it may lead to undesirable effects in the teaching of psychoanalysis. Annie Reich refers to the mistaken view that any wrong interpretation or any mistake in managing the analytic situation should be regarded as an expression of countertransference. This, she said, has led to the erroneous idea that the principal task of the supervisor is to point out countertransference difficulties to the student and to concentrate on the complications that arise in the relationship between student and instructor, rather than teaching the supervisee how to apply the principles of psychoanalysis to the very intricate patterns of clinical data. It is as though there were a tacit assumption that the young analyst was born with an inherent knowledge of psychopathology and "correct interpretation." What causes him to make mistakes, then, is countertransference, rather than lack of knowledge and experience.

None of these considerations should be taken to indicate that I recommend disregarding the role of the subjective elements in how the analyst arrives at an understanding of the patient. Quite the contrary. Beres and I (1974; Arlow, 1979) have considered the matter in great detail, and I will refer to our views only briefly. There are two aspects of the process of interpretation: a subjective, aesthetic one; and an objective, cognitive one. The aesthetic component begins with empathy, that is, a transient identification that enables the analyst to understand what the patient is experiencing. Empathy gives way to intuition, a process of organizing the data afforded through empathic experience, together with all that the analyst has learned about the patient. This organization takes place outside the realm of consciousness. The end result of the intuitive process becomes manifest to the analyst as a result of his intermittent introspection. What appears in consciousness as a result of introspection is a form of inner communication.

The insight the analyst has gained as a result of the process of empathy and intuition does not, however, necessarily appear in the form of an interpretation. The form the insight takes, as it appears in consciousness, differs with the analyst's style and the nature of the patient's conflicts. In effect, the analyst's associations represent a commentary on the patient's productions. Occasionally they do take the form of a neatly formulated interpretation. They may appear, however, in the form of the memory of another patient, a paper one has read, a joke, a line of poetry, a personal recollection. Not the least among these inner communications is the analyst's affective response to the patient's material. It is striking how in this volume Drs. Stein, Kernberg, and Gedo at one time or another describe the feelings they had in response to the patient's material, even though they may not have expressed their feelings to the patient. Dr. Stein speaks about a sense of sheer ingratitude. Dr. Kernberg mentions something about a state of confusion, a sense of futility; and Dr.

Gedo tells of his own patient's violent reaction and his bemused response to the patient's productions. All of these constituted inner communications, facilitating the analyst's understanding. The inner communication was not, however, the final interpretation, but a clue, a signpost, pointing in the direction where the correct interpretation was to be found and formulated.

This is an important methodological point. The analyst's response is not evidence. It is not part of the data, but rather a signpost indicating to him the emergence in his awareness of what is going on in the patient. Sometimes this takes the form of an affective response, but it is not necessarily countertransference. It is, in fact, the way people ordinarily respond to each other. Our understanding of any kind of communication goes beyond what is contained in the precise verbal components transmitted to us by another person, patient or otherwise. The correct interpretation comes to the analyst's mind as a free association. This is the most common experience and represents the aesthetic aspect of the patient-analyst interaction. However, before the interpretation is communicated to the patient, it should be subjected to cognitive examination. How this is done, and the criteria appropriate to the process, goes beyond the scope of this discussion. Here the point of divergence between most of the American analysts and the South American Kleinians, for example, becomes clear. The latter, relying on projective identification, make direct interpretations of the patient's manifest productions. The point is that one has to learn to appreciate one's inner responses, not to look on them as unwanted countertransference reactions, but as part of a gradually developing process of insight in the analyst concerning the nature of the patient's unconscious motivations, disguised and distorted by the defense function of the ego.

In our work with difficult patients, we are frequently subjected to transference reactions expressed in the most intense and violent manner. What the therapist experiences under these circumstances is in effect a transference assault. The intensity of the patient's strivings perforce evokes powerful defensive measures in the therapist. If the therapist feels that he must be completely opaque and respond only like a mirror, mistakenly thinking that he should have no subjective response, he is really rationalizing guilt emanating from the intensity of his own defensive reaction to the patient's assault. This may impede his capacity for identification with the patient and interfere with the process of empathy, thus making impossible an important route in the understanding of the patient's unconscious motivations. The therapist's intuitive capacity becomes immobilized, and he may respond with a frozen silence or withdrawal. In such a setting, the analyst may tend to disregard the important principle that his affective and cognitive responses to the patient's assault really represent commentaries on the patient's material and should afford him clues or signposts indicating where a proper comprehension of the patient's strivings may be achieved. Having striven so hard himself to become a civilized human being by denying, mastering, repressing, or sublimating primitive drive strivings, the therapist may be hard put to appreciate the reality and the intensity of the patient's transference motivations. In the clinical setting, it may seem unfathomable to some therapists that patients could really lust so strongly for sex or violence.

In some respects the nature of psychiatric training has an important bearing on the therapist's ability to master situations of this sort. Here the medically trained psychiatrist, who has spent some years with deeply regressed and psychotic patients in mental institutions, may have a definite advantage. He has seen the raw, primitive instinctuality which in later clinical experience he laboriously and speculatively tries to reconstruct from hints and images contained in subtle behavior, symptoms, dreams, fantasies, and parapraxes. Unless one has personally observed a self-destructive patient struggling against all restraints, attempting to bash his head against a wall, or has witnessed the violence of a catatonic furor, it is difficult to fathom the intensity of the instinctual potential.

In reflecting on the transference-countertransference interaction, the therapist must always be aware that he is under the constant scrutiny and study of the patient. Nothing escapes that observer, and what the patient may not respond to at one moment of the transference assault may be filed away in his memory for use on another occasion, at another time.

Most countertransference reactions that I have observed in students under supervision have not been of the nature of blind spots. Quite the contrary. In my experience, countertransference distortions most often are dynamically determined by a persistent, rather than a transient, identification with the patient and his instinctual strivings or defenses. If one observes the patterns of intervention employed by the supervisee caught in a countertransference reaction, one will be struck by the fact that the timing and the content of the interventions are directed towards diverting the flow of the patient's associations away from the transference towards some other figure or topic. Most often it takes the form of prematurely introducing the original infantile object, an interpretation that is essentially correct but dynamically ineffective because, for purposes of defense, it has been introduced at a time when it is not relevant. In fact, under these circumstances, most of the interventions made by the therapist safeguard him from the eruption of anxiety that would be occasioned by the emergence within him of forbidden impulses and fantasies that he shares in common with his patient or that the patient's material evokes in him.

There are many ways in which the patient elicits clues concerning the therapist's countertransference vulnerability. One of the most effective means is prolonged silence. This places the burden of intervention on the therapist and, for the most part, enables the patient to get a good sampling of the spontaneous fantasy productions that his silence may have occasioned in the therapist.

There are several classic situations in which countertransference reactions can be determined by the nature of the analytic setting. This is especially true of training analysis or when analyzing people who are therapists or in fields closely allied to psychotherapy. Dr. Stein's (this volume) example of massive acting out is a classic one, and I suspect that the patient he used as an illustration was probably a member of the psychological healing profession or an allied field affording some contact with the analytic community. Victory through failure, defeating the analyst by massive acting out or persistent pseudostupidity is typical of this interaction.

Patients may set countertransference traps for their therapists through gossip, spreading poisonous tales, misconceptions and, as an analytic observer once commented, pursuing a pattern of behavior that may be called "analytic blackmail." A common trap of this sort is set when the patient comes for a second analysis after having failed at his first attempt with another therapist. He may draw the second therapist into criticizing the former therapist. It is striking how often in the first interview one sees glaring errors and omissions in the previous therapist's work, only to find later in the course of one's own work with the patient that similar traps and difficulties have been prepared for him. Such unconscious manipulation on the part of the patient threatens the analytic equipoise and places a burden of testing on the ethics and integrity of the therapist. A proper ethical stance by members of the analytic community becomes an essential requirement in establishing an appropriate atmosphere in which analytic work can be conducted. Accordingly, internecine struggles and splits within societies and institutes, in addition to the usual elements of professional envy, may be factors governing how the patient attempts to manipulate the transference-countertransference interaction and immobilize the therapist in a defensive countertransference stance.

It is important to recognize indicators of countertransference reactions. Within the setting of the analytic situation, these responses are well known. Essentially they relate to the loss of the analytic stance. The usual phenomena are the blind spots that are picked up in supervision, a sense of confusion over long periods of time when the analyst is unable to grasp the flow of the associations, that is, he has lost his empathic contact with the patient. More dramatic, of course, are those examples of excessive emotion, loss of control, irritability, sleepiness, or boredom within the hour.

There are, however, a number of indicators outside the analytic session which the analyst might do well to pay attention to as indicators of possible countertransference involvement with a patient. Recurrent thoughts about the patient outside of working hours, characterized by mood changes, especially of depression, are usually indicative of some disturbance. If the patient appears in the manifest content of the analyst's dreams or if there are intrusive fantasies in which the patient figures, there is reason to look into the matter. More subtle, but perhaps equally significant, is the tendency to recount events or to talk to others about the nature of the patient's problems or the analytic experience even without betraying any confidence. Just a need to articulate continuing responses to the analytic session, particularly in nonprofessional situations, is an important sign.

Unfortunately, the limitations of space prohibit me from doing justice to the rich clinical presentations. Dr. Gedo's experience with students in supervision is very striking. The material, to begin with, indicates the wisdom of one of Loewenstein's (1957) maxims. He said that one of the things that every analyst should think about in connection with transference-countertransference is this: When a certain mood is aroused in the analyst, when certain feelings appear either during or after a session, the analyst should always ask himself whether this was indeed the reaction that the patient had *intended* to stimulate in the therapist. In other words, we must always contemplate the possibility that unconsciously we may be completing a scenario arranged for us by the patient, a scenario representing an attempt to actualize a transference fantasy. When there has been a persistent countertransference reaction, considerable doubt necessarily falls on the validity of the reporter's observations. The objectivity of the observer during such times may be suspect. Thus, for example, in the case of the patient who dishonestly arranged for an unrealistically low fee, one can understand and sympathize with the therapist's chagrin. Nevertheless, the material may organize itself around more than the transference-countertransference interaction. That patient is, in effect, a swindler, and I suspect that his behavior may represent an example of a character perversion, that is, a pattern of behavior in which an earlier trend to act out castrating fantasies during homosexual activity may have been replaced by a pattern of swindling and deceiving. To be sure, the student who responded violently to the idea of having been fooled may have suffered narcissistic mortification and/or a counterdefensive response to her own wish to steal. I would have enjoyed the opportunity to discuss in much greater detail the rich material of Dr. Gedo's second illustration. I suspect that we are dealing in that instance with an example of the psychology of the exception, and the interpretive work, of course, would have to be sustained by careful examination of the clinical data.

Dr. Kernberg's chapter puts to the fore a new and hitherto unreported clinical phenomenon. The pattern of a patient who cannot accept dependence on the analyst is puzzling for two reasons. First, dependency as it is understood here differs from the way it is usually understood. Ordinarily we think of dependency as representing the behavioral pattern related to a set of specific fantasy wishes, of reliance on a nurturing object, usually connected with ideas of oral protection and gratification, and where separation anxiety is a dominant presenting clinical manifestation. The patients Kernberg describes seem to be more of the type who have difficulty engaging in the process of interaction with the analyst; they belong not only to a different category from the usual dependent patient, but may represent examples of a new syndrome entirely. It is possible that these patients represent not one syndrome but different aspects of those patients who find themselves unable, for various reasons, to form a working relationship with the analyst, a difficulty that might be related to different unconscious fantasies and conflicts. We are all acquainted with the patient who cannot accept an interpretation unless it is phrased in his own words or who resents an interpretation because he feels he had thought of it first and had not mentioned it—or even the patient who feels angry with Freud because he had the same ideas, but Freud got around to writing them down first. These fall within the spectrum of the narcissistic personality and the affront to one's sense of omnipotence, but I think they represent different facets of a wide range of obstacles to engaging in the analytic situation.

I have one further thought, which was stimulated by Dr. Aronson. The difficulty encountered in treating a case is not always proportionate to the nature of the psychopathology or to the level of regression. Sometimes a particularly stubborn resistance, or character trait, or unresolved transference from a previous analysis may form the core of what turns out to be an insurmountable obstacle. It is appealing but hazardous to try to identify the difficult case with a more primitive type of conflict or psychopathology.

REFERENCES

Arlow, J. A. (1979). The genesis of interpretation. *J. Amer. Psychoanal. Assn.* Suppl., *27*:193–206.

Beres, D., & Arlow, J. A. (1974). Fantasy and identification in empathy. *Psychoanal. Quart. 43*:4–25.

Heimann, P. (1950). On countertransference. *Internat. J. Psycho-Anal. 31*:81–84.

Kohut, H. (1971). *The Analysis of the Self: A Systematic Approach to the Psychoanalytic Treatment of the Narcissistic Personality.* New York: International Universities Press.

Loewenstein, R. (1957). Some thoughts on interpretation in the theory and practice of psychoanalysis. *The Psychoanalytic Study of the Child,* 12:148. New York: International Universities Press.

Reich, A. (1951). On countertransference. *Internat. J. Psycho-Anal.,* 32:25–31.

——— (1960). Further remarks on countertransference. *Internat. J. Psycho-Anal., 41*:389–395.

Strachey, J. (1934). The nature of the therapeutic action of psychoanalysis. *Internat. J. Psycho-Anal.,* 15:127–159.

CHAPTER SEVEN

Countertransference in the Selection of Brief Therapy

Samuel Perry and Robert Michels

A characteristic of contemporary psychoanalysis is that its duration is not time limited. It is never brief, but, much more important, its length is determined by internal processes rather than by external constraints. It continues until it is over. This feature of psychoanalysis is one of its greatest strengths—and one of its greatest problems. The inevitable question, asked at least since the day of Ferenczi and Rank, is: Can goals similar to those achieved by psychoanalysis be attained in a shorter time and with less frequent sessions?

While investigators in outcome research struggle with this question, psychoanalysts interested in the new brief therapies also ask questions that are less related to cost effectiveness and more related to therapeutic process. Specifically, how do the characteristics of these brief treatments, as opposed to characteristics of the patient and psychoanalyst or psychotherapist, determine transferences and countertransferences? How do these transferences compare in nature, intensity, and meaning with those that develop in psychoanalysis? And should these transferences be interpreted? Avoided? Or sometimes one and sometimes the other? Just as brief therapy uses basic tenets derived from psychoanalysis, is there something we can now learn from studying brief therapy that will help further our understanding of the transference and countertransference issues of psychoanalysis? The authors in this section approach these questions from different perspectives and at times present differing views, but in one area they all agree: changing the time frame from the traditional arrangements of psychoanalysis to those of brief therapy changes the experience of both participants, including the transference and countertransference features of the relationship.

In this chapter we illustrate how countertransference problems can influence the selection of brief therapy. Also, as a way of introducing other chapters in this section, we present a transference-countertransference paradigm that occurred in a brief therapy and comment on how subsequent authors might view this clinical material. Before approaching these specific tasks, we begin by examining some general myths associated with brief psychoanalytic psychotherapy. Because of their historical and clinical implications, these myths are worth correcting.

One myth is that brief therapy is a recently conceived child, or perhaps even the stepchild, of psychoanalysis. The reverse is closer to the truth. Most of the early cases that led to the development of our basic model of psychoanalysis were relatively brief. In fact, the psychoanalytic movement was quite mature before what we would today consider psychoanalysis (Valenstein, 1979) took its place beside treatments of shorter duration. Since psychoanalysis was in part genetically derived from the rich clinical experiences of these briefer treatments, the new brief therapies* cannot be dismissed as illegitimate offspring. They are part of our heritage and, like their predecessors, can generate valuable psychoanalytic insights. In many ways it would be more appropriate to think of contemporary psychoanalysis and modern brief psychoanalytic psychotherapy as two derivatives of a common, undifferentiated matrix—the early cases of Freud and his immediate followers.

This first myth is related to a second, that the new brief therapies were conceived as a response to pressure from consumers and third-party payers for a psychoanalytic treatment that was more available and less costly. Such is not the case. The impetus for these new approaches has not been primarily fiscal, nor, despite the label "brief therapy," is the main concern treatment duration. Instead, today's innovative brief therapists are far more interested in perfecting those therapeutic processes that remove symptoms or catalyze character change. Their search is not so much for a shorter treatment as for a more effective one. In this regard, the new brief therapies are consistent with Freud's decision to establish a time limit for the treatment of the Wolfman.

A third myth is even more clinically relevant: that brief therapy was conceived as yet another attempt to find a way of using psychoanalytic concepts for those patients who do not have the attributes necessary for psychoanalysis. Again, quite the opposite is true. Brief therapy is not principally part of the historic trend that has recom-

---

*We will use the term "brief therapy" to include many approaches (Sifneos, 1972; Mann, 1973; Castelnuevo-Tedesco, 1975; Bellak, Small, 1978; Davaloo, 1978; Small, 1979; Wolberg, 1980; Malan, 1976a,b). As we have discussed elsewhere (Frances, Clarkin and Perry, 1984), these therapies differ in their duration, approach, process and goals, but for purposes here of considering countertransference reactions they are sufficiently similar to place under one rubric.

mended "active technique" (Ferenczi & Rank, 1956), "corrective emotional experience" (Alexander & French, 1946), "parameters" (Eissler, 1953), "psychoanalytic psychotherapy" (Tarachow & Stein, 1967), "auxillary egos" (Kernberg, 1982), or "transmuting internalizations" (Kohut, 1977) for those not capable of participating in a "proper" psychoanalysis and fully reaping its benefits (Stone, 1954). On the contrary, the major advocates of brief therapy, however else they may differ, prescribe methods that have stringent enabling factors and often have therapeutic goals that are almost as ambitious as those of psychoanalysis (Perry, Frances, Klar & Clarkin, 1983). Psychotherapists who have witnessed the videotaped cases of Davanloo (1978), read the transcribed sessions of Malan (1976a), or studied the cases of Sifneos (1976) can appreciate the ego strength required to absorb the treatment's direct confrontations and to weather the intense transferential storms.

The very fact that many patients suitable for the new brief therapies *are* analyzable poses a special problem for the psychoanalyst. For those inclined to view psychoanalysis as "the best possible whenever possible," the decision to recommend another kind of treatment is usually based on limitations in the patient, such as lack of motivation, psychological mindedness, and impulse control, or practical constraints, such as financial resources. But when the enabling factors for "analyzability" (Bachrach and Leaff, 1970; Perry et al., 1983) are present and there are no practical obstacles, the question of whether or not to recommend psychoanalysis is not so easy to answer. The question is no longer can the patient be analyzed, but rather should he be? Because the indications for selecting among psychoanalysis and alternative psychotherapies are so poorly defined (Waldhorn, 1967; Tyson and Sandler, 1971), clinical judgment must determine whether any treatment other than a full analysis is likely to be as effective, or even more effective, in achieving the desired goals.

It would be reassuring if this clinical judgment were based on a direct experience with both psychoanalysis and brief therapies, or at least on a thorough knowledge of the techniques used in each. It would be even more reassuring if this clinical judgment were supported by well-controlled outcome research comparing the various approaches. But such is not the case. Most psychoanalysts are not familiar with the specific approaches of brief therapy, and the research on treatment selection of dynamic therapies in general (Luborsky and Spence, 1978; Parloff, 1979; Smith, Glass and Miller, 1980; Frances et al., 1984) and psychoanalysis (May, 1973; Kernberg, Burstein, and Coyne, 1978) or brief therapy (Malan, 1976b;

Butcher and Koss, 1978; Strupp, 1980) in particular, is confusing and inconclusive regarding their relative indications. The clinician is therefore forced to base much of the decision on intuition—and it is here that individual preferences, previous training, and unavoidable biases (conscious and unconscious) are likely to be most influential.

In informal discussions among colleagues at workshops on brief therapy or at psychoanalytic meetings, these biases are freely exposed. Brief therapists (Strupp, 1975) argue, for example, that psychoanalysts confuse passivity with neutrality and thereby fail to engage the patient actively, to generate an intense emotional atmosphere in the treatment, and to make the mutative transferential interpretations traditionally advocated by Freud (1914) and Strachey (1934) and recently reviewed by Gill (1979). As a result, the therapeutic process is diffused while analyst and patient ineffectively, or at least inefficiently, circle around the central themes. Psychoanalysts (Schafer, 1973) counter these arguments by contending that brief therapy does more than control the therapeutic process; it controls the patient as well and in doing so, subtly deprives the patient of the confidence and autonomy that can come only from finding one's own way through the maze of a well-established transference neurosis. Furthermore, the limited duration of the treatment not only risks leaving large and perhaps malignant areas of the patient's character unexplored but also precludes the arduous but necessary working through, the "assimilation" (Bibring, 1954), that only time can provide.

Informal discussions that stereotype and polarize brief therapy and psychoanalysis often include thinly disguised comments regarding countertransference problems in those representing the opposing view. For example, advocates of psychoanalysis may suggest that brief therapists have little tolerance for ambiguity and uncertainty and that they cannot sustain attachments or that they need to impose their wills on others; advocates of brief therapy may contend that analysts are so frightened of acting on any impulses, either aggressive or libidinal, that they have retreated into a paralyzing self-consciousness and a passive therapeutic stance, which they then rationalize as being the necessary—and traditional—requirement for a "real" psychoanalysis.

No doubt these opinions are sometimes true, but they are seldom based on convincing evidence. More often, such presumptions about unconscious motivation come from reading between the lines of case presentations or from responding to the manner and style of the therapist. Recognizing the hazards of such long distance analysis, one is tempted simply to ignore these speculations. But since the prescription for psychoanalysis or brief therapy is at best based on clinical judgment and since such judgments are inevitably influenced by biases, we have chosen a different tack. Rather than dismissing the various unsubstantiated views about countertransference problems, we see these speculations as a stimulus to survey our own experience for data that might be relevant to a discussion of how unconscious factors can affect treatment selection.

We do this by presenting two vignettes from supervision (which have been slightly modified to maintain confidentiality). In the first, brief therapy was clinically indicated and was prescribed but, because of countertransference problems, was conducted half-heartedly by the therapist; in the second, brief treatment was not indicated but was inappropriately recommended, again in response to unconscious forces in the therapist. The consideration of treatment selection extends the discussion beyond the traditional boundaries of the term countertransference to encompass unconsciously derived prejudices for or against a type of treatment, prejudices that are not necessarily related to the therapist's conscious and unconscious responses to a particular patient. We conclude with a situation in which a countertransference problem (as narrowly defined) evolved in a brief treatment as a response to the patient's transference. This vignette also serves as an introduction to other issues of transference and countertransference discussed in the following chapters on brief therapy.

The first case involved a female fourth year medical student assigned for brief therapy to a psychiatry resident, who was also a female and also in her fourth year. During the opening phase of supervision, the resident could not have been more enthusiastic about enriching her therapeutic armamentarium by learning the techniques of brief therapy. She acknowledged that since she was a candidate in psychoanalytic training, psychoanalysis was her first love but she believed that her assigned patient could "profit" from one of the new brief therapies. To support this contention (and perhaps to gain favor with her supervisor), she read his papers on the enabling factors and contraindications for focal dynamic therapy and cited them when she explained how the patient's presenting complaint of anxiety about leaving her parents upon graduation from medical school met one of the indications: circumscribed intrapsychic conflict precipitated by a pending stress.

The first few weeks of the treatment suggested that the resident's clinical assessment was correct. Seen twice a week, the patient rapidly formed an intense maternal transference that was almost palpable and that facilitated "here and now" interpretations, such as how the patient's anxiety towards the end of sessions or before long holiday weekends was linked to unrecognized fears of separating from the therapist. To complete the "interprative triad" (Malan, 1976b) this anxiety could be related to separating from her parents upon graduation and then be traced genetically through dreams and fantasies to repressed memories of the patient's childhood experience when her mother had been placed in a tuberculosis sanitorium for an extended period of time.

However, despite the resident's initial enthusiasm and the suitability of the patient for focal dynamic therapy, both the therapy and the supervision went "flat" within a few weeks. Process notes, reported lifelessly, indicated that separation issues were being avoided by the patient and diffused by the resident who, though she knew better, continued to explore material that was neither affectively nor dynamically related to the central conflicts.

The supervisor's enthusiasm was waning as well, a fact that became inescapable when he scheduled an analytic patient at the designated supervisory hour. At first the supervisor suspected that this slip was only a reaction to the resident's general oppositionalism and her refusal to assume the focused and actively engaged stance required for brief therapy; but further self-analysis revealed the misscheduling also had a more specific meaning. In contrast to the plodding tone of supervision, the analytic patient was deeply committed to her analysis.

The supervisor told the resident that he suspected that her recent difficulties in the treatment and in supervision were due in part to a devaluation of the therapeutic task. He wondered if the resident (like the supervisor) might not secretly be wishing that her hours were being filled by a psychoanalytic case. Though this possibility was initially denied, the following week the resident recognized that her disappointment and guilt stemmed largely from being directed by the supervisor to give such a lovely and capable patient "something less than the best."

Of course, an argument could be made that the reluctance of the resident to administer a focal dynamic therapy was not based on a countertransference problem but rather on a different (and perhaps correct) clinical opinion. She would not be the first to question the wisdom of using a brief therapy with a patient who was capable of participating in a psychoanalysis (Clarkin and Frances, 1982; Binder, Strupp, and Schact, 1983; Frances et al., 1984). But even given the nature of the supervisory relationship and the limited availability of unconscious material, sufficient evidence surfaced over time to confirm that the resistance to conducting brief therapy was at least in part due to countertransference problems. For instance, during one supervisory hour the resident mentioned, almost as an aside, that she had had a strange dream of giving birth to the patient, who was delivered fully grown and wearing an intern's outfit, stethoscope and all.

The supervisor suggested that the resident might want to explore the dream in her own analysis, where more of the latent personal determinants could be revealed; but the manifest content strongly suggested that the resident was not sure whether she wanted to be the surrogate mother, responsible for the care of an infantilized patient, or she wanted the patient to be an adult who could treat ("doctor") herself (and perhaps also the resident). In the resident's mind, brief therapy and psychoanalysis symbolized these extremes. She would often fail to clarify a point for the patient, explaining in supervision that because treatment would soon be stopping, the patient should learn to do the work on her own. In contrast, at one point the resident jokingly referred to her own treatment by saying, "I'm in my third year of analysis, and I'm not even up to the age of two."

This link in the resident's mind between brief therapy and self-sufficiency versus psychoanalysis and nurturing was further complicated by another countertransferential difficulty: her sympathetic identification with the patient. One manifestation of this problem occurred when, hearing the resident describe sessions from her process notes, the supervisor often could not discern whether the resident or the patient was talking (who was "delivering" whom).

As a result of this confused identification, the resident became first tearful and then openly defiant when after three months of treatment the supervisor recommended that a termination date be set for early spring, about three months away. Pleading that the treatment should continue until both she and the patient were graduated in June, the resident could not accept the recommendation. The supervisor pointed out that the clinical material suggested that the patient was prepared to work through the separation and, furthermore, that by setting the date on the basis of therapeutic needs rather than external circumstances, the patient would more likely realize that her fears of separation were due to transferential feelings rather than the combination of the actual loss of the therapist and graduation from medical school. These explanations were to no avail, and during of the fourth supervisory hour devoted to this issue, the resident stormed out of the office, proclaiming that *her* analyst would never be so cruel as to abandon one of her patients!

With the help of supervision and her own analysis (and perhaps also with the help of the patient), the resident did terminate the brief therapy within a couple of weeks of the suggested time. The final session, in both treatment and supervision, was quite moving as both the patient and the resident expressed appreciation for being encouraged to grow by learning to distinguish real from irrational fears.

The resident's conscious and unconscious attitudes affected not only the process of therapy, but also her judgment regarding the selection of therapy. Left on her own, she doubtless would have chosen psychoanalysis as the treatment of choice for this medical student, a choice that would have been influenced largely by unconscious factors.

The second case involved a 59-year-old businessman referred by his internist to a junior psychiatry attending, who, in turn asked for supervision. He explained that he believed the patient was a perfect candidate for a time-oriented therapy, a known interest of the supervisor. The psychiatrist added that because he was regarded by colleagues primarily as a researcher in psychopharmacology, most of his referrals were "drug patients," and he was interested in enlarging his therapeutic repertoire. He felt that his new patient had no recent mood or vegetative symptoms warranting medication and would probably be better suited for one of the psychosocial treatments.

Times and fees were arranged, and weekly supervision began. The first few meetings were mainly spent by the supervisor listening to the therapist discuss the different kinds of brief therapy—their theories, techniques, and reported outcomes. Though these sessions had more the feeling of a seminar than a supervisory hour, the supervisor believed the psychiatrist, reflecting both his training and his temperament, needed to overcome his skepticism and anxiety about any "talking cure" by reviewing the literature on the topic. The supervisor was wary of prematurely interpreting this behavior as a resistance to discussing what was happening in the treatment.

By the fifth supervisory session, more than a month had passed and still only glimpses of the therapy itself had been revealed. Those glimpses suggested that paralleling the supervision, the psychiatrist was assuming a "didactic" approach with the patient, who was being told what he felt and was being instructed not to act on those feelings—for instance, that he was "not accepting the limitations of growing old" and should "try to enjoy retirement." These instructions, phrased more like commands, were characteristically followed by reminders to the patient that the twice weekly treatment was going to stop, as prearranged, in just four months—as though the threat of termination would be sufficient to force the patient to change.

At this point, the supervisor became more directive and pointed out that the psychiatrist still had not discussed what it was the patient wanted to change. In fact, this goal had not yet been explored in the treatment. On the basis of very sparse information (primarily comments by the referring internist), the psychiatrist had assumed the patient's difficulties to have begun when he sold his very successful business. On hearing this, the supervisor advised the psychiatrist to spend the next few sessions taking a more detailed history. To this straightforward recommendation the psychiatrist responded by becoming uncharacteristically contentious. He argued that at this point history-taking would be a "distraction" and deflect attention from using the time-oriented treatment to work out "separation from the patient's business and life [*sic*]." The supervisor disagreed and reminded the psychiatrist that a dynamic understanding of the patient based on an adequate history, was an essential tool even in time-limited therapy. The psychiatrist heard the remark (correctly) as somewhat patronizing, and the supervisory hour ended on a discordant note, the first of many.

From the information presented so far, one might conclude that the problems in the brief therapy were due not so much to countertransference difficulties in the psychiatrist as to his being an inadequate psychotherapist. After all, not all problems are caused by countertransference. But as supervision proceeded, more compelling evidence accumulated to confirm that the psychiatrist's behavior in the therapy and in the supervision was dictated by unconscious responses to the patient—and that his responses were directly related to why a brief therapy had been selected in the first place. For example, after several more suggestions by the supervisor, the psychiatrist "remembered" to ask the patient what exactly had made him ask the internist for a psychiatric referral. Even then, the psychiatrist admittedly had trouble "hearing" the patient's response: the scribbled process notes were either illegible or unintelligible fragments.

With the prodding of the supervisor and with constant encouragement to have the psychiatrist obtain more history, the scattered pieces of the puzzle were found and pieced together. A more complete picture of the patient then began to emerge. The man was not at all concerned about retirement. In fact, he had decided to sell his business after separating from his second wife; he realized that his consuming drive for absolute perfection and corporate acquisitions had destroyed, perhaps irreparably, his relationship with his children and first wife and now was about to destroy the relationship with his second wife and stepchildren. The patient was concerned that he would be forced to endure his twilight years alone, crippled by a harshly critical attitude toward himself and others. He saw psychotherapy as a last chance to work out these difficulties, the character problems he had pushed aside over the years because of "business pressures."

After this more complete view of the patient was obtained, the supervisor raised the possibility with the psychiatrist that a brief therapy might not be the treatment of choice. The supervisor explained that the patient had longstanding character problems that were not well circumscribed in a single section of his personality and were not merely a response to a specific current situation. Further, the patient had not responded to two other brief therapies in his earlier years, which also suggested that an open-ended, exploratory treatment of longer duration might now be indicated.

Consideration of any approach other than a time-oriented brief therapy was most upsetting to the supervisee. With an emotional outburst that was quite uncharacteristic of his usual manner, he claimed that he had been deceived; he accused the supervisor of breaking the contract and of being "a closet analyst." The supervisor suggested that the psychiatrist's strong feelings indicated that certain issues had still not come into view and that they needed further examination. The psychiatrist found this oblique reference to possible countertransference problems unacceptable. He left the session abruptly, did not pay his last bill, and did not return the supervisor's calls.

This case was chosen for discussion not only because the data are so clear but also because additional information that was obtained, fortuitously, regarding both the patient and the psychiatrist revealed the specific way unconscious factors can influence the selection of a brief therapy:

A few weeks after the therapist's abrupt termination of supervision, the patient discontinued the time-oriented treatment and entered psychoanalysis with one of the supervisor's colleagues, who, knowing the supervisor's research interest in differential therapeutics, confidentially reports that after three years the analysis is proceeding slowly but beneficially. The patient has returned to his second wife and for the first time has taken some enjoyable vacations with his own children.

The follow up on the psychiatrist is more relevant to our discussion. Three months after his stormy departure, the psychiatrist called to ask if the supervisor would be willing to see him in therapy. Taken aback, the supervisor explained over the phone that under the circumstances he did not think it wise but that he would be pleased to see the psychiatrist in consultation to discuss the matter personally. The psychiatrist agreed.

Two consultative visits shed light on the unconscious origins of the conflicts that had interfered with the psychiatrist's treatment. When he was in postgraduate training and preoccupied with staking out a research career, his father retired and died shortly thereafter. Though he attended the funeral, the psychiatrist allowed himself no time to mourn his father. However, over the past few weeks (concomitant with the patient's stopping treatment and four years since the month of his father's death) the psychiatrist had been thinking of his father, recalling their cold and critical relationship and yet feeling guilty that he had not sat shivah but instead had returned to his research. These feelings of remorse and guilt were behind his considering psychiatric treatment now.

These revelations added a meaningful dimension to the psychiatrist's choice to work with the patient in psychotherapy and yet avoid an intimate attachment. For him, the selection of a time-oriented therapy represented a compromise between an opportunity to become involved with his patient-father (saving him from the plight of retirement) and an opportunity to confront and control the inevitable separation.

There was yet another irony in why this psychiatrist had selected a brief therapy for his patient—and why he later asked the supervisor, whom he had experienced as enraging and demeaning, to become his therapist. A couple of months before supervision began, the psychiatrist had attended a conference on brief therapy that was given at a resort area. He originally planned the week more as a vacation than as an educational experience, but to his surprise he became quite absorbed by the clinical material, particularly the videotaped illustrations, and elected to attend the small workshops. These proved to be quite traumatic. The workshop leader was apparently tactless and humiliating in pointing out the participants' limitations, and the psychiatrist left the conference feeling demeaned. The subsequent decision to conduct a brief therapy—and later to seek an enraging supervisor for a therapist—was in part motivated by an unconscious need to overcome feelings of shame and impotence.

The psychiatrist accepted the supervisor's referral to a colleague and was seen in twice-weekly psychotherapy for several months; then, at least partly for professional reasons, the psychiatrist left to accept a higher position in another city. Before departing, he called the supervisor-consultant to say thanks and goodbye. He also mentioned that his drug reasearch was going well and that he had decided that being a psychotherapist was not his "cup of tea."

These two vignettes illustrate how unconscious factors can influence the choice between psychoanalysis or brief therapy. We are wary of any global speculations concerning how specific conflicts determine the preference of one treatment over another. Such conjectures risk being little more than projections of one's own wishes and fears (such as the need to control, avoidance of separation, inability to engage and act). As stated earlier, we agree with others (Kernberg, 1965; Racker, 1968; Sandler, 1976; Epstein, 1981) that the concept of countertransference is most useful when defined as an individual therapist's specific reactions to a specific patient.

We are aware that by concentrating on the role of these factors in treatment selection, we have ignored the role of the patient's transference in the process. Patients usually participate, and often have the final say in, what treatment is chosen, and often this choice is based on an initial transference response to therapist's presentation of a particular mode of treatment. In the course of either a psychoanalysis or a brief therapy, the transferential reasons for the choice should come into view. There are times when this might lead to a decision to change the prescription, although we must keep in mind that all changes, right or wrong, are determined partly by unconscious, irrational reasons. The situation is more of a problem when the therapists's initial unconscious responses have significantly influenced the treatment selection—although here too there is the possibility that during the course of the treatment these unconscious conflicts will be recognized and modified by self-analysis, personal therapy, or supervision (Searles, 1965).

The following chapters in this section continue to examine how the characteristics of brief therapy influence transference and countertransference. Whereas we have described how unconscious forces can effect treatment selection, subsequent authors concentrate more on how transference and countertransference can effect the therapeutic process. To facilitate this shift of focus and to introduce some of the issues these authors discuss, we now present a transference-countertransference paradigm that developed during the course of a brief therapy.

A young man, self-described as "a starving artist," sought consultation because of a marital crisis. His wife had "accidentally" become pregnant for the first time, allegedly because of a misfitted diaphragm. She wanted to have the child, but he wanted her to have an abortion. In fact, he had wanted out of the marriage soon after he entered it but had been unable to share these feelings with his wife for fear that she would become too upset. With the prospects now of being forever trapped with a woman he did not love, he was in a panic. A twice-weekly brief therapy was arranged with the specified goal of understanding and resolving his need to be so overprotective of his wife that he could not even consider sharing with her some of his longstanding doubts about their relationship. Only when this problem was overcome would he be able to deal effectively with the current crisis.

The historical precipitants of his problems were not difficult to uncover. The patient's father was remembered as an inept laborer who could neither provide for his large family nor care for his overwhelmed and depressed wife. That responsibility was assumed by the patient, who from an early age comforted his mother at her bedside. Later, during his adolescence, when the father was killed in an accident at work, the patient arranged for his mother's psychiatric hospitalizations and tried to protect her from life's inevitable stresses and disappointments.

By the third session, the patient realized that he was needlessly assuming the same overprotective stance with his wife, who, by his description, was socially withdrawn and somewhat naive but not the mental cripple he feared. However, this insight was not mutative. On the contrary, from the beginning of treatment, he became even more solicitous at home, preparing the meals, managing the finances, and scheduling his wife's obstetrical appointments so that she would not feel any burden or distress. Of note, his behavior within the therapeutic situation was the opposite of that in the marital relationship. In a passive and depressed manner, he would present his plight and describe in detail the chronic dissatisfactions with his wife and then expect the therapist magically to make everything all right.

In the fifth session, the patient reported a dream that revealed other unconscious transference determinants of his behavior. He dreamt that both he and the therapist had been drafted into a foreign war; one of them was killed (he was not sure which one), and the other returned with jewelry to console the widow. The patient's first association was to the "jewelry," which reminded him of his mother's wedding ring and other valuables that had been stolen during one of her hospitalizations. He then recognized that at one level, the dream expressed his wish to "leave the scene" (like the father) and have the therapist (like the patient) remarry his wife-mother and take on the responsibility. He also realized that his passive behavior in treatment stemmed in part from an identification with his depressed mother and his hope of being rescued by the therapist.

The therapist inquired about the other elements in the dream, specifically, about the death in a foreign war and the fact that valuables had been stolen. The patient had no immediate associations then, but he began the following session, the sixth, by stating that on the way to the therapist's office he had worried that the appointment hour might have been unexpectedly changed and no one would be there. He then became quite tearful. Fruther exploration of this fantasy and of the dream brought into view a heretofore unexplored dynamic, a deep yearning for his deceased father ("stolen" and "valued") as well as his unconscious guilt for assuming the father's place.

Other dynamics could also be described, but the point to be made here is that within a relatively brief period of time, catalyzed both by the marital crisis and by the regression within the therapeutic situation, an intense and multifaceted transference had developed. Furthermore, analysis of this transference had exposed a previously unappreciated intrapsychic meaning of the patient's behavior.

Meanwhile, time was ticking away and the possibility of an abortion would soon be over. This fact, coupled with the patient's transference, was producing a countertransferential response that went unrecognized by the therapist until he made a slip when discussing the case with a colleague. The therapist, intending to convey the therapeutic dilemma of when and how to intervene, inadvertently referred to the patient—not the situation—as "a ball buster." The colleague pointed out this slip and asked what it was about the patient that was at all castrating, for he had been described as rather mild mannered and not even passively aggressive. Self-analysis disclosed that the countertransference was directly related to the patient's transference. The therapist was aware of his wish to assume an authoritative stance with the patient and give advice about what to do; he had not been aware that the therapeutic necessity of maintaining a more neutral stance was unconsciously experienced as being reduced by the patient to an unmanly position. This conflict was reminiscent of the infantile wish to be the man of the house and the fear of castration that would result if that wish were put into action. In effect, the patient and therapist were both unconsciously struggling with similar Oedipal conflicts; each wanted to be the father and yet each was frightened and guilty about assuming that role. As in the dream, it was not clear who was killing whom.

An appreciation of this transference-countertransference paradigm redirected the dynamic focus of the brief therapy and led to a favorable outcome. Instead of continuing to explore how the patient was overprotecting his wife in the same way that he had overprotected his mother, the therapist focused on the patient's yearning to have and to become a father and his fear and guilt of again acting on that infantile wish. Because the therapist was more aware of his own fear of acting authoritatively, he became more confident and incisive in making his interpretations. After a period of delayed mourning for the lost father, who was no longer devalued, the patient felt far more capable of being a husband and father himself and actually looked forward to having the child, though he was appropriately worried about his financial situation. He began to share his concerns with his wife, who responded by being more supportive, nurturing, and capable. In addition, the patient realized that he had been assuming the same passive role in his profession that he had taken in the transference: he had been afraid to assert himself and instead had been waiting in the wings, hoping to be recognized and "adopted" by a senior artist. By the time treatment terminated after three months, he had sought a teaching position and was planning a long delayed exhibition of his work.

Presented with this condensed vignette, what might the authors in the following chapters have to say about the transference and countertransference in this brief therapy? Dr. Allen Frances, who outlines the indications for transference interpretation in focal dynamic therapy, would no doubt be interested in what systematic studies might guide the therapist in this situation. He also would be interested in whether the transference distortions constituted a resistance and an impediment to the therapeutic alliance and whether the conflicts revealed in the transference were a reflection of the conflicts responsible for the patient's chief complaint. Dr. James Mann, who discusses the time-limited model of brief therapy, would be particularly interested in whether the termination date was set in advance (it was not) and whether by so doing the therapist might have encouraged the necessary grieving over the lost father and unnurturing mother. Dr. Milton Viederman might have considered for this patient in crisis a specific type of brief treatment, what he terms a psychodynamic life narrative. This intervention emphasizes the primary, or fundamental, transference; the presumed, nonpathological, infantile substrate of trust and relatedness that is at the core of all doctor-patient relationships. Although Dr. Viederman would certainly want to understand this patient's transference, he might not choose to interpret it but rather to use this understanding to achieve a specific therapeutic goal, such as helping the patient cope with becoming a father. A psychodynamic life narrative might thereby foster a sustained therapeutic transference response. In contrast, Dr. Roy Schafer might wonder if a future analysis would reveal, for example, that the patient's assumption of the father role was actually a fragile reaction formation against the unrecognized rage towards his own father and mother.

Despite these different points of view, the authors of the following chapters all agree that brief therapy is an important and valuable treatment and that a psychoanalytic understanding of transference and countertransference is essential. There are differences on how to use this understanding but agreement that the understanding is necessary if the therapy is to be conducted effectively. The differences are revealing. To learn more about the role of these treatments, Dr. Frances wants us to study the effect of various types of brief therapy on various types of patients in various types of situations, while Dr. Schafer wants us to analyze individuals after brief therapy in order to understand what the brief therapy really meant. Whereas Drs. Frances and Schafer agree that brief therapy should focus on a central pathogenic conflict, Dr. Mann and, to a considerable degree, Dr. Viederman see brief therapy as creating rather than discovering the central foci of treatment.

Whatever their differences, it becomes clear in the following chapters that as these psychoanalysts return to the study of treatments similar to those that gave birth to psychoanalysis, they develop new strategies that can enrich our understanding of old problems.

REFERENCES

Alexander, F., & French, T. M. (1946). *Psychoanalytic Therapy, Principles and Applications.* New York: Ronald Press.

Bachrach, H. M., & Leaff, L. A. (1970). Analyzability: A systematic review of the clinical and quantitative literature. *J. Amer. Psychoanal. Assn.,* 26:881–90.

Bellak, L., & Small, L. (1978). *Emergency Psychotherapy and Brief Psychotherapy, 2nd Ed.* New York: Grune & Stratton.

Bibring, E. (1954). Psychoanalysis and the dynamic psychotherapies. *J. Amer. Psychoanal. Assn.,* 2:745–770.

Binder, J. L., Strup, H. H., & Schact, T. E. (1983). Countertransference in time-limited dynamic psychotherapy. *Contemp. Psychoanal.,* 19(4):605–623.

Butcher, J. N., & Koss, M. P. (1978). Research on brief and crisis centered therapies. In: *Handbook of Psychotherapy and Behavior Change, 2nd Ed.,* ed. S. L. Garfield & A. E. Bergin. New York: Wiley.

Castelnuevo-Tedesco, P. (1975). Brief psychotherapy. In: *American Handbook of Psychiatry, 2nd Ed.,* ed. S. Arieti. New York: Basic Books, pp. 254–268.

Clarkin, J. F., & Frances, A. (1982). Selection criteria for the brief psychotherapies. *Amer. J. Psychother.,* 36:166–180.

Davanloo, H. (1978). *Basic Principles and Techniques in Short-term Dynamic Psychotherapy.* New York: Spectrum Press.

Eissler, K. (1953). The effect of the structure of the ego on psychoanalytic technique. *J. Amer. Psychoanal. Assn.,* 1:104–143.

Epstein, L. (1981). Countertransference and its use in judgment of fitness for analysis. *Contemp. Psychoanal.,* 17:55–68.

Ferenczi, S., & Rank, O. (1956). *The Development of Psychoanalysis.* New York: Dover.

Frances, A., Clarkin, J., & Perry, S. (1984). *Differential Therapeutics in Psychiatry: The Art and Science of Treatment Selection.* New York: Brunner/Mazel.

Freud, S. (1914). Remembering, repeating and working-through, *Standard Edition* 12:145–156. London: Hogarth Press, 1958.

Gill, M. M. (1979). The analysis of the transference. *J. Amer. Psychoanal. Assn.,* 27(Supp):263–288.

Kernberg, O. F. (1965). Notes on countertransference. *J. Amer. Psychoanal. Assn.,* 13:38–56.

——— (1982). Supportive psychotherapy with borderline conditions. In: *Critical Problems in Psychiatry,* ed. J. O. Cavenar & H. K. Brodie. Philadelphia: Lippincott.

Kernberg, O. F., Burstein, E. D., & Coyne , L. (1978). Psychotherapy and psychoanalysis: Final report of the Menninger Foundation's Psychotherapy Research Project. *Bull. Menn. Clin.,* 36:3–275.

Kohut, H. (1977). *The Restoration of the Self.* New York: International Universities Press.

Luborsky, L., & Spence, D. (1978). Quantitative research on psychoanalytic psychotherapy. In: *Handbook of Psychotherapy and Behavior Change,* ed. S. Garfield & A. Bergin. New York: Wiley.

Malan, D. H. (1976a). *The Frontier of Brief Psychotherapy.* New York: Plenum Press.

——— (1976b). *Toward the Validation of Dynamic Psychotherapy: A Replication.* New York: Plenum Press.

Mann, J. (1973). *Time Limited Psychotherapy.* Cambridge, MA: Harvard University Press.

May, P. R. (1973). Research in psychotherapy and psychoanalysis. *Internat. J. Psychiat.,* 11:78–86.

Parloff, M. B. (1979). Research in psychotherapy and psychoanalysis, *Internat. J. Psychiat.,* 11:78–86.

Perry, S., Frances, A., Klar, H., & Clarkin, J. (1983). Selection criteria for individual dynamic psychothe'apies. *Psychiat. Quart.,* 55(1):3–16.

Racker, H. (1968). *Transference and Countertransference.* New York: International Universities Press.

Sandler, J. (1976). Countertransference and role responsiveness. *Internat. Rev. Psycho-Anal.,* 3:43–47.

Schafer, R. (1973). The termination of brief psychoanalytic psychotherapy. *Internat. J. Psychoanal. Psychother.,* 2:135–148.

Searles, H. F. (1965). Oedipal love in the Countertransference. *Collected Papers on Schizophrenia and Related Subjects.* New York: International Universities Press.

Sifneos, P. E. (1976). *Short-term Psychotherapy and Emotional Crisis.* Cambridge, MA: Harvard University Press.

Small, L. (1979). *The Briefer Therapies, 2nd Ed.* New York: Brunner/Mazel.

Smith, M., Glass, G. V., & Miller, T. I. (1980). *The Benefits of Psychotherapy.* Baltimore: Johns Hopkins University Press.

Stone, L. (1954). The widening scope of indications for psychoanalysis. *J. Amer. Psychoanal. Assn.* 12:567–594.

Strachey, J. (1934). The nature of the therapeutic action of psychoanalysis. *Internat. J. Psycho-Anal.,* 15:127–159.

Strupp, H. H. (1975). Psychoanalysis, "focal psychotherapy," and the nature of the therapeutic influence. *Arch. Gen. Psychiat.,* 32:127–135.

______ (1980). Success and failure in time-limited psychotherapy. *Arch. Gen. Psychiat.,* 37:947–954.

Tarachow, S., & Stein, A. (1967). Psychoanalytic Psychotherapy. In: *Psychoanalytic Techniques: A Handbook for the Practicing Psychoanalyst,* ed. B. Wollman. New York: Basic Books.

Tyson, R. L., & Sandler, J. (1971). Problems in the selection of patients for psychoanalysis: Comments on the application of the concepts of indications, suitability and analyzability. *Brit. J. Med. Psychol.,* 44:211–229.

Valenstein, A. F. (1979). The concept of "classical" psychoanalysis. *J. Amer. Psychoanal. Assn.,* 27 (Supp):113–136.

Waldhorn, H. (1967). Indications for Psychoanalysis, in *Kris Study Group Monograph,* ed. E. Joseph, New York: International Universities Press.

Wolberg, L. (1980). *Handbook of Short-Term Psychotherapy.* New York: Thieme-Stratton.

CHAPTER EIGHT

Transference Interpretations in Focal Therapy: When Are They Indicated?

Allen Frances

Within the relatively narrow compass of focal therapy, is it possible to interpret the transference, and how important to treatment outcome is interpretation in this specific type of technical intervention? The literature contains three seemingly contradictory answers. Some authors (Malan, 1963; Sifneos, 1972; Mann, 1973; Malan, 1976; Davanaloo, 1978), present the "radical" view that transference interpretation is the single most crucial technique for promoting change. Others (Berliner, 1941; Deutsch, 1949; Pumpian-Mindlin, 1953), the "conservatives," believe that transference interpretation is indispensable in psychoanalysis but out of place in focal therapy. A third group (we might call them "skeptics") (Rosenzweig, 1936; Frank, 1971; Shapiro, 1971; Sloane, Staples, Cristol, Yorkston, & Whipple, 1975; Strupp, 1975) argue that the nonspecific interpersonal features shared by all psychotherapies are more important in producing change than are specific treatment techniques. In summary, there are those who think that interpretation of the transference is essential to focal therapy, those who advise against it, and those who say it does not matter much what is said specifically as long as doctor and patient are engaged in a meaningful therapeutic relationship.

This debate has both a narrow and a more general importance. Research defining the effects of transference interpretation in focal therapy will no doubt improve technique in this modality of treatment. More broadly, for better and worse, this investigation has become a testing ground for psychodynamic psychiatry and a paradigm for clinical research into psychotherapy process and outcome. Psychoanalysis and long term exploratory psychotherapy are difficult to study systematically because of their complexity and long duration. Not surprisingly, clinical researchers prefer to use data derived from the more convenient study of focal therapy to validate or invalidate psychodynamic hypotheses. Any reasoning by analogy from focal therapy to psychoanalysis suffers from the obvious weakness that the different psychodynamic treatments differ in what are likely to be essential ways. Nonetheless, focal therapy is the first psychodynamic treatment to receive careful scientific scrutiny, and its elucidation is bound to influence opinion about more general questions in psychodynamic psychiatry.

This chapter reviews the evidence supporting the three contradictory positions mentioned above, reconciles them, and discusses clinical situations in which each is most applicable. Two cases are described briefly—one in which transference interpretations seemed necessary and effective, another which progressed quite nicely with interpretations that never involved the transference.

THREE VIEWS

The Radical View

Not long after Freud had recognized transference as a complication of the "talking cure," he realized that he had accidentally discovered a phenomenon of great technical power. The sources of a patient's neurosis were made available by repetition in the immediacy of the current transference situation and not just by remembering (Freud, 1914). Strachey's (1934) enormously influential paper "The Nature of the Therapeutic Action of Psychoanalysis" settled for many analysts that the ultimate instrument in their work with patients was in *mutative interpretation* of the transference neurosis. Strachey offered three arguments to support his hypothesis that transference interpretations are unique in producing profound intrapsychic change: (a) in analysis, the point of emotional urgency available for interpretation is most likely to be the transference neurosis; (b) the distortions in the patient's perception of the analyst are the only ones that can be demonstrated with certainty; and (c) the patient's unrealistic superego can be modified only by the gradual introjection of the realistic images of the analyst which result from transference interpretation.

Even if these arguments were to be accepted for psychoanalysis, they cannot easily be applied to brief therapy. The first notion travels especially badly—in brief therapy, the point of emotional urgency often involves events occurring in the patient's outside life, not the therapist's. Furthermore, although it has become a basic tenet of psychoanalytic technique, the special effectiveness of transference interpretations has never received scientific testing and confirmation. Schafer (1973) argues that such testing is in principle impossible and that questions about analytic technique are not answerable by methods of behavioral science. We will not take up this interesting argument, but instead will review such studies as are available.

The current leading contributors to the focal therapy literature (Malan, 1965, 1976a,b; Sifneos, 1972; Mann, 1973; Davanloo, 1978) all support the notion that transference interpretations are the most crucial of its technical interventions. Malan has studied the question in a clinically sophisticated research enterprise. During the past twenty years, he and his colleagues at the Tavistock Clinic conducted two separate investigations of a total sample of 60 focal treatments and obtained follow ups that extend, in some cases, to more than ten years. Malan (1963, 1976a,b) concluded that the most important technical procedure in producing enduring psychodynamic change was the thorough interpretation of the transference. Successful outcome correlated significantly, but fairly weakly, with early interpretation of the transference and careful exploration of the patient's feelings about termination. Of all types of transference interpretation, the most important seemed to be those linking the patient's transference feelings to his relation to parents (T/P link).

Malan (1963, 1976a,b), somewhat optimistically, suggests that these findings constitute validation of dynamic psychotherapy. Severe methodological limitations restrict the authority of this conclusion. Malan's naturalistic design did not allow for control groups, precise definition of the treatment, and sufficient measurement of possibly pertinent patient variables. His ratings of treatment process scored therapists' notes, which had been dictated from memory after therapy sessions—a data source that is subject to considerable and systematic bias. Most of the process and outcome ratings were not made blind. Malan's measures of psychodynamic change are creatively operational, but remain controversial and vulnerable to attack—from one side as too subjective and unscientific, from the other as too superficial and unpsychoanalytic.

Because there was no control group, it is impossible to know for certain whether focal treatment had any effect whatever on the patients, even on those who did well. Furthermore, as Malan (1963, 1976a,b) acknowledges, correlations do not imply causality. Although T/P interpretations correlated with psychodynamic change, we cannot conclude that they caused the improvement. It is equally plausible, within Malan's design, that causality flows in the other direction; that is, good outcome patients may cause, or at least allow, their therapists to make transference-parent linking interpretations (or retrospectively to report having done so). The therapists in this study, analytically oriented, would be naturally inclined to make transference interpretation and were not blind to the hypotheses. Despite these reservations, Malan's research is of considerable interest. Although he does not conclusively prove transference interpretations to be specifically helpful in focal therapy, his findings confirm Strachey's (1934) hypothesis and the clinical experience of many leading practitioners of focal therapy.

The Conservative View

Most psychoanalysts, particularly those with little experience in focal therapy, tend to regard it conservatively and perhaps with a jaundiced eye. Therapists whose professional practice consists primarily of psychoanalysis follow a model that requires considerable therapist passivity, encourages the development of a regressive transference neurosis, and avoids premature transference interpretations. Change is not expected to occur quickly or without considerable working through. Those analysts may have occasion to conduct nonanalytic treatments but tend to do so in a markedly trimmed down fashion. Psychodynamic understanding is applied, but transference interpretations and reconstructions are avoided. Any treatment short of analysis is regarded as a poor compromise, unlikely to produce profound character change, and indicated only when circumstances demand it (patient in crisis, lacking resources, or unsuitable for psychoanalysis). This point of view contrasts with the radical position that focal therapy can include the basic analytic technique of transference interpretation, can produce enduring characterological change, and is sometimes the treatment of choice.

There is no scientific research to support the conservative view, but there is also little doubt that it is appropriate for many patients who do not meet the stringent selection criteria often suggested for focal therapy. It is likely, nonetheless, that conservative authors are unnecessarily cautious in adapting psychoanalytic techniques, including transference interpretations, to other treatment settings. It is also quite possible that nontransference interpretations are mutative and that conservative practitioners promote more intrapsychic change in their patients than they claim or realize.

The Skeptical View

Skeptics, as defined here, accept that psychotherapy works but question whether its beneficial affects are attributable to any of the specific technical interventions so cherished by their practitioners. This hypothesis, stated by Rosenzweig (1936) almost fifty years ago, has been championed convincingly by Frank (1971) and recently has received a variety of interesting research confirmations. Sophisticated reviews of the literature on psychotherapy outcome, aggregating results from hundreds of controlled studies, fail to demonstrate any specific advantages or indications differentiating one modality of treatment from another (Luborsky, Singer, and Luborsky, 1975; Smith, Glass, and Miller, 1980). If one accepts that therapies as different as the behavioral, psychodynamic, and rational emotive all produce essentially equivalent results, then it seems of little consequence whether psychodynamic interpretations are made primarily within or outside the transference. The burden of proof now seems to rest squarely with those who believe in the specific effect of different treatments. Nonetheless, the available psychotherapy outcome research is so weak, even in its aggregate, that this remains a wide open question requiring furhter, more refined study. Outcome research has been deficient in ways that limit our ability to answer questions about specificity:

1. The purpose of most available controlled studies has been to determine whether one or another competing treatment is superior in some global way. More sophisticated statistics and measures (and a larger sample are necessary to determine the specific advantages and disadvantages of particular treatments for specific patients.
2. Outcome measures tapping symptom relief can be put in specific and reliable form. Outcome measures for the change attempted in psychodynamic treatments (e.g., intrapsychic, characterological change) are more difficult to put into operational form and, perhaps, are inherently less precise. Is it possible that specific treatment effects do occur, but manage to elude our current measurement tools.
3. Until very recently, patient diagnosis was so unreliable and nonspecific as to obscure specific differences in results.
4. The treatments being studied are difficult, but not impossible, to package in a reproducible manner which would ensure that the patient receives specific interventions in the way they are meant to be delivered.

It is clear that most available outcome research has been insufficiently specific in purpose and design to determine whether different treatments are differentially effective. Recently, several studies have been performed that avoid some or most of the pitfalls listed above. We will discuss only two, both of which failed to demonstrate the efficacy of specific interventions. Even these have design and measure problems and will, in any case, certainly require extensive replication.

An interesting, but inconclusive, study was reported by Strupp and Hadley (1979). Experienced, psychodynamically oriented therapists were compared with college professors in their ability to promote change in brief psychotherapy. The subjects were male college students who on MMPI scored high on depression, psychasthenia, and social introversion. Results achieved by professional and lay therapists were essentially equivalent, and it was patient, not therapy, variables (Strupp, 1980) that best predicted outcome. The evidence against specificity provided by this study would be convincing if there were not serious problems in its method of patient selection, definition of treatments, outcome measures, and sample size. The most telling weakness resulted from difficulties in patient recruitment, which forced the investigators to advertise for subjects. Patients in this study may thus differ in important ways from true and unsolicited patients. It is also unclear whether college professors would have done as well treating patients who were not students—what kindly professors have to offer depressed and lonely students in a campus counseling setting may have been quite specific for this population.

Sloane et al. (1975) conducted a beautifully designed study comparing results achieved by experienced behavioral and by psychodynamic therapists in brief treatments of nonpsychotic outpatients. Both treatment groups were significantly more improved than a waiting list control group, but were virtually indistinguishable in outcome and in patients' perceptions of what had occurred during therapy. If replicated, this study presents telling evidence against the notion that specific interventions matter a great deal. Its weaknesses reflect the state of the outcome research art (i.e., the relatively uncontrolled treatments, target symptom oriented measures, and small sample).

That available research supports the skeptical position means only that specific differences have yet to be demonstrated and does not prove their nonexistence. In the meantime, no one has recommended that patients be assigned to treatment techniques based on a coin flip. Even if it turns out that nonspecific treatment conditions are much more influential than expected, specific interventions must still be chosen to meet specific patient needs and tastes, as best these can be perceived. On the other hand, the available data certainly do provide a useful antidote to anyone afflicted with therapeutic dogmatism.

DISCUSSION

Systematic research designed to determine the effects of transference interpretation has only just begun. Because the early results are necessarily inconclusive, we are forced to rely on clinical judgment in conducting current work. None of the three positions we have reviewed is supported by very compelling data, and it is perhaps not even very plausible to assume that any one would be applicable to all clinical situations. The three views are easily reconciled if we accept that all are sometimes true and none is always true. In some focal treatments, transference interpretation may be indispensable; in others, it will be unnecessary or potentially harmful; and there may be times when the fine points of technique do not matter one way or the other. We will specify, on clinical grounds and tentatively, those situations in which each position seems most useful. The following suggestions are specific to focal therapy and cannot be generalized to the very different treatment environments that characterize psychoanalysis and long-term exploratory therapy.

Transference interpretations in a focal therapy are most likely to be appropriate under a preponderance of the following conditions:

1. The patient has developed emotionally immediate transference distortions directed toward the therapist, and this has become the point of urgency for the treatment.
Z. The transference distortions onstitute resistance and are an impediment to the therapeutic alliance.
3. Interpretation of the transference distortions appears to strengthen the therapeutic alliance.
4. Conflicts revealed in the transference relationship with the therapist are a reflection of the conflicts responsible for the patient's chief complaint and the patient's nuclear conflict.
5. The patient is sufficiently endowed with personality attributes that make transference interpretation possible (psychological mindedness, intelligence, affect modulation, frustration tolerance, impulse control, ability to simultaneously participate and observe, and so forth)
6. Treatment is of *sufficient duration* to allow exploration of a manageable transference paradigm.

The analysis of transference is probably unnecessary or inadvisable to the extent that: (a) the patient fails to develop particularly strong or meaningful transference distortions about the therapist, and the major resistances that evolve are not within the transference; (b) the patient's intrapsychic conflicts instead find expression in current dealings with significant others outside the treatment situation; (c) the therapeutic alliance is weakened by transference interpretations and not sufficiently established to tolerate this challenge; (d) the patient is poorly endowed with the factors that enable transference interpretation; and (e) the treatment is too brief for even a partial analysis of transference distortions. In these situations, such interpretations as are made will elucidate the patient's transference to people other than the therapist and resistances that do not involve the transference.

It is impossible at this point even to guess the characteristics of those patients most influenced by general aspects of the therapeutic relationship and for whom the specific use or avoidance of transference interpretation is peripheral to treatment outcome. One suspects, however, that the nonspecific benefits of the therapeutic relationship are most important for patients who are in crisis situations and/or at developmental transition points.

Thus far, we have considered only those attributes within the patient that might determine whether the interpretation of the transference becomes possible. We must now complicate this picture by acknowledging that the real attributes of the therapist as these are revealed in the interaction with the patient, serve as triggers to some of the patient's potential transference reactions and may suppress others. This is particularly true in brief therapy. In an example described later, Mr. B. is almost completely reasonable and realistic in his dealings with a male therapist but might well have experienced important transference distortions to his therapist had she been female.

As mentioned earlier, many investigators generalize from findings concerning focal therapy to make broader statements about psychodynamic treatment and theory. Such jumps should inspire caution. Given our current data, there is no way of knowing whether transference interpretations have the same, or even similar, impact when they are offered in the different contexts of focal, long-term, and psychoanalytic treatments. The transference available for interpretation seems to be quite a different phenomenon in each setting. In focal therapy, transference reactions directed toward the therapist are equivalent to transference reactions the patient displays toward significant others in his everyday life. In contrast, the transference regression occurring in psychoanalysis allows for the recovery of previously submerged paradigms. Also different in the two treatments is the nature and timing of transference interpretation. In focal therapy, these are made early, based on incomplete data, and occur in a less emotionally charged field. In this context, transference interpretations are more likely to be heard (and to be given) as an aid to intellectual understanding and problem solving. This can be enormously useful but probably has an impact different from the transference interpretations made within analysis.

Much of the controversy surrounding focal therapy has resulted from a misunderstanding, shared by supporters and critics alike, that this treatment is a replacement for, or competitor to, psychoanalysis. Analysts are skeptical of claims that any brief treatment will quickly, and relatively painlessly, produce the same sort of change they know to be more difficult and time consuming. We do not at this time have sufficiently sensitive measuring instruments to differentiate the effects of focal therapy from those of psychoanalysis. Nonetheless, there is every reason to continue to believe they are different and to try to demonstrate this with more sophisticated research designs and instruments.

CASE ILLUSTRATIONS

I will present two brief examples of focal therapy—in one, transference interpretations seemed crucially important; in the other, they seemed unnecessary. These are, of course, no more than illustrations of the issues involved and are not intended as proofs. Firm conclusions can be drawn only from controlled study, not from anecdotal report. Alternatative lines of interpretative approach will undoubtedly occur to the reader, as they did to me. Focal therapy requires no more than the meaningful exploration of one conflictual area and makes no claim to comprehensiveness.

Case 1

Ms. A., an attractive, unmarried, twenty-four year old nurse, presented with slashed arms and fears that she was going crazy. Her boyfriend had recently ended their relationship after several days of bitter argument. The patient had experienced insomnia, unbearable restlessness, and tension and hatred for both the boyfriend and herself. She concluded that relief would come only with the infliction (fortunately mild) of self-mutilation and pain.

During initial sessions, the patient talked about herself with emotion and some insight. Soon, however, she became consistently silent and finally admitted that she did not believe in psychiatry. A bit of exploration made clear that this shift in behavior was a specific manifestation of transference resistance—the patient had quickly, and erroneously, concluded that the therapist did not like her and was finding her unworthy of his efforts. She had remained quiet about her doubts in order not to disturb the therapist or hurt his feelings. These issues were examined during the middle stages of this twenty-two session brief therapy. Her fears of hurting the therapist recalled her longstanding fears of harming people she cared for—e.g., her boyfriend, mother (who had recently died of cancer), hospital patients (she feared she might kill them accidentally), and a younger brother addicted to drugs. Beneath the fear of hurting, she began to recover her anger towards people for the demands or disappointments they inflicted upon her. Ms. A.'s assumption that the therapist did not like her seemed to be a projection of her own harsh self-condemnation and intolerance for destructive fantasies. In addition, she had experienced her parents as clearly favoring her brothers, and she had easily become convinced that the therapist would find his other, especially male, patients, more interesting.

This intelligent, highly motivated, and psychologically minded woman responded to transference interpretations with new and emotionally meaningful material. She was gradually able to correct distortions in her view of the therapist and to gain perspective about herself. In this process, she became more accepting to her aggressive fantasies and less likely to project self-condemnation onto the therapist or important people in her current life. She also seemed more tolerant of defects in others, especially in her father. As termination approached, Ms. A. became less constricted and began to express shy, fond feelings to the therapist. Her difficulty in experiencing warm, and also sexual, feelings towards him reminded her of similar problems with her boyfriend, which had been the occasion of their bitter fight and separation. Traced further, she recalled a time when she had been quite close to her father, but their comfort with one another had ended with her puberty. In part, then, her anger towards men was seen as a means of avoiding tender and sexual feelings that she experienced as both inherently wrong and also leading to ultimate abandonment.

On three-month follow up, Ms. A.'s dress and manner had become more comfortably feminine, her range of emotions was wider, and she was happy. She had begun a new relationship with a man that seemed less inhibited in its tender and angry expression. I felt convinced that the attention to and interpretation of the transference were necessary to establish the therapeutic alliance with this patient, to shed light on her intrapsychic conflicts and interpersonal difficulties and to promote specific changes.

Case 2

Mr. B. was a successful, forty-year-old business executive forced into treatment by his wife, who threatened divorce unless he immediately changed his behavior towards her. He was bewildered by her dissatisfaction, had no idea how he might be contributing to her unhappiness, and assumed that she must be "high strung." Nonetheless, Mr. B. loved his wife, wanted to preserve his marriage, and invited the psychiatrist to tell him what he was doing wrong so that he could try to change. Mr. B., a practical-minded, no nonsense sort of fellow, wanted (and needed) fast results but was initially quite skeptical about psychotherapy.

Throught this twelve-session focal treatment, Mr. B. related to the therapist in a generally friendly and cooperative, if somewhat controlling, manner. Because his major resistances were characterological and major transference distortions were directed towards his wife, it was in these areas that interpretations were made. It was soon pointed out to Mr. B. that he was a methodical, perfectionistic man, so preoccupied by detail as to leave little room for spontaneity in his treatment or his life. His constricted expression of feelings, especially tender ones, was immediately apparent. Mr. B. noted with surprise that these were indeed the very things his wife had complained about, although he had never before taken her observations very seriously. He now became able to notice ways in which he criticized, frustrated, and intimidated his wife.

When Mr. B. eventually became curious about the reasons for his behavior, the therapist asked him to explore previous experiences with women. Mr. B. immediately and emotionally described his mother as domineering, demanding, critical, and impossible to manage. He discovered that he had been engaged in a lifelong struggle to fend her off and to control his own loving and dependent desires to be cared for and controlled by her. This conflict had been repeated with his wife and had taken the color out of their relationship. Interpretation of transference distortions towards his wife, and in his current dealings with his mother, helped Mr. B. to respond more freely and realistically in both relationships. On follow up, the marriage had improved considerably and his compulsiveness was less prominent. He remained friendly, cooperative, and somewhat controlling with the therapist.

CONCLUSIONS

The current state of accumulated research evidence and clinical experience should discourage any tendency to therapeutic dogmatism about the specific methods and effects of focal and other forms of psychotherapy. One cannot argue convincingly that focal therapy requires transference interpretations, that it precludes them, or that it does not matter either way. Flexibility is required in meeting the particular needs of any given patient with what seems to be the optimal intervention. In the absence of scientific guidelines, decisions about what is optimal rely on informed clinical judgment and intuition. Certain tentative and unsupported clinical indications for and against transference interpretation in focal therapy have been outlined in this chapter.

REFERENCES

Berliner, B. (1941), Short psychoanalytic psychotherapy: Its possibility and its limitations. *Bull. Menn. Clin.* 5:204–211.

Davanloo, H. (1978). *Basic Principles and Techniques in Short-Term Dynamic Psychotherapy.* New York: Spectrum.

Deutsch, F. (1949). Applied Psychoanalysis. New York: Grune & Stratton.

Frank, J. D. (1971). Therapeutic factors in psychotherapy. *Am. J. Psychother.,* 25:350–361.

Freud, S. (1914). Remembering, repeating and working through. *Standard Edition,* 12:145–156. London: Hogarth Press, 1958.

Luborsky, L., Singer, B. & Luborsky, L. (1975). Comparative studies of psychotherapies: Is it true that "Everybody has won and all must have prizes"? *Arch. Gen. Psychiat.,* 32:995–1008.

Malan, D. H. (1963). *A Study of Brief Psychotherapy.* London: Tavistock.

Malan, D. H. (1976a), *The Frontier of Brief Psychotherapy.* New York. Plenum Press.

Malan, D. H. (1976b). *Toward the Validation of Dynamic Psychotheraphy: A Replication.* New York. Plenum Press.

Mann, J. (1973). *Time Limited Psychotherapy.* Cambridge, MA: Harvard University Press.

Pumpian-Mindlin, E. (1953), Considerations in the selection of patients for short term therapy. *Am. J. Psychother.* 7:641.

Rosenzweig, S. (1936), Some implicit common factors in diverse methods of psychotherapy. *Am. J. Orthopsychiat.,* 6:422–425.

Schafer, R. (1973), The termination of brief psychoanalytic psychotherapy. *Internat. J. Psychoanal. Psychother.* 2:135–148.

Shapiro, A. K. (1971), Placebo effects in medicine, psychotherapy, and psycho-analysis. In: *Handbook of Psychotherapy and Behavior Change* ed. A. E. Bergin & S. L. Garfield, New York. Wiley, pp. 439–473.

Sifneos, P. E. (1972). *Short-Term Psychotherapy and Emotional Crisis.* Cambridge: Harvard University Press.

Sloane, R. B., Staples, F. R., Cristol, A. H. , Yorkston, N. J., & Whipple, K. (1975), *Psychotherapy versus Behavior Therapy.* Cambridge, MA: Harvard University Press.

Smith, M. L., Glass, G., & Miller, T. I. (1980). *Benefits of Psychotherapy.* Baltimore: Johns Hopkins University Press.

Strachey, J. (1934). The nature of the therapeutic action of psychoanalysis. *Internat. J. Psycho-Anal.* 15:127–159.

Strupp, H. H. (1975). Psychoanalysis, "focal psychotherapy," and the nature of the therapeutic influence. *Arch. Gen. Psychiat.* 32:127–135.

Strupp, H. H., & Hadley, S. W. (1979). Specific vs. nonspecific factors in psychotherapy: a controlled study of outcome. *Arch. Gen. Psychiat.* 36:1125–1136.

Strupp, H. H. (1980). Success and failure in time-limited psychotherapy. *Arch. Gen. Psychiat.* 947–958.

CHAPTER NINE

Transference and Countertransference in Brief Psychotherapy

James Mann

It is relatively easy to present a review of the role of transference in brief psychotherapy as it appears in the literature. One may find every conceivable position elaborated and illustrated. The extremes are supported at one end by the Rogerian therapists, for whom transference does not exist, and at the other by therapists who advocate interpreting transference from the first moment of interaction to the last; from those who recognize but choose to ignore any transference reactions to those who choose to recognize and promote only positive transference. (Small, 1971).

In this regard, Malan (1976) reviews the opinions of some of the more important contributors to brief psychotherapy. He describes conservative, intermediate, and radical views of the transference. Typical of the conservative stance is that of Straker (1968), who speaks of the aim of brief psychotherapy as providing ego support with concurrent exploration of current external interpersonal, family, and intrapsychic conflicts. Problems and characteristic defenses are clarified, but transference interpretations are avoided where possible. The intermediate stance is represented by Bellak and Small (1965) who write:

> . . . in brief psychotherapy positive transference is sought and maintained from the beginning to the end. It is not "permitted to develop" but rather is encouraged and elicited . . . . The positive transference is fostered and taken for granted. The emergence of a negative transference is avoided as much as possible and referred to only on rare occasions when it can, in a helpful way, be related to other manifestations or when it stands in the way of therapeutic progress. (p. 11)

They add that they will not analyze defenses likely to arouse negative feelings unless these can be dealt with readily and easily for a constructive purpose.

Wolberg (1965) takes the position that:

> transference reactions are dealt with rapidly with the object of avoiding a transference neurosis. While the latter may release the deepest

> conflicts, there is no time available for the essential working through. If a transference neurosis develops without intention, this must be dissipated as soon as possible. Resistance is managed by active interpretations [p. 154].

It is reasonable to question the appearance of a transference neurosis in any form of brief therapy and even in long-term psychotherapy if it is considered to be a phenomenon arising only in psychoanalysis and all of whose complex, intense, and regressive components are the consequence of the psychoanalytic process.

Malan (1976), Sifneos (1972), and Mann (1973) are the radicals who share Menninger's concept of the "triangle of insight," connecting transference, the patient's current external relationships, and relationships with past significant figures. In contrast to Malan and Sifneos, Mann's transference interpretations—although including the past, the present, and the therapist—are not couched in libidinal and aggressive developmental terms even though these may be expressed unknowingly but very clearly by the patient. All three agree that in brief psychotherapy, powerful transferences, both positive and negative, are aroused and must be dealt with rather than avoided and further that, as in any analytic therapy, it is the positive and negative transferences and their interpretation that constitute the essential therapeutic leverage.

Malan (1976) and Sifneos (1972) interpret transferences from the start and throughout the course of treatment on the basis of their position that the presenting problem is oedipal in nature. They maintain that within the span of treatment, interpretations can rapidly be deepened to the point of making direct oedipal interpretations of both positive and negative feelings in the patient's responses to the therapist. In the particular method of time-limited psychotherapy that I have developed, presenting problems are not approached as Oedipal but rather as distorted images of the self arising out of conflict, both Oedipal and pre-Oedipal. Transference interpretations are almost never made early but rather sometime around the mid-point of treatment where there is serious resistance, and they are always made in response to both positive and negative feelings as the work of the termination phase. I go into further detail later in this chapter.

Of great interest is that there is very little said about countertransference in brief psychotherapy. Small (1971) says nothing on the subject despite his extensive review. Neither Sifneos (1972) nor Malan (1976) address this subject. Bellak and Small (1965) make some general remarks. Under the heading of Professional Resistance, they say:

> Resistance to the idea of brief psychotherapy by members of the profession arises from our identification with and reverence for the analytic process. . . . To many well trained therapists a procedure which does not develop, interpret and work through transference is not treatment. . . . The goals of brief psychotherapy are not analytic goals; the methods, therefore, are modifications [p. 13].

Later they add: "Because of the emphasis on positive transference (in their method), the selection of the proper therapist for each patient assumes great importance. The factors that may be involved include the therapist's age, sex, most comfortable role and cultural suitability" (p. 41).

Wolberg (1965), in response to a question about which characteristics in the therapist will block reconstructive therapy answers: "Unresolved hostilities, needs to maintain too dominant and authoritarian a status in the relationship, and detachment . . . a therapist will be limited by his own personality and ways of working . . . it is silly to deify and glamorize techniques . . . one has to devise and improvise as one goes along with each patient" (p. 197). Further on he alludes to countertransference as arising out of the therapist's idiosyncratic attitudes, unknowing communication of the therapist's values and intentions overtly as well as nonverbally, and the therapist's unknowing reactions to the patient's reactions to him.

Although a good deal of attention is given to the role of transference in brief therapy, it is apparent that, for some reason, countertransference is barely considered. The question is why this is so. Is it that the problems of countertransference in brief therapy are simply like those in any kind of psychotherapy and are therefore taken for granted? Should we expect different or, in some respects, more or less intense countertransference problems because we are dealing with a different form of psychotherapy? Is the fact of brevity in brief psychotherapy a sufficient reason to expect particular emphasis of any kind on the nature of countertransference? These are difficult questions because brief therapy really includes a wide variety of tactics and techniques. First of all, what is brief therapy? Is it one session, two, ten, fifty, a year, two years? Is the standard of brief therapy determined by how long it lasts as compared with long-term psychotherapy or psychoanalysis? If the latter is true (and in some instances I suspect that it is), then the time range of brief therapy extends from one session to two years. Are there any differences in countertransference responses if brief therapy is only of several sessions' duration or, in the extreme instance, of two years' duration? Is there some way we can find out?

I propose that the method of brief therapy that I have devised—time-limited psychotherapy—because of its clearly defined structure and process, may cast light on this question and, by extension, may clarify some of the other brief therapies. To do this requires some elaboration of the method and its process, with particular emphasis on the transference and countertransferences that arise and must be managed.

The core of time-limited psychotherapy lies in two elements: first, the duration of treatment, which is limited to 12 sessions with the date of the final 12th meeting announced in the first treatment session; and second, the particular means for selecting the central issue that will be the guideline through out treatment. The first treatment session begins at the point at which sufficient evaluation of the patient's problems and history allows the therapist to formulate a central issue, present it to the patient as the work to be accomplished, and gain the patient's agreement to the central issue and to 12 sessions in which to do the work. The patient is given every opportunity to raise questions or to object to the total treatment proposal. Firm objection rarely occurs. When it does, the problem is likely to be an error in case selection.

The process that the time limit and the particular kind of central issue set in motion illuminates the relationship between time, affects, and self-image, and of treatment as a desire for reunion as opposed to separation with the resultant conflict responsible for a distorted image of the self.

The patients we treat suffer unconscious conflicts and treatment must aim to uncover and expose the unconscious elements not only for the purpose of turning them to the light of day (or reason) but, more important, to subject them to reality and the test of the appropriateness or inappropriateness in terms of the patient's present status in life, which differs from what it was when the conflicts had their genesis. In the usual practice of brief therapy, attention is directed to what appears to be that among the patient's presenting complaints which seems to carry greatest weight in the present distressed state. The complaint selected usually is already heavily buttressed by long-standing and now even reinforced defenses.

In our patients, rigidly held conceptions about the self have their parallel in the conviction that nothing about the self can change. A negative self-sameness persists even in the face of reality evidence to the contrary. The central issue formulated directs the attention of the patient to this kind of fixation about the self and circumscribes the area of work for the twelve sessions. In delineating the patient's history, we look for those painful events in his life that have recurred, those that have a history over time. Further, we seek to learn how the patient managed and adapted to those painful, recurrent life events. Recurrences of course need not be similar factually; they may be totally similar symbolically and therefore also similar in the response and management of them by the patient. From the patient's hsitory then we extract the privately felt, rarely verbalized *present and chronically endured pain. It is the kind of pain that is an important statement about how one feels and has always felt about the self.* The present and chronically endured pain is the affective component of the statement by the patient to himself that he has been victimized. The victim in us is the child in us, and the child as victim tends to become elaborated as a guiding fiction in the life of the adult. In adulthood we continue to respond to events that have the same early meaning to us in the way we responded when we were children. The statement of the central issue in terms of the present and chronically endured pain spans the patient's experience from the remote past to the immediate present and into the expectable future. *With very few exceptions, therefore, the central issue as formulated by the therapist in time-limited psychotherapy will be very different from the problems that the patient states are his reasons for seeking help.* Further, because the variety of affects available to all mankind is limited, the present and chronically endured pain can be identified in all patients of all classes, irrespective of education and socioeconomic status.

The goal of time-limited psychotherapy is to foster as much as possible the resolution of the present and chronically endured pain, the persistent negative self-image. The patient's symptoms or complaints will be diminished or relieved through the resolution of the central issue. Symptom relief becomes a byproduct of the process, and not the goal. The time limitation, in combination with the central issue of the patient's adaptive efforts and his feelings about himself, brings to the forefront of the treatment process a central dynamic, namely, *the wish to be as one with another but the absolute necessity to learn how to tolerate separation and loss without undue damage to one's feelings about the self.* The statement of the central issue in our terms is, in effect, a paradigm of the transference that will ensue. Its aim is to enable the patient to move into and to experience affectively the origins and vicissitudes of the pain that has led to a maladaptive self statement and resultant maladaptive behavior. Time does not permit extended clinical examples, but perhaps the following will illustrate the statement of the central issue as I have defined it.

1. "You have tried very hard all your life but what hurts you is the feeling that you are stupid and a phony." (A depressed 42-year-old woman who suffered an acute disorganizing experience in conflict with her husband whom she thinks she may divorce.)

2. "You seem to be a decent sort of man and you have tried to please others, yet you feel and have always had the feeling that you are not wanted." (A 25-year-old man depressed and given to unpredictable and impulsive fights with his wife.)

3. "You are a big man who has achieved very successfully, and yet when you are alone you feel helpless." (A 35-year-old man with an acute phobia.)

4. "You are a man who has always been a scrapper. You have been successful and you are aware of your competence. However, what troubles and hurts you and always has are the feelings about your self as being small, inferior, and bad." (A 38-year-old man with the presenting complaint of mounting anxiety verging on panic in certain business situations.)

This kind of central issue reveals something the patient has never fully allowed himself to know and which has always been a source of pain. It is brought to light in an empathic and nonthreatening manner. The therapist knows and recognizes the strenuous efforts of the patient to overcome his pain, that despite his best efforts, the pain continues, and that it is precisely this which lies hidden behind the complaints or symptoms that have brought the patient for help. It is this kind of statement of the central issue that creates a tremendous sense of optimism in the patient that he can be helped and gives rise to a rapid working alliance and positive transference. The customary defenses of the patient have been bypassed and anxiety decreased; the therapist, by his statement, has come to the side of the patient and has not brought to the center of attention the conflicts of the patient with significant others. These will emerge later in a setting of trust and continuing positive transference. The transference is usually experienced in terms of father or mother or some other early substitute parent. In some cases, positive transference will prevail until the termination phase. In others, ambivalence and latent or overt negative transference will appear at and shortly beyond the mid-point of the 12 sessions; in still others, negative transference may appear by the third or fourth meeting. In the latter instance, interpretation of the transference is made in order to overcome the resistance. In all instances, the initial positive transference provides an unusual amount of personal data, so much that the interpretations that will follow, whether in response to positive or negative transference, will be based on solid factual information and not on guesswork.

The most common instance is that in which the positive transference prevails until the termination phase, the last three, sometimes four, sessions. No effort is made to interpret the early positive transference. Rather, my aim is to use all the sessions preceding the termination phase as data gathering in preparation for what I know is coming, namely, the reaction to termination, which, as I have already noted, is going to be an experiential repetition of the central issue. The patient will once more feel stupid and phony, or unwanted, or helpless or inferior and small. In the termination phase, interpretations of the negative transference will undo the negative self-image by virtue of a process that is insightful, cognitive, and experiential.

The structural model of time-limited psychotherapy makes the process intensely affective for both patient and therapist. The emotional life of the patient is at a substantial boil from the first session to the last, and the impact of the patient's feelings and the necessity for the therapist to keep abreast, even ahead, of what is transpiring in the patient places considerable strain on his own capacity for keeping his transference and countertransference under control. In fact, I believe that it is the therapist's countertransference that becomes the major issue in undertaking this kind of therapy, as well as in bringing treatment to an appropriate close in the time agreed upon.

It is true that once a therapist becomes comfortable in the mode of treatment he regularly employs, it is difficult to change gears, to work more rapidly, to endure the anxiety of something new and different in process although not at all different in content. The commitment to any kind of brief therapy, however short or long, implies an obligation for the therapist to be of help over a brief period of time. Uncertainty about one's competence to do this creates a readiness to feel guilty as treatment goes on. A positive transference usually makes treatment sufficiently comfortable to make one wish to continue, whereas negative transference stimulates guilt and the feeling that one must do more and give more. Brief therapy is often most attractive to beginning or young therapists who have not yet adapted to some particularly comfortable mode of working and to whom helping patients quickly is also very appealing. Suffice it to say that brief therapy is, I believe, more difficult than long-term therapy and requires experience in long-term therapy as a prerequisite. Personal analysis always provides an increment to the therapist's skill, understanding, and ability to manage transference and countertransference.

The most overt countertransferences are observable in those who consider doing time-limited psychotherapy and in those engaged in it. The idea of setting a clear, brief time limit is anathema to some therapists. The many apparently reasonable and theoretical objections that may be raised are, for the most part, rationalizations in the service of anxiety about establishing a termination point from the start. The narcissistic gains in having patients become dependent on us are felt to be aborted from the start. But there is something more important at stake. I have already noted that time-limited psychotherapy induces a process that is intensely affective for both participants. As a result, major countertransference problems arise as the termination phase approaches. You will recall my earlier statement about the central dynamic of tolerating separation and loss without undue damage to one's feelings about the self. I believe that this holds true for all of us—therapists and patients alike. The intense reaction of the patient to the termination of time-limited therapy reverberates in the conflicts around this same issue in the therapist, and it is in this phase of treatment that conscious and unconscious moves are made by the therapist that will prolong treatment. A common conscious consideration is something like this: This patient has come a long way thus far . . . Of course he has other problems . . . Could I not do more for him with some more time?

Terminations are always difficult in any kind of therapy. We have not only to endure the patient's anger and grief—we also have to endure our own, even more so in any kind of brief therapy. I believe that this accounts for the very sparse literature on termination in brief therapy, even though any kind of brief therapy presumably has set limited goals. It is difficult to stay with our limited goals, and it is easier to let the patient say when he has had enough and let it go at that or to add more sessions, or to leave the duration of treatment ambiguous, or to invite the patient to return—almost anything but to deal intensively and actively with the powerful responses of the patient to the meaning of the end.

Objections to brief psychotherapy as an effective goal-limited modality can no longer be sustained. Neither can negation of the appearance of powerful positive and negative transferences in brief therapy. I have tried in this brief review to point up the importance of dealing with the positive and negative transferences even as one must do in long-term therapy or in psychoanalysis. I have also noted some of the countertransference responses peculiar to time-limited psychotherapy and possibly applicable to all varieties of psychotherapy in which the therapist commits himself to a short period of time in which to be of help.

REFERENCES

Bellak, L., & Small, L. (1965). *Emergency Psychotherapy and Brief Psychotherapy.* New York: Grune & Stratton.

Malan, D. H. (1976). *The Frontier of Brief Psychotherapy.* New York: Plenum Medical Book Co.

Mann, J. (1973). *Time Limited Psychotherapy.* Cambridge, MA: Harvard University Press.

Mann, J., & Goldman, R. (1982). *A Casebook in Time Limited Psychotherapy.* New York: McGraw Hill.

Small, L. (1971). *The Briefer Psychotherapies.* New York: Brunner/Mazel.

Sifneos, P. (1972). *Short Term Psychotherapy and Emotional Crisis.* Cambridge, MA: Harvard University Press.

Straker, M. (1968). Brief Psychotherapy in an Out Patient Clinic: Evolution and Evaluation. *Amer. J. Psychiat.* 124:1219.

Wolberg, L. (1965). *Short Term Psychotherapy.* New York: Grune & Stratton.

CHAPTER TEN

The Psychodynamic Life Narrative: Its Implications as a Transference Cure

Milton Viederman

INTRODUCTION

What is described in this chapter is a brief psychotherapeutic intervention, that I call the *psychodynamic life narrative.* Originally developed to treat depression in physically ill patients, it represents the encounter of a psychoanalyst with a special patient population, the physically ill. Although it is not primarily interpretive in nature or designed to foster insight, at least as it pertains to unconscious conflicts, the intervention must be understood in psychoanalytic terms. It is an application of psychoanalytic theory to a situation that does not involve psychoanalytic treatment per se. Although it evolved in a consultation-liaison setting, it has implications that go beyond the treatment of the physically ill, particularly to individuals who are experiencing other life crises. However, even in this regard, the experience of working with patients in a general hospital highlights life cycle issues that are sometimes obscured in psychoanalytic work with character disorders. It is the intention of this chapter to demonstrate the richness that psychoanalysis as a theory can bring to work with patients in a general hospital.

The psychodynamic life narrative is a brief psychotherapeutic intervention that functions, in part, as a transference cure.[1] Such cures are usually considered adventitious and unfortunate complications

---

*This chapter is an expanded version of "The psychodynamic Life narrative: A psychotherapeutic intervention useful in crisis situations. *Psychiatry,* 46:236–246, 1983. Adapted by permission.

[1]The idea of a psychodynamic life narrative is not to be confused with what Schafer (1978) has called the Psychoanalytic Life History. This is the product of analysis, the integrated view that the patient evolves of his participation in his own life experience *and the role of conflict and wishful fantasy, guilt, etc.* in his developmental experience as it relates to his current life. This is never presented to the patient in a comprehensive way but on some level is what the patient and analyst have arrived at at the end of analysis.

of insight-oriented therapy. However, the idea of mobilizing the transference, rather than interpreting it, adds a powerful tool to the psychotherapist's armamentarium. The use of the Psychodynamic life narrative with patients who are physically ill or in crisis has been described in previous papers. (Viederman, 1983; Viederman & Perry, 1980). Though considerable attention was devoted to possible therapeutic modes of action, it was only later and after use with patients other than those afflicted with physical illness that it became apparent that the special power of the intervention could be understood as a transference cure.

In many ways, the intent and presumed therapeutic effect of the psychodynamic life narrative are diametrically opposite to those of brief, focal psychotherapy, as it has been described by Mann (1973), Sifneos (1972), Davanloo (1978), and Malan (1976). It has many of the characteristics of crisis intervention and is most effective with those patients who become depressed in response to an important event in their lives that has disrupted a previous relatively comfortable homeostatis. Though based upon psychodynamic principles, the primary intent of the psychodynamic life narrative is not to foster insight as it pertains to repressed intrapsychic conflict; rather, it offers a construct to a patient who is experiencing depression or other symptomatic responses to a major life crisis. This construct, when presented to the patient, mobilizes an idealizing transference and thereby offers a latent and uninterpreted transference gratification, which reciprocally increases the power of the construct and may include unconscious transference fantasies of a continued relationship with the therapist.

Though the technique was evolved in working with the physically ill it can be applied in a variety of situations, to people who are experiencing other types of crises in their lives, particularly crises of involution and old age, and even in situations where the critical crisis occurred many years before and left residual symptoms (see Case 2 later). However, because the predicament of the physically ill patient was so central in the development of this intervention, much of the discussion centers on its use in that situation.

This chapter describes the psychodynamic life narrative and discusses its usefulness as it relates to the ingredients of crisis in the physically ill. Two illustrative cases are described. These are followed by a discussion of the logic of the efficacy of the psychodynamic life narrative. Emphasis is on the presentation to the patient of a organizing construct defining his current predicament in relationship to his past and the formation of a silent, idealizing transference that facilitates the patient's assimilation of the construct.

THE CRISIS OF PHYSICAL ILLNESS AND THE PSYCHODYNAMIC LIFE NARRATIVE

It is not surprising that the development of this intervention should have occurred in the context of work with patients in the crisis of physical illness. This crisis may be viewed as having three characteristics: (a) psychic disequilibrium with confusion and uncertainty, (b) regression with intensified transferences, and (c) a tendency to examine the trajectory of one's life. These characteristics make the patient not only more vulnerable, but potentially more responsive to intervention.

Patients respond to the disequilibrium evoked by significant and disruptive challenge with regressive attempts to reestablish the comfort and safety previously experienced with parental figures. This regression fosters intense transference responses and reactivates old conflicts. As important as psychic disruption and regression is the third element, namely, "that the crisis of physical illness forces the patient to take stock of his life, to examine where he has been, where he is going, and what expectations now will or will not be fulfilled." (Viederman & Perry, 1980, p. 174). This is accentuated by the real or imagined threat to his life. According to Viederman and Perry (1980):

> Under normal circumstances an adult has some sense of the trajectory of his life, a perception of what has happened, what the future will be, what he has come to value, and what he seeks for satisfaction, security and self-esteem. This includes fantasies—conscious and unconscious—of what he one day, ideally, will become, with the implication that the future offers the potential to fulfill dreams that have not yet come true. A 'life crisis' occurs when the person becomes aware that a fantasied life trajectory will not be realized. A shift has occurred and the perception of one's life trajectory must be modified. . . .
>
> Physical illness can cause such a shift and have a profound impact on the perception of one's relationship to the world. The self-examination of one's life trajectory can no longer be accomplished comfortably over time or defensively relegated to the future. Illness forces a painful confrontation that cannot be disavowed so easily [p. 179].

As a result, the patient may be forced to cope prematurely with what Erikson defines as the normative life crisis of old age, the struggle with integrity vs. despair and disgust. Erikson (1959) emphasizes that integrity is "the acceptance of one's own and only life cycle and of the people who have become significant to it as something that had to be and that, by necessity, permitted no substitutions." On the other hand, despair is associated with "an unconscious fear of death," and "expresses the feeling that time is short, too short for the attempt to start another life and try out alternate roads to integrity" (p. 98). Any crisis that demands a changed perception of oneself in relationship to the world is likely to evoke such an examination.

THE CONCEPT OF THE PSYCHODYNAMIC LIFE NARRATIVE

It is with these considerations in mind that the psychodynamic life narrative has a particular logic as a therapeutic device. The narrative consists of a statement to the patient that places his emotional response to the precipitating event in the context of his life trajectory. The statement "explains" what this illness means psychodynamically to this particular person at this particular time. The patient's emotional response is viewed as a natural result of his personal psychology rather than an inevitable consequence of the current experience per se. Although the statement is based on the psychodynamic formulation that evolves from the consultation, only certain parts of this formulation are presented to the patient.

The narrative is designed to be ego syntonic, and, therefore, it specifically avoids the interpretation of substantial, repressed conflict. Because such a narrative is usually given after two or three interviews, this abbreviated and parsimonious statement will be oversimplified but its very simplication provides a cohesive structure. Hence, the narrative has some of the characteristics of an inexact interpretation (Glover, 1955). It is intended to offer cognitive structure based on preconscious elements, to create order out of chaos, and specifically to support intellectualizing defenses in part by organizing a coherent account of the patient's current experience of himself and his plight in relationship to the past. In this respect, by avoiding the interpretation of defense, it is the very opposite of what is intended in brief focal psychotherapies. Moreover, self-esteem is solidified by emphasizing past strengths, supporting coping mechanisms that have been effective in the past, and, where applicable, by pointing out that the current response is understandable because previous adaptive modes can no longer be used. The narrative, thereby helps the patient to accept his current state as part of his life cycle and as "something that had to be and that, by necessity, permitted no substitutions" (Erikson, 1959, p. 98).

The presentation of the psychodynamic life narrative also takes into consideration another characteristic reaction in the situation: the regression, with its intensified transference wishes, in particular the wish for an omnipotent and protective parent. To gratify these wishes and reinforce positive past experiences, the narrative is presented in an active, engaging, and enthusiastic manner. A bland, neutral approach may be construed by the patient as a lack of interest and a rejection, but the construction of a life story presented with vigor can convey a fascination to the patient, an interest that carries with it affirmation and hope and a special type of relatedness to the therapist. It is to be emphasized that this mode of intervention involves deviation from the traditional stance of neutrality and, to a certain extent, anonymity. Moreover, the patient is explicitly offered the opportunity for further consultation if the need arises, a maneuver that has important implications, particularly as it solidifies the fantasy of a continuing relationship with the therapist.

EXAMPLES OF THE PSYCHODYNAMIC LIFE NARRATIVE

The clinical vignettes presented here are intended to illustrate the form, tone, and language of the psychodynamic life narrative. Much material obtained during a consultation is of interest but not pertinent to the thrust of the narrative as presented to the patient. It goes without saying that individual life experiences are much more complex than are the narratives presented here; and the depressions that these patients experienced have ramifications that go beyond the explicit statements.

Case No. 1

This patient was a skilled carpenter in his late thirties who had weathered hemodialysis and a transplant very successfully. When he developed an aseptic necrosis of the femur—a complication of prednisone—and could no longer work, he became depressed and was referred for consultation.

The patient was a black man, raised on a farm in the South. He described how hard both his parents had worked to support their large family. He particularly remembered his father's long hours of toil in the fields, which "just showed how much he cared for us." These childhood memories of his active, toiling father surrounded by respectful children contrasted sharply with his current inability to work and the adolescent rebelliousness of his own children. With these issues in mind, he was told the following toward the end of the second session:

"It seems pretty clear why you are depressed. For most of your life you have worked hard to give to your children all the support and love your father gave to you. As long as you could work, you could see yourself as a good father. Even when you got sick and needed dialysis and then a transplant, you kept your spirits up because you could work—but now this difficulty with your legs has hit you. Just when you want to give your teenage children a good image to look up to, you find yourself sick, frustrated, and angry at your kids, who are going through a stage when they need to rebel and put their father down. And yet, as I listen to you describe your life, it is certain that if this leg problem had not occurred, you would be at work this very moment. Your children know you better than I, so I'm sure they must realize what a good provider you can be and how much you care about them."

With this statement, the patient put his present situation in perspective and ceased to view himself as a total failure at work and at home. When he was next seen, his depression had significantly improved (Viederman & Perry, 1980, p. 181). The patient's appreciation of my authority strongly suggested a paternal transference.

Case No. 2

The patient was a 64-year-old married man, the father of two sons, who was referred by his physician son for evaluation of long-standing depression. He had had polio at the age of six, with permanent paralysis of some of the muscles of one leg; a bleeding peptic ulcer at the age of thirty; two coronaries, one at thirty-eight and one at forty-five; and bypass surgery at the age of fifty-eight. However, it became apparent that the depression had been precipitated by the loss of a substantial amount of money on the stock market ten years earlier. The patient came only at the insistence of his son, as he was very disinclined to see a psychiatrist.

Mr. F was a ruddy, vigorous, well-dressed, active and engaging man, who had a marked limp and walked with the support of both a brace and a cane. Though he did not appear depressed, he complained of depression and indicated that his only source of pleasure at the present time was his business. He no longer enjoyed trips or social activities at home and had a vague uncertainty and lack of security that he had never before experienced.

Toward the middle of the second session the patient was told the following:

"It is becoming increasingly clear what this depression is about. It started very clearly when you had this financial reversal ten years ago, and yet certainly it doesn't have to do with the reality of the loss because you have emphasized how comfortable you are financially. Clearly it had some speical meaning to you. You've told me that you were a very active, ambitious kid, the favorite son, endowed, as your father said, with all the intelligence in the family. And then all of a sudden you got polio and began to recognize that you were damaged and would never be quite right. It was painful for you to be put in the special class with the crippled kids, and you decided that you were going to overcome this. Your fantasies of being a perfect athlete were part of this, and, even more important, the fantasy of being a millionaire with a chauffeur. You had decided that you would compensate for that sense of defectiveness and you have been very successful in doing it—in fact, you achieved this dream, at least as far as money is concerned. I guess you would have been quite successful even if you hadn't had polio—but the need to compensate certainly helped."

At this point the patient interrupted and indicated that he was skeptical about whether he would have been as successful had he not had polio.

I went on: "And so you continued in this very successful way, through a heart attack and an ulcer, until you had this reversal. It was as if that whole sense of overcompensation had punctured, this fantasy of being a millionaire with a chauffeur, and you could no longer trust yourself, you no longer could believe you were the man you thought you were. This was certainly accentuated by the message that your father had sent to you loud and clear, 'Never depend on anyone, never be indebted to anyone. Money is your best friend.' So, when you did have this reversal and went to this close friend of yours, whose father you had helped financially and he turned you down, this was a real confirmation of what your father had said and you've never really recovered from this. You've been really depressed and hesitant to fully go out in the world ever since. Moreover, this has certainly been accentuated by the sense that your oldest son is the financial dynamo in the family, having earned more than you."

The patient responded by saying: "You know, there's another thing. I've always considered myself slightly superior to everyone else until that moment when I fell apart financially. Take my driving, for example. I am probably the best driver in the world—always know where the other cars are. I drive fast, but in 45 years I have never had a single accident. I even take pride in talking myself out of traffic tickets. And you know how I do it? By using my bum leg. When I was stopped by a cop last time, I got out of the car and hobbled up to him and he immediately started to protect *me.* I told him I'd never gotten a ticket before. He could look at my special license to see that. He said, O.K., Mr. F, but be careful in the future. I feel a sense of power and exhilaration when this happens. Power has been an important thing in my life."

The patient entered the third session in an exuberant mood, indicating that he had had an exceptionally good time on vacation in the Caribbean and that he did not remember ever having enjoyed a vacation so much. His wife was delighted with his interest now in planning a new vacation. Even more striking to him, however, was that, for the first time in his life, he had put on a bathing suit and gone swimming in the pool in spite of his severely deformed leg (interesting in light of his compensatory fantasy of becoming an athlete). He stated that he felt minimal self-consciousness and experienced this as a triumph. He added, jokingly, that at the airport, he for the first time and without any sense of shame had asked the stewardess for a courtesy wheelchair. He took particular pleasure in the fact that in so doing he was able to avoid waiting to go through customs. The patient reviewed some of the issues we had discussed during the previous session and was pleased to hear that he could return if any difficulties ensued (Viederman, 1983, p. 238–239).

It is difficult to define precisely the specific transference configuration in this case. The patient indicated that he had never in his life spoken so openly to another person and was quite unable to associate this experience with any previous one. He stated openly, however that he idealized doctors with whom he could establish rapport and spoke of a positive relationship with a surgeon at the time of his bypass surgery, when he felt that the doctor would see him through the experience. Pertinent is the fact that during the course of the consultation, I received a telephone call from one of the local television channels asking me to comment on an important international event that had been occurring at the time. The patient had referred the news people to me through an acquaintance, with the fantasy that this would make me very successful, as had been the case in a previous situation with a friend of one of his sons. Clearly, the patient wished to establish my future as if I were one of his sons. Another aspect of the relationship, though never overt, seems important. Early in his adult life, a strong, older man had offered moral support at a critical time and had been experienced as a mentor in a way that his own, less successful, father had been unable to do. There were suggestions in the tone of our relationship during the third session that he experienced me in a similar way.

THE THERAPEUTIC ACTION OF THE PSYCHODYNAMIC LIFE NARRATIVE

In the preceding cases, the personal logic of the depression was elucidated in the first two sessions and presented to the patient in a coherent statement, which, while placing current conflicts in the context of historical antecedents, emphasized past strengths, thereby increasing self-esteem. A number of elements contribute in varying degrees to the therapeutic efficacy of this intervention, but in all cases the uninterpreted transference plays an important role.

Creation of Order: Presentation of A Life Trajectory

The crisis situation that leads to depression also leads in many cases to confusion and chaos, particularly if the crisis is an acute and highly disruptive one. In this regard a psychodynamic life narrative offers a clarity and logic to the patient's response at a time when he is struggling against a sense of hopelessness, powerlessness, and confusion. It offers a sense of control in the face of an implacable fate. Moreover, the narrative has special usefulness because it is presented at a time when the patient is struggling to reconcile himself to an altered life trajectory.

But what of the accuracy of a statement based on such limited information? Clearly, the narrative is an oversimplified account that could be contradicted by additional material obtained from memories, fantasies, dreams, and transference material as they evolve in a longer treatment. Schafer (1978) and Ricoeur (1977), address this problem as they argue that even psychoanalysis, in its effort to reconstruct early life experiences, never succeeds in obtaining an accurate reproduction of those formative years. Past events and previous fantasies become important because of their meaning in relation to the current life experience and not because of an essential historical veracity. Narrative "truth" changes over the course of time and of treatment. For the patient, a construction (rather than reconstruction) has the value of offering a reasonable and therefore meaningful integrating perspective on his life that is concordant with the current experience of himself. The psychodyanmic life narrative does not impose truth; instead, it presents a coherent explanation of what the precipitating situation means to the patient at a moment in time and in the context of his present conscious and preconscious view of the past.

The Supportive Nature of the Psychodynamic Life Narrative: Solidification of Defense

In presenting to the patient a cognitive, ego-syntonic "explanation" of his current reaction, the intent is to minimize conflict and to encourage intellectualizing defenses. The narrative may be viewed as an incomplete interpretation or, more accurately, a clarification. It integrates and organizes preconsciously experienced thoughts and feelings and does not involve interpretations that the patient would experience as ego-dystonic or that would evoke anxiety or guilt. It is designed to help the patient view himself in a way that facilitates the approximation of his ego ideal, and in this respect it solidifies self-esteem, which is consistently impaired in a depressive response to crisis. In short, this is a covering statement rather than an uncovering statement. The manifest involvement, activity, and engaged stance of the therapist convey a personal interest in the patient that is also supportive of self-esteem. This intervention is viewed as a type of supportive therapy, though it differs very clearly from some aspects of the supportive therapy suggested by Kernberg (1982) for work with borderline patients. Kernberg defines supportive therapy as follows:

> Supportive therapy is defined by the nonutilization of interpretation as a technical tool, the partial utilization of clarification and abreaction, and the predominant use of suggestion and environmental intervention: . . . while the therapist is acutely aware of and monitoring the transference resistances as part of his technique in dealing with character problems and their connection to the patient's life difficulties, transference is not interpreted, and the use of suggestion and environmental intervention implicitly eliminates technical neutrality as well. In conclusion, psychoanalysis, expressive psychotherapy, and supportive psychotherapy may be defined in terms of the variation within the paradigms of (1) the principal technical tools (clarification and interpretation vs suggestion and environmental intervention); (2) the extent to which the transference is interpreted, and (3) the degree to which technical neutrality is maintained. (p. 183–184)

It is important to emphasize that Kernberg's description of supportive therapy is to be diffentiated from the therapeutic use of the psychodynamic life narrative. Kernberg's intervention is directed toward a different patient population, has different goals, and utilizes different techniques, namely, the interpretation of primitive ego defenses when they present major problems for the therapeutic relationship. Kernberg's stance has important elements of clarification *and* of interpretation in his emphasis that the therapist's function is to acquaint the patient with his primitive defenses and their effects upon his evaluation of reality and his decision-making process although clearly he does not recommend consistent and general interpretation of transference. The psychodynamic life narrative may also be viewed as a supportive therapy. It does not utilize interpretation of the transference and it violates technical neutrality in the following respects: (a) its utilization consistently solidifies defense and decreases anxiety and depression by offering a "reasonable" and ego-syntonic construct, designed to raise the patient's self-esteem; (b) it is designed, in some situations, to alleviate guilt by emphasizing the appropriateness of guilt-evoking impulses, thereby diminishing the intensity of superego pressure; and (c) it casts the therapist in the role of a gratifying object, allied with the patient in his struggle against the painful reality. In short, there is the support of defenses, a mitigation of superego pressure, in some situations, and the experience of the therapist as a gratifying, real object.

TRANSFERENCE IMPLICATIONS

This discussion addresses two levels of transference manifestations: (a) the more usual transference phenomena as they are manifested in the psychotherapies and in the transference neurosis of psychoanalysis, and (b) what has been called the fundamental, or primary, transference as elaborated by Greenacre (1975) and Stone (1961).

Transference reactions (and the transference neurosis as it evolves in the psychoanalytic situation) are defined by the specific configurations of the patient's representational world of self and objects. Experienced or wished for relationships with important figures are re-evoked in the treatment situation. If not interpreted, they remain unconscious, but unlike the "fundamental transference," they can achieve consciousness and be resolved through interpretation. These transference projections are mobilized by the use of the psychodynamic life narrative. The activity and manifest warmth of the therapist's response seems to evoke positive and idealized transferences. These transferences may be composite in that they may represent the condensation of a number of good object-representations. The transferences are not interpreted and are not manipulatively evoked but evolve spontaneously as the therapist actively engages the patient. It is in this respect that they are gratifying, although they are authentic and do not represent a contrived "corrective emotional experience."

This range of manifest transference reactions is to be differentiated from "fundamental" or "primary" transference, as elaborated by Greenacre (1975) and Stone (1961), among others. Greenacre states: "By basic transference I mean the existence of an almost undifferentiated, dependent confidence, which has its origin in the relationship of the infant to the mother, and also provides the matrix out of which the transference neurosis may emerge (p. 704).

Stone (1961) states in a similar vein:

> There is a "legitimate transference gratification . . . in making interpretations we are gratifying transference wishes, whether in one of myriad possible archaic references, such as the wish for the tolerant acceptance of excreta or the desire to be given food, or, in my view, in gratifying a more "mature" wish of childhood, underlying and essential to the initial genuine viability of the analytic situation: a wish for tolerance and for sympathetic understanding, for help in mastering the baffling and challenging outer world of living and inanimate objects and forces, the pressures of somatically experienced discomforts and urges, and most of all the mastering of a dark and mysterious inner pyschic world. Without the support of this component of latent transference I am skeptical that the adult, rational, clinical need, supported by unconscious, irrational transference expectations and fantasies could sustain many analytic situations. . . [pp. 49–50].

This primary or fundamental transference is a substrate on which all effective psychotherapies rest. This concept implies that patients capable of entering into a psychoanalytic relationship have developed in their early life experience, particularly in the mother-child dyad, the background of trust sufficient to permit the establishment of a trusting object relationship in which a transference neurosis can develop. This level of transference is the infrastructure of the analytic relationship and is in itself never analyzed. It originates genetically in the earliest preverbal developmental phases and relates to attachment behavior and to the ultimate sense of safety and security to permit object relations to develop even though they may subsequently be affected by neurotic conflicts and inhibitions. It is this substrate of trust that distinguishes what Freud (1914) called the transference neuroses from the narcissistic neuroses. It is this early experience which creates the "background of safety" (Sandler, 1960), which protects the infant against his most primitive fears of disorganization and disintegration in a chaotic world. A trusting and protective umbrella with this developmental origin is a prerequisite for intimate object relations and is a background for all meaningful psychotherapeutic relationships.

The physically ill regressed patient in a state of psychic disequilibrium evoked by a threatening outside world approaches the therapist in a state of wishful expectation that he can find the benevolent and omnipotent parent of previous times. The therapist responds by understanding and tactfully and appropriately communicating his understanding of the patient's predicament through the psychodynamic life narrative. In so doing, he gratifies the patient in a way reminiscent of the early mother-child relationship, and a sense of oneness with a nurturing figure is reinforced. In psychoanalysis, as Stone (1961) has pointed out, the capacity of the patient to tolerate ego-dystonic interpretations rests on the previous substrate of a trusting relationship. The brief therapy I have described, is designed to be ego syntonic and to convey to the patient the sense that he is understood. This enhances the positive transference of which I have spoken.

> By presenting a narrative that spans a patient's life, the therapist conveys a sense of having known the patient over time. . . . Like the good parent who has a perspective on the child—where he has been and what he is becoming—the therapist captures in the life narrative the quality of a shared experience over time and becomes in the crisis situation a reassuring, parental figure. This conveys a sense of protection and hope to the patient.[2]
>
> The therapeutic action of this enhanced positive transference may also be related to the concept proposed by Ornstein and Ornstein of the "curative fantasy". They describe a universal fantasy "to have past hurts undone and all frustrated wishes fulfilled" These include fantasies of finding idealized good objects. The Ornsteins explain how this "infantile expectation" can be activated in the regressive situation of the therapeutic relationship and how this hope for cure motivates the patient. Similar infantile expectations of finding good objects and being cured are no doubt activated by the regression during a crisis situation. The psychodynamic life narrative, by enhancing this positive transference, supports these wishes and rekindles the childhood hope for repair of damage done. This hope can be instrumental in relieving the suffering evoked by crisis [Viederman & Perry, 1980, p. 184].

In the analytic situation, the latent transference that Stone (1961) describes never becomes conscious; hence, it persists even after the

---

[2]The concept described in this extract has been elaborated by Loewald (1960) in his discussion of the parallel between the function of the analyst in the psychoanalytic situation and the role of the mother with the developing child.

termination of the most lengthy and exhaustive analysis. One must infer that this echo of the earliest benevolent relationship with the protective parent persists and may take the form of an unconscious expectation that in the event of some terrible life disaster, a good object will be available to offer a modicum of protection and relief. This concept, evolved by Stone in his consideration of the psychoanalytic situation has implications that go beyond psychoanalysis as a treatment per se. By extension, it implies that the nurturant mothering experience is the substrate on which all adequate object relations are built and that it continues to have a powerful influence throughout our lives. Both Erikson (1959) and Benedek (1970) commented on this issue when they spoke of basic trust and confidence. The protective fantasy associated with this is present in all of us, is activated regressively in a state of crisis, and becomes the context in which the psychodynamic life narrative is presented and has its effect.

It is not surprising that these thoughts should have evolved in the context of working with the physically ill, where the dangers of bodily disintegration and annihilation are ever present. Some researchers have commented on the difficulties of analyzing patients with serious physical illness (Discussion Group, 1980), and there is evidence to suggest that even when such analyses can be instituted, the ever present specter of death may prevent the patient from working through a normal termination and separation. One might say that the umbrella of protection that the relationship with the analyst affords cannot be relinquished under these circumstances.

TRANSFERENCE CURE AND ITS IMPLICATIONS

The effectiveness of the psychodynamic life narrative, at least from the point of view of transference, suggests that it may be viewed as a special type of transference cure.

Oremland (1972) has presented the most comprehension classification of transference cure and flight into health. He views the transference cure as a product of the relationship with the analyst, and the three levels he describes represent varying capacities for object relatedness. All must be considered resistances in view of the fact that they operate against understanding and substitute a therapeutic change for understanding. The most primitive form, which occurs early in the treatment "brings about massive repressive and suppressive mechanisms . . . [in order to ward off] . . . the threat of the relationship to the therapist" (p. 66). This occurs early in the treatment, is a reflection of a great deal of fear, expectation of criticism, and usually implies rather primitive mechanisms of projection, splitting and denial. The second, higher level transference cure reflects an identification with the analyst who is idealized. This represents a defense against jealousy and ultimately against loss. This identification implies that the analyst is taken in to avoid the pain of separation. The highest level of transference cure is most persistent and easily reinforced through life experiences. In this situation, symptoms are relinquished and "improvement is unconsciously experienced as the condition for acceptance and love" (p. 69).

Oremland's formulation has pertinence to the psychodynamic life narrative. However, one should deemphasize the issue of resistance and focus rather on gratification. His second and third categories are most applicable with certain modifications. In his second category, he focuses on the improvement in part as a defense against jealousy and in the third, as a *condition* for love. Neither circumstance applies to the psychodynamic life narrative. What is pertinent, however, is Oremland's description of the patient's identification with the idealized analyst as a defense against loss and his statement that the analyst is "taken in to avoid the pain of separation" (his second category). With the psychodynamic life narrative not only is the therapist "taken in," but the therapist's construct is also taken in and assimilated under the powerful influence of an idealizing transference that increases the ego's integrative capacity. Furthermore, it seems that the symptoms are relinquished not so much as a condition for acceptance or love, but in the context of an atmosphere perceived by the patient as loving. The therapist's presentation of himself as a real object, coupled with the explicit statement that the patient is free to return for future consultations, tends to reinforce an internal representation of the good, protective object and to encourage the fantasy of availability of a protective person in the outside world who can be helpful in relieving future pain ("curative fantasy object"). This engenders or reawakens a sense of confidence that, if necessary, required relief can be obtained in the future.

It is most important to emphasize that the idealizing transference I have described is not the same as the primitive idealization described by Kernberg (1982) in his work with borderline patients who utilize defensive splitting. The idealization here is reflective of an early gratifying relationship with an integrated good object. But why does this idealizing transference not lead to ultimate disappointment? There are at least three factors that would contribute to this:

1. The intervention probably works best when the person has had a predominantly good early maternal relationship. This permits the

mobilization of a good and gratifying transference object rather than a defensively idealized one. This also implies a previous relatively healthy emotional equilibrium.

2. The patient is in a regressive state, and it is in the context of this regression that he receives gratification. The gratification is immediate and relieving and tends to undo the degree of regression in the context of symptom resolution.

3. Finally, and not least important, the availability of the therapist for subsequent consultation encourages the maintenance of a continued, if fantasied, relation with the therapist.

In summary, an important part of the therapeutic action of the narrative relates to transference gratification and, hence, is a transference cure. A cognitive construct is presented to the patient. This structure offers a new perspective on him in relationship to the world. The patient experiences the gratification of being understood at a moment in crisis. This contributes to the development of a silent, idealizing transference, which increases the power of the cognitive structure and facilitates its assimilation. Hence, the cognitive structure and the idealizing transference act upon each other in a reciprocal way, each increasing the power of the other. The loving aspect of the transference gratification from the powerful transference figure places value on the patient's self representation and brings it in closer proximity to the ideal-self representation, or, on a higher level, the ego ideal.

In no situation is the transference actually interpreted. It is likely that both manifest transference and fundamental transference, or primary transference, are important therapeutic influences. Unfortunately, it is difficult to obtain evidence of the action of these two categories of transference reaction. The latter is inferential and by definition unavailable to consciousness. The former, ultimately available to consciousness, could be revealed in long-term follow up, though, of course, it is questionable whether brief contact would permit confirmation of its therapeutic action.

GOALS AND IMPLICATIONS OF THE PSYCHODYNAMIC LIFE NARRATIVE

The psychodynamic life narrative was viewed originally as a type of crisis intervention designed to alleviate depression in patients undergoing the crisis of physical illness and to help them reestablish their previous emotional equilibrium. In its extension to other crises of the life cycle, its goal is to create a powerful bond between patient and physician in order to relieve dysphoric symptoms and in some situations to influence the patient's behavior.

It is important to emphasize that in a crisis individuals are not only vulnerable, but susceptible to significant change. There is considerable evidence to suggest that important personality changes, reflective of changes in the representational world (modification of self and object representations as well as ideal self and object representations), can occur during periods of crisis in a facilitating environment, one that solidifies the individual's view of himself as worthy, loving, strong, and capable of overcoming adversity.

One need not be limited to clinical experience to find examples of profound and rapid personality change in situations of crisis. Ingemar Bergman's (1960) film *Wild Strawberries* reveals such a change in a 76-year-old man during a single day in his life, a day on which he was to receive a Golden Jubilee Award for 50 years as a physician and a day on which he revisits his past in fantasy and reality under the catalytic influence of a chance encounter with admiring young people.

I have emphasized that this intervention is a clarification rather than a true interpretation. Yet, to the extent that it has meaning to the patient, it involves insight, for it offers a new ordering and perspective of the world. The degree to which its effectiveness is dependent on transference gratification, and the degree to which it is actually integrated as something that changes the patient's perception of himself, will vary from patient to patient.

A CONSIDERATION OF THE PSYCHODYNAMIC LIFE NARRATIVE IN RELATIONSHIP TO THE PSYCHOANALYTIC VIEW OF HUMAN BEHAVIOR

Does the apparent ease and rapidity of change possible with the Psychodynamic Life Narrative do violence to the psychoanalytic theory of behavior? Depression, in particular, as described by Freud (1917/1957) presumes antecedent intrapsychic conflict related to ambivalence, fixation at the anal-sadistic level, and elements of narcissistic object choice. Guilt then becomes a central focus of the melancholic conflict. Although everyday clinical experience repeatedly confirms these observations in a certain group of depressive patients, Bibring's formulation (1961) presents a model of depression that lends itself more readily to understanding the changes that have been observed in the above described cases. Bibring emphasizes that depression is primarily a product of damaged self-esteem rather than a result of guilt about unresolved ambivalence toward a lost object. With this shift in focus to the problem of self-worth, any narcissistic injury, such as physical illness, can lead to a state of helplessness and powerlessness in the ego with resultant damaged self-esteem and depression, reflective of a discordance between the ideal self-representation and the self-representation itself. Joffe and Sandler (1965) view depression in a similar way.

Yet there is a persistence in Freudian psychoanalytic thinking that the indignities that fate imposes on the individual inevitably lead to the re-emergence of the rage, guilt, and persecutory phantoms of infantile life. These fantasies emerge with considerable regularity in our work with troubled neurotic patients. Though they may well be universal, one must not presume that they inevitably dominate the responses of individuals confronted with adversity. Contributing to the final common pathway of behavior are other influences such as effective conflict resolution, internalized good objects, and the like. These forces may lead to the development of traits and attitudes that evoke predominantly benevolent perceptions of the world, hopefulness, recognition of self-worth, courage, and the ability to accept one's fate. The quality of the individual's response to adversity will ultimately be determined by the balance of these forces. Need anticipation of death always evoke demons? Voltaire's comment on his deathbed when he was approached by a priest and asked to choose God and renounce the devil is reported to have been, "Father, I thank you and acknowledge your concern but this is hardly the time to make new enemies." Individuals do make peace with death and suffering. Is it not presumptuous of us, as analysts, to assume that persecutory devils must regularly dominate the experience of one's confrontation with a noxious fate or, more neutrally, what Camus called "the tender indifference of the world"? The analytic generalization of the inevitability of this rageful and fearful response to the world may be the product of the experience of the consulting room. In the world about us there exist multitudes not only of the unanalyzable but also of the unanalyzed—one must admit a predominant majority.

Does such a view present a defensive and hence distorted view of the human experience, reflective of what might be considered a general countertransference response? Certainly powerful countertransference responses are evoked in work with the physically ill. Most often such responses lead to disturbances in the relationship with the patient and have negative therapeutic effects. Does the wish to "cure" (recognizing the limitations of one's success under any circumstances) represent countertransference in this situation? Often therapeutic zeal leads to difficulty in the psychoanalytic situation, where the required mode of conducting an analysis involves understanding and not the analyst's wish for patient change. This is not the case in working with the physically ill, where the goal is to alleviate suffering. The opportunity to observe individuals who face adversity with remarkable equanimity, courage, and integrity readily convinces anyone working in such a situation that at the very least the possibility for such adaptation exists. In the face of these observations, belief in the possibility of significant modification of dysphoric responses does not necessarily imply defensive denial of reality or participation in a hypomanic flight from depression.

But what of the validity of these observations based as they are on limited contact with a patient already involved in an idealizing transference? Can one trust data obtained without the use of the analytic instrument? It is undeniable that the nuances of the patient's character structure, the nature of his unconscious fantasy world and its associated conflictual base, is not available for observation. However, to demand evidence of change from an instrument that is inapplicable in the special circumstances of the crisis of physical illness is to exclude the possibility of making observations in such a situation. Of central importance to the person in crisis is the patient's feeling state, his conscious awareness of the experience, and the behavior reflective of the above two elements. One must conclude that although the nature of the data available is clearly different from that of the psychoanalytic situation, what can be observed is not to be minimized or discarded.

Initially, it was a source of some astonishment to me that the intervention described could have a powerful impact. However, upon continued reflection, it became apparent that there is a logic to its effectiveness and that this logic might well be applied to a further understanding of aspects of psychotherapeutic change.

REFERENCES

Benedek, T. (1970). The family as a psychologic field. In: *Parenthood: Its Psychology and Psychopathology*, ed. J. Anthony & T. Benedek. Boston: Little, Brown & Co., pp. 109–136.

Bergman, I. (1960). Wild strawberries. In: *Four Screenplays of Ingmar Bergman*. Boston: Simon & Schuster.

Bibring, G. (1961). The mechanism of depression. In: *Affective Disorders*, ed. P. Greenacre. New York: International Universities Press, pp. 13–48.

Davanloo, H. (1978). Basic principles and techniques. In *Short-Term Dynamic Psychotherapy.* New York: Spectrum.
Discussion Group, American Psychoanalytic Association. (1980, December). *Reaction to Congenital and Acquired Loss of Bodily Parts,* New York.
Erikson, E. H. (1959). Identity and the life cycle. *Psychological Issues,* Monog. 1, p. 179.
Freud, S. (1914). On narcissism: An introduction. *Standard Edition,* 14:67–102. London: Hogarth Press, 1957.
——— (1917). Mourning and melancholia. *Standard Edition,* 14:237–258. London: Hogarth Press, 1957.
Glover, E. (1955). The therapeutic effect of inexact interpretation. In: *The Technique of Psychoanalysis,* ed. E. Glover. New York: International Universities Press.
Greenacre, P. (1975). On reconstruction. *J. Amer. Psychoanal. Assn.* 23:4.
Joffe, W. G. & Sandler, J. (1965). Notes on pain, depression and individuation. *The Psychological Study of Child,* 20:394–400.
Kernberg, O. (1982). Supportive psychotherapy with borderline conditions. In: *Critical Problems in Psychiatry,* ed. J. O. Cavenar & H. K. Brodie, Philadelphia: J. B. Lippincott, pp. 180–202.
Loewald, H. W. (1960). On the therapeutic action of psycho-analysis. *Internat. J. Psychoanal,* 41:1–18.
Malan, D. H. (1976). *Toward the Validation of Dynamic Psychotherapy: A Replication.* New York: Plenum Press.
Mann, J. (1973). *Time-Limited Psychotherapy.* Cambridge, MA: Harvard University Press.
Oremland, J. D. (1972). Transference cure and flight into health. *Internat. J. Psychoanal. Psychother,* 1:61–75.
Ornstein, P. H. & Ornstein, A. (1977). On the continuing evolution of psychoanalytic psychotherapy. Reflections and predictions. *The Annual of Psychoanalysis,* 5:329–370.
Ricoeur, P. (1977). The question of proof in Freud's psychoanalytic writings. *J. Amer. Psychoanal. Assn.,* 25:805.
Sandler, J. (1960). The background of safety. *Internat. J. Psycho-Anal.* 41:352–356.
Schafer, R. (1978). *Language and Insight.* New Haven: Yale University Press.
Sifneos, P. E. (1972). *Short-Term Psychotherapy and Emotional Crisis.* Cambridge, MA: Harvard University Press.
Stone, L. (1961). *The Psychoanalytic Situation.* New York, International Universities Press.
Viederman, M. (1983). The psychodynamic life narrative: A psychotherapeutic intervention useful in crisis situations. *Psychiat.,* 46:236–246.
Viederman, M., & Perry, S. (1980). Use of the psychodynamic life narrative in the treatment of depression in the physically ill. *Gen. Hosp. Psychiat.,* 3:177–185.

CHAPTER ELEVEN

Discussion of Transference and Countertransference in Brief Psychotherapy

Roy Schafer

There is an old story about the practical joker who sent the same anonymous telegram to a dozen friends chosen at random. The telegram read, "Flee! All is discovered!" And they all left town at once. Psychoanalytic practice demonstrates repeatedly that serious physical illness or impairment and other reversals of fortune carry the same message and provoke the same response as the joker's telegram. Fate is everyone's practical joker.

Freud pointed out that Fate is the superego projected into the world at large. In this way, Fate stands for the omniscient, accusing, and persecutory infantile parental imagoes. But flight from a hostile Fate in the external world and from the hostile superego figures in the inner world is not possible, except to a limited extent through the use of defensive measures. Prominent among these defensive measures are manic denials of painful external realities, incoporation of magically benign figures such as doctors and ministers, and paranoid projection of the sinister internal figures. These figures are projected through demonic personification of the symptoms of illness or handicap and through fantasies of jealous gods. But because these defensive measures are limited in effect, some amount of helplessness will be felt by the afflicted—and with that, depression. Subjectively, it will then seem true that one stands condemned for one's infantile "sins" and "shortcomings"—condemned unconsciously, if not consciously, as a ruthlessly greedy devourer, a sadistic withholder or mess-maker, an incestuous masturbator or castrate, and the like.

On the basis of analytic evidence of this sort, one ought to try to understand Dr. Viederman's physically ill and depressed patients as being caught up in these fantasies. Given their ominous or malignant circumstances, they could be expected to welcome a benign, magical figure who offers to collude with them in their defensive efforts by speaking out strongly, and not altogether incorrectly, in support of their virtues, virtues they can no longer affirm independently. And yet an analyst will also assume that in their regressed condition these patients can extend only an ambivalent welcome to the doctor; for they have, they feel, been confirmed in their mistrust of both Fate and their presumably benign parental figures. There is rage to contend with as well as needfulness.

Consequently, Dr. Viederman's approach, when it works, would also have to be understood as a way of subduing the hostile side of this ambivalent reception, that is, the negative transference to the doctor. How might this disarming be accomplished? Let me mention three enabling factors. The first is projection, through which the patients now believe that the colluding doctor bears the burden of their superego guilt. Like Christ, he takes the sufferers' guilt on himself. If he says they are fine people, and even seems to offer them a special relationship, then let their sins be on his conscience. It is part of his goodness to assume that burden and imply that forgiveness. Then the good doctor can be incorporated as a benign imago that will refute the self-reproaches and neutralize the persecutory internal imagos—shout them down, as it were. This is what Strachey (1934) brought out in his classic paper on transference, and it should be a central factor in Dr. Viederman's explanation of his own good results as transference cures.

What we are confronting here is mental magic. As mental magic, its results are inherently unstable, even though continuing contact with the doctor, if only in fantasy, can sometimes fortify and sustain the magical gains over considerable time. Additionally, if the patient's premorbid ego was reasonably strong and if the medical crisis or illness passes, the patient's need for this mental magic may diminish and normal self-esteem regulation may then be re-established. In any case, it is probable that incorporating the benign doctor serves more functions than just avoiding the pain of separation that Dr. Viederman singled out for emphasis in his discussion.

The second enabling factor may be defined by drawing on Winnicott's (1971) contribution to psychoanalysis. One may view the Psychodynamic Life Narrative as providing for the creation of a shared illusion between doctor and patient like that between parent and infant. This shared illusion is not altogether fantastic; it takes account of real factors. Nevertheless, it is a slanted story that is legitimated and buttressed by the exaggerated influence of the doctor in his role of rational, scientific, objective authority. He offers the equivalent of the parent's kiss of the painful area that conjures away the child's hurt through its affirmation of goodness and victimization. After all, many other people, family and friends among them, attempt to support a mixture of denial, repression, projection, and reality testing when dealing with these depressed patients—and often enough they fail. The idealized doctor with his Life Narrative offers something extra in the intermediate zone of illusion and may thereby get better results.

The third enabling factor might be called situation-specific countertransference. Let me put it as a question: When working with physically endangered patients and their relatives, how much does the doctor, for his or her own personal reasons, need to succeed in reducing depression and increasing self-esteem? Dr. Viederman mentions that the success of his approach seems to depend on the vigor and enthusiasm with which the Life Narrative is communicated. He seems to be referring to an eagerness that extends beyond neutral professional dedication to the patient's welfare. I doubt that every one of us could do well what he can do well. I, for one, could not, as my countertransference predilections go in other directions. If a situation-specific countertransference of this sort is an enabling factor, it follows that the patient would want to buck up in order to be loved by the doctor. I refer here to the third of the factors in transference cures covered by Oremland in the paper Dr. Viederman reviewed. The patient will do it for the conditional love of the doctor. And in terms of Glover's (1931) discussion of the therapeutic effects of inexact interpretation, the way to please is by developing a less disturbing and less obvious substitute neurosis—perhaps a phobic avoidance of tabooed depression and the adoption of a manic posture. At least one of Dr. Viederman's patients—the one who made the triumphant trip to the Carribean—seems to exemplify this kind of change.

I have indicated that the preceding part of my discussion depends not primarily on evidence that may be gathered by an approach such as Dr. Viederman's; but rather on evidence of reactions to illness and help that have been gathered in full-scale analyses. That is the only kind of evidence an analyst can fall back on to understand phenomena of this kind. But one must be convinced about psychoanalysis in the first place. The word is *convinced,* not *dogmatic.*

Dogmatic appears in Dr. Frances's chapter when he speaks of therapeutic dogmatism. Dr. Frances makes it clear when he discusses variables that he is a convinced analyst. Nevertheless, I think he is inconsistent in one important respect in his otherwise excellent methodological review of research and practice in the brief therapies. The inconsistency—perhaps ambiguity is the better word—is this: he fails to distinguish sharply enough between therapeutic dogmatism and confident assertion of a psychoanalytic point of view. Therapeutic dogmatism would be evident were a therapist to insist that the same approach be foisted on every patient. That position is certainly to be rejected as dogmatic. But it is not dogmatic to consistently raise analytic questions and advance analytic conjectures about what might be going on unconsciously in any brief therapy; nor is it dogmatic to go on to assert that by its very nature a brief therapy cannot fully reveal all the unconsciously significant factors at work in it. One cannot even make that claim for full-scale analyses, however informative they are in comparison to brief therapy.

Dr. Frances, however, seems to say that better research methods applied to brief therapy are needed to settle questions of this sort. I say that as a convinced analyst he could assert something else: although one may do useful descriptive research on the outcome of brief therapy, one cannot, in principle, carry even the descriptive approach too far, the data being so sparse, and one cannot hope to begin to settle psychodynamic issues of any depth outside the analytic situation. The kind of research he discusses is a version of applied psychoanalysis in that it extrapolates from analysis to brief therapy. Applied analysis is useful in raising questions and establishing new data for analytic consideration; it cannot test analytic hypotheses. Thus, although Malan's research is of interest to analysts, its use to cast doubt on the analytic theory of the therapeutic process can only be greeted with skepticism; and this would be so even if Malan's research design were flawless—which it is not. It may well be that a certain kind of situation-specific countertransference is controlling his entire approach: this would be a countertransference that implausibly simplifies the minds of his patients and culminates in an implausible simplication of the theory of therapy.

Countertransference plays a prominent part only in Dr. Mann's chapter. Dr. Mann is especially illuminating in that he centers attention on countertransferences specific to, or inherent in, the practice of time-limited therapy. The factors he mentions are mainly three: guilt; thwarted narcissistic gratification with respect to the dependence of patients; and anger, grief, and the problems (associated with these affects) of tolerating separation and loss with no great damage to one's self-feeling. Disturbance of the therapist's self-feeling is, Dr. Mann points out, the same problem that faces the patient and must be dealt with carefully in the critical termination period of his version of brief therapy. As such, it can greatly endanger the success of the therapy. There are less structured analytic brief therapies than Dr. Mann's, and there are other views of the crucial dynamics in brief therapy than his, but rather than dwell on these variations, let me extend the discussion of countertransference in brief therapy. I want to do so not only to give this important topic its due in this chapter but also because countertransference is a major and frequent source of disruption, confusion, and ineffectiveness in this work.

Dr. Mann mentions the therapist's guilt over not offering an open-ended therapy to the patient, and he pointed out the guilty therapist's tendency to prolong the therapy to no good purpose. There are other disruptive ways for the therapist to betray guilt in this situation. The therapist might introduce a seductively apologetic tone, a defensive "I'm doing the best I can" tone or an "It's not my fault we're so limited" tone; he or she might even introduce a demanding or accusatory tone that is intended to extort collaboration and progress from patients or punish them for failing to get "all better." Leaving aside individual colorations in this respect, one may say that this guilty countertransference is likely to be based on the assumption that the therapist is morally obliged to heal the patient completely or, at least, in the moderate version proposed by Dr. Mann, obliged to be of help. One major source of this assumption is the therapist's reparative needs. These are needs that commonly play a large part in the choice of a therapeutic career. Reparative needs involve some combination of reaction formation, atonement, and undoing, and they are closely related to unconscious infantile sadistic wishes, fantasies, and deeds. On this basis it may be all too urgent for the therapist to prove that he or she is a healer of damaged parents and children, including the self-as-child.

Brief therapy inherently thwarts these reparative needs. Here, as Dr. Mann says, the therapist's own analysis may significantly reduce this urgency. From the patient's standpoint, however, the guilty therapist is a narcissistic manipulator, one who burdens them with his or her own needs for reassurance. In response, patients may submit and compliantly try to be good, insightful, and responsive; alternatively, they may rebel in a negative transference that, with some real justification, is intended to ward off the demands of yet another narcissistic parental figure who claims to be concerned only with the child's best interests. And since the guilty therapist is likely to interpret the rebelliousness as stemming *only* from the patients' conflicts, he or she will tend to confirm the patients' feelings of "badness" and unworthiness.

Before continuing, I would like to express two reservations about Dr. Mann's discussion. First, it would be more exact to say, not that it is the therapist's obligation to be of help, but that it is the therapist's obligation to do the best that he or she can under very limiting conditions; for not every patient is helped by brief therapy—or any therapy. To feel obliged to get results is to increase the chance of feeling and expressing countertransference guilt.

My second reservation has to do with the initial decision on the therapist's part to offer only brief therapy. In my observation, it makes a great difference whether, on one hand, the therapist has unilaterally decided that that is all the patient needs—as Sifneos (1980) says in one of his transcripts—or, on the other hand, the constraint of time-limit is imposed on the therapy by such factors in reality as heavy clinic case loads or the patient's inability to stay or pay for long. Not that the therapist should defensively hide behind these reality constraints in order to ward off the patient's disappointment and hostility at being offered so little—these must be dealt with—but rather that the unilateral decision that that is all the patient needs exposes the therapist to increased countertransference guilt. It seems to me that in this presentation Dr. Mann tends too quickly to brush aside the objections raised as mere rationalizations, even though he acknowledges that there are some good grounds for objecting. Dr. Mann does not make it clear how, in his approach, the decision is made to offer only time-limited therapy. Much hinges on the basis of this decision.

There are, I believe, other countertransference hazards built into the brief therapy situation. Another hazard lies in the thwarting of the therapist's needs to be omniscient and omnipotent. These needs, like the reparative needs, are shared by all therapists to one degree or another. The threat of helplessness and imperfection that looms over any therapeutic attempt looms all the more over brief therapy. Having only a limited time in which to work, the therapist is tempted to answer too quickly the question of where the patient's major problems lie—for example, that they are primarily oedipal—and to decide too quickly how these problems are to be remedied. The daring and questionable assumption that one can and should achieve definite results in a clearly specified sector of the patient's personality will go unexamined. From this perspective, the patient is likely to be seen, unconsciously, as a threat to the therapist's self-esteem, and to the extent that this is true, the patient is in danger of being manhandled by unwarranted and confining interventions or else implicitly abandoned as a poor risk. In either case, the patient's masochism and needs for authority and symbolic castration may be gratified enough to produce a symptomatic change for the better that only seems to be based on insight and working through.

Freud observed that therapists who can deal effectively with patients are likely to mount the same resistances as their patients once they become patients themselves. But if this is the case, as it seems to be, if should be no surprise that these resistances play a part in their therapeutic work too. Thus, a major correlate of the therapist's needs for omniscience and omnipotence is resistance against the recognition of imperfection and imperfectibility in his or her clinical work. One wants to believe that anything can be understood and anything can be changed for the better. These beliefs amount to denials of the psychoanalytic insight into the strength of defenses and the unconscious dread on which the defenses are based. This dread, or terror, stems from the infantile danger situations that Freud designated as loss of the love object or of its love, castration, and superego condemnation. From other standpoints, one could speak also of the danger of loss of self, and of paranoia, depression, murderous or suicidal rage, and devastating humiliation and shame.

All of the foregoing relates to brief therapy in the following way: through what may be called countertransferential therapeutic zeal, the therapist tries to deny how difficult it is to bring about change based on true and insightful modification of defenses and how magically conceived and unstable many of the apparent benefits of brief therapy are likely to be. The unyielding patient is a threat to the overeager therapist's defenses. As a result, the therapist may make excessive claims for the penetration and the results of brief therapy. In this respect, I would mention that even Dr. Mann's careful analytic account of this method includes what I would consider an excessive claim: in one place he says that his method helps "bypass the patients' customary defenses." It is questionable whether customary defenses can ever be bypassed, for they are too important to the patient and too pervasively applied by him or her. Rather than thinking of end runs around defenses, I would suggest instead thinking that under certain transferential conditions, the patient may re-align important defenses in a compromise move that allows some limited exploratory work to be done and some limited change to occur for reasons that combine irrational repetition and rational change. To some extent this seems to be true in every treatment approach, but it is especially true in brief therapy.

Dr. Mann also mentions the therapist's countertransferential difficulty with loss and separation. To his remarks on this factor I would add this: if one does a lot of brief therapy, one has to deal with frequent and often many simultaneous terminations; and this state of affairs is likely to induce grief reactions in the therapist that in their sheer quantity exceed his or her conscious tolerance. A likely way of coping with this difficulty is defensive detachment or aloofness and working by formula rather than individual "feel." Another likely way of coping is to be intent on achieving up-beat or manic endings to the therapy. From the analytic standpoint, one such manic ending is the shared illusion of analytic cure in *circumscribed areas of the personality*—so-called focal analysis. The analytic method is holistic; that is, it is guided by the conviction that every important aspect of the personality is closely related to, or implied by, every other aspect. In practicing analysis, one would not believe it possible to analyze a circumscribed sector adequately. That a limited analytic approach can alleviate suffering is not in question; what is in question is the correctness of regarding this alleviation as a product of adequate and coherent analysis.

What follows from all of these considerations concerning transference, countertransference, and therapeutic benefits that are partly magical, limited, unstable, and unknowable directly? Contrary to what you might expect, not a counsel of despair. Having done a great deal of brief psychoanalytic therapy myself, and having supervised even more of it, I am impressed by its effectiveness. It is often effective in helping patients regain the psychic equilibrium they had before they became patients. It may even improve that premorbid equilibrium by helping the patients for the first time to recognize and see the ramifications of some of their characteristic vulnerabilities and some of their major assets. Alsto, they may get to realize some of the ways in which they have, on the basis of their inner conflicts, characteristically played an active and significant part in bringing on their own troubles. And they may with some clarity be able to place these conflicts within a more coherent life history than they previously had available. Even though they do not resolve the basic conflicts, even though their major defenses are not fundamentally altered, and even though magical transference factors are probably at work in their improvements, the brief therapy patients may be able to moderate their passive view of themselves as victims, as Dr. Mann (1973) rightly emphasized, and they may also moderate their absolute view of themselves as bad or unworthy. They may moderate these views just enough to tip the scales and, impressively, begin to function in a somewhat more resourceful, adaptive, and happy way. They are then in a better position to invite and get more positive responses from family members and others in the environment or, at least, to end some of the dreadful interpersonal stalemates that played a part in their becoming psychotherapy patients in the first place. It seems that even a slight tipping of the scales can make a big difference. To say that the stability of that change will necessarily remain open to question, at any rate by convinced analysts, is not to say that the therapy is pointless or unhelpful.

Each of the contributors to this volume has addressed himself to this achievement and each has shown how psychoanalytic understanding of the therapeutic process, especially of the roles of transference and/or countertransference in it, can enhance the design, execution, and assessment of clinical and research strategies. Being candid about the indefinable and the irrational and unstable, as well as rational and stable factors, in effective therapeutic work is one of the hall marks of the psychoanalytic approach. The contributors have been most instructive and stimulating in this respect.

REFERENCES

Glover, E. (1931). The therapeutic effect of inexact interpretation: A contribution to the theory of suggestion. In: *The Technique of Psychoanalysis.* New York: International Universities Press, 1955.

Strachey, J. (1934). The nature of the therapeutic action of psychoanalysis. *Internat. J. Psycho-Anal.* 15:127–159.

Winnicott, D. W. (1971). *Playing and Reality.* New York: Basic Books.

CHAPTER TWELVE

Analytic Work By and With Women: The Complexity and the Challenge

Helen Meyers

Alongside the cultural and social changes in attitudes about women, there have been, since the work of Freud (1924, 1925, 1931, 1933) and his immediate followers (Deutsch 1944; Bonaparte 1934), far reaching changes in psychoanalytic concepts of the psychology of women. Moving from the days when only single voices were raised in dissent (Horney 1924, 1926; Jones, 1927), in the last ten years there has been an explosion of important contributions and revisions in our understanding of female psychology and female development (Schafer, 1974; Strouse, 1974; Blum, 1976). Concurrently, interest has grown in taking a new look at clinical work with and by women and the technical aspects involved, such as transference and countertransference issues. Cases of female patients and reports by female analysts have, of course, filled the analytic literature from its beginning, but they have focused on the particular individual countertransference and transference phenomena, not on general issues of the impact of gender as such.

In fact, the gender question per se seems not to have come up in the writings of such eminent female analysts as Jacobson or Annie Reich, although Freud (1931) himself felt that, as a man, he was at a disadvantage in analyzing women compared with his female colleagues. The impact of the gender of the therapist is currently a much debated question. Is there an impact? If so, how much? And what is its nature? Obviously the actual gender of patient or therapist, or rather the unconscious fantasy related to it, is at most one of many variables. Theoretically, in a well-conducted analysis as a whole, the analyst's gender, like all other reality issues, should have little effect, since all transference paradigms are eventually established and worked through. However, my own clinical experience and discussion with colleagues and supervisees leads me to believe that the gender of the analyst does affect the treatment, but only in certain ways, namely, the sequence, intensity, and inescapability of certain transference paradigms in both therapy and analysis. In this essay, I spell out the details of some of these transferences. The gender of the therapist probably makes more of a difference in dynamic therapy, which is more reality linked, with less regression than analysis and where not all transferences are established and worked through. The same would apply to incomplete analyses. Chasseguet-Smirgel (1984) and others have suggested that the effect of gender is probably greater with more regressed patients who have a less secure sense of self identity, are not sure of their sexual identity, and who need, therefore, to cling more concretely to the reality of the sex of the analyst as an organizer.

At the same time, concentration on the gender issue can lead to blind spots and countertransference problems on the part of the therapist, which I also try to describe in these pages. And the therapist's theoretical framework in relation to female psychology will have its impact on the process. Therapists can deal only with what they can hear, and what they hear is informed by their own theoretical stance and training, as well as their bias and character.

We might best, then, approach these rather complex issues by focusing our exploration on three areas within the general framework of our topic. One area might be called a form of transference and countertransference expectation, or anticipation, by the prospective patient in relation to gender, derived from unconscious fantasies prior to starting treatment. This would play a role in the choice of a male or female analyst by a woman about to enter treatment.

The second area concerns the actual transference and countertransference aspects established during the analysis that relate to the gender of the patient and analyst. Parenthetically, let me mention here that my use of these terms is fairly traditional. Transference refers to the reworking, or new version, in the current treatment situation of old infantile conflicts, defenses, internal object relations, and unconscious fantasy. Similarly, countertransference, in the narrow sense, refers to the analyst's or therapist's reaction to the patient or the patient's transference, related to the therapist's own infantile unresolved conflicts and internalized object relations. From the more total point of view, countertransference includes all interferences in the analytic posture, from those reactions predominantly unrelated to the patient, such as the analyst's preoccupation with other issues, to those presumably less related to the analyst's past but specifically created by the patient's pathology.

The third focus narrows the exploration to issues specific to women, such as pregnancy in the patient or the analyst.

All take place in an arena of new values, the feminist movement, the sexual revolution. What is the impact of these cultural changes on treatment of women? Do we see differences in transference and countertransference issues? Are they real or apparent? Is it too soon to tell?

EXPECTATIONS AND CHOICE OF MALE OR FEMALE ANALYST

This area seems most affected by cultural changes in the role and image of women. More women come to women for treatment nowadays than before. Women used to prefer men as analysts. Consciously, men were respected as professional, intelligent, strong, and capable. Men were "real" doctors. Women were devalued and not to be trusted. Sometimes awareness of difficulties with mother and greater ease with men, or pride in being accepted among men, played a conscious part in the woman's choice of a man as analyst. Unconsciously, of course, there were and are other issues. A wish for successful union with the oedipal father, or support from the good preoedipal father, has often been a motive for seeking out a man. Fears of retaliation from the competitive oedipal mother, or expectations of deprivation or punishment from the nongiving or controlling preoedipal mother, have been reasons for avoiding a woman in the sensitive, vulnerable patient-therapist relationship. Conscious devaluation and avoidance of women often has been the defense against this unconscious image of a strong punitive mother or against the recognition of unfulfilled longings for love from the early mother.

Some women have, of course, always come to women based on a variety of conscious and unconscious fantasies: They have avoided the "noncaring, nonempathic" male, who would not and could not understand because he was a man and because the woman would not let him know her. They have fled the "dangerous" male—seen as aggressive and sexually threatening because of their own guilt and fear of their erotic wishes as well as fear of retaliation for their anger and penis envy. They have consciously searched out women therapists as role models to supply "understanding," empathy, and sympathy, for support from a "better" mother or replacement of a lost mother, and to work out problems of separation or battles with the early mother. Unconsciously such choices often involve the infantile wish for the support of, identification with, or even merger with the powerful preoedipal mother, the need to work out guilt and competition with the oedipal mother, or even a need not to get well with an "inferior, defective" woman. These motivations have not changed. Nevertheless, more women today look for treatment with female therapists than ever before, either self-referred or referred by other therapists. Why this increase?

A number of cultural factors present themselves. There is a greater number of well-trained female therapists. Professional women are enjoying greater prestige in general. The relationship between women has acquired new importance and meaning. The search for a role model for today's woman's apparent conflict between career and home, motherhood and self-realization, has become more urgent. There is escalation in the conscious concern that men cannot understand or be sympathetic to female needs and strivings—particularly in regard to feminist issues—and a comcomitant unrealistic expectation that women *will* understand and empathize. Patients with this last expectation sometimes are very disappointed and angry when automatic agreement on attitudes is not forthcoming from their female therapist. They accuse the therapist of betrayal or destructive countertransference, and often threaten to leave treatment. This conscious confrontation often really stands for the female patient's unconscious transference experience of the therapist as the competitive oedipal rival or the depriving preoedipal mother and reflects a repetition of the infantile struggle. Or an angry outburst at lack of agreement can be the result of panic experienced by the patient who had unconsciously chosen the therapist in order to provide a mirroring selfobject for completion or maintenance of a sense of self; here, lack of concordance is experienced as loss of this needed reflection and therefore the threat of loss of self.

What about internal psychic shifts in the new generation of women that would contribute to chosing a female therapist? These are more speculative. A change in the parents' feminine image to one of more assertiveness and completeness will be internalized in the female child's self-representation and may be reflected in lessened penis envy in terms of its culturally determined aspects and less need for submission to, or identification with, the "powerful" male. This will encourage more positive relations with women, who are no longer internally conceived of as fundamentally helpless and defective. Easier maternal acceptance of female sexuality may lessen some of the added complications of the oedipal competition and permit greater comfort between women, who also may need less to be devalued defensively. Paradoxically, the same greater interest in women therapists by young women nowadays may also reflect the opposite of the foregoing. Greater freedom, changing values, changes in roles and family caretaking patterns may create confusion in the parents that may be reflected in the child in lack of clear identifications, problems in ego ideal, or a search for a solid preoedipal mother for completion and repair of self-identity. These women will then seek out female therapists.

REFERRALS

Referrals to female therapists also are more frequent today. It is interesting that, while patients tend to be referred to a man simply because he is thought of as a good therapist by the referrer, others are sent to a female therapist specifically because she is a woman, that is, for a particular conscious reason that seems to make a female therapist desirable. The reason may be idealizing, such as the traditional notion of greater female empathy or women's greater skill with difficult preoedipal material. Or it may be devaluing, such as the idea that women accept lower fees or that "a little mothering" rather than therapeutic skill is all that's needed for a particular patient. But it almost always takes the female gender of the therapist into special consideration. More and more, female training analysts are specifically requested for consultations or reanalysis for patients whose previous therapists were male. The idea is that certain issues may not have been addressed with a male therapist but will come to the fore in the transference with a woman, as I describe later.

WOMEN'S REASONS FOR SEEKING TREATMENT

What are the reasons given by women for coming to treatment? They run the gamut of problems today as they did in the past: depression, anxiety, and phobias; patients' dissatisfaction with work, with relationships, with their sexual life, with themselves. Perhaps one hears a vagueness in their complaints more frequently today than before, a sense of emptiness, a lack of direction, related to the problems in sense of self alluded to earlier.

Much has been said about the predicament of today's woman in striking a balance between work and home, power and love, personal and professional priorities. Many, though not all, women do raise these issues in treatment. For some women who raise these issues, the presented struggle between work and home, this problem of priorities, is a spurious issue. They talk of ambition yet exhibit chronic dissatisfaction at work and complain of inability to find the right career, which they claim they want but see as conflicting with their wishes for family life. It is only much later in treatment that it becomes clear that this was not the conflict. These women want no career at all but get their satisfaction from "traditional female" pursuits. However, they cannot let themselves become aware of such attitudes, which are in shameful conflict with their conscious, often strongly feminist, value systems. It is often quite difficult for them to deal with this discrepancy between the conscious and the unconscious aspects of their ideal self-image.

Other women come with problems in both their work and their relationships: this young woman cannot finish her thesis and cannot maintain a satisfactory love relationship; that woman is not quite the success in her career that she wants to be, nor is she gratified in her marriage. They seem to understand the problem to be a conflict between career, or masculine strivings, and femininity—as conflicting identifications or conflicts in their ego ideal, but they don't want to give up either. They say they have come to realize that as women they cannot really let themselves succeed at their career and, if they try, they will be found out as inadequate and "wanting." These are intelligent women, well read and well versed in current literature. Many have been in previous treatment, which has led to this "understanding." But treatment has been of only limited help. The problem is that sometimes this insight is only part of the story. In some of these cases, the apparent conflict between two opposing needs and wishes is a rationalization in the service of defense; underneath is the woman's inability to let herself succeed at either area. Both areas represent the same battlefield, and success in either represents the same aggressive, competitive success over and destructiveness toward the oedipal or preoedipal mother. As such, it is forbidden and punishable by the internalized mother. These women thus do not let themselves succeed fully either in love relationships or at work. They guiltily punish themselves with lack of success and satisfaction and with additional torturous self-derogation of inadequacy.

Other women do not experience these priorities as conflictual at all. These women do well in both areas. Whatever problems they have lie elsewhere. Such women have been referred to as "superwomen" (Epstein 1984), but actually they are more common than would be expected from the popular literature. This phenomenon relates to a little explored aspect of feminine psychology. Much has been written about women's sense of defectiveness related to their awareness of anatomical differences and to culturally derived self-concepts of inferiority. Far less has been said about women's basic security and high self-esteem based on early identification with the all-powerful, competent mother and on their sense of inborn creativity and productivity as potential mothers. These factors may even contribute to a secret overevaluation of women by men, with all its consequences of envy and compensatory devaluation of women by men (Kestenberg, 1968; Chasseguet-Smirgel, 1976). This chapter, however, is not the place for a thorough discussion of this topic.

TRANSFERENCE AND COUNTERTRANSFERENCE ASPECTS RELATED TO GENDER OF THERAPIST OR PATIENT

What does happen in treatment? Do the patient's anticipated transference situations become established according to the sex of the analyst, one kind with a man, another with a woman? The answer is both yes and no. Let us examine this apparent contradiction. The variables in individual patients are so numerous; their character, dynamics and environment so individually different; and the variables in the therapists so many, depending on character, background, experience, training, and style, that gender and cultural variables can play only a part and are difficult to tease out. In the long run, I am convinced, as mentioned in the beginning, that in a complete analysis it doesn't matter whether the analyst is a man or a woman. All significant early object relationships are reexperienced in a new version in the transference; all unconscious fantasies are transferred onto the analyst, so that at one time or another the analyst is reacted to as father, mother, brother or sister, regardless of the actual gender of the analyst. A frequent problem indeed is that this is overlooked. The oedipal father image behind the maternal figure is often missed in the transference with the female analyst, a subject on which I expand later.

On the other hand, the gender of the therapist does affect the course of treatment. As I suggested earlier, the therapist's gender affects the sequence, intensity, and inescapability of certain transference paradigms in both therapy and analysis. Certainly the earliest transference reactions tend to be influenced by the therapist's gender, as well as by other reality factors. I am thinking of several male patients who started with explosive erotic transferences with female analysts, whereas in similar cases with male analysts such maternal transferences did not develop for years. Many of my patients, of either sex, start with a strong mother transference reaction—be it a mother image that is depriving, punitive, or invasive, loving, or seductive. Only later will I be responded to as the competitive successful father or any other paternal object. But there is more than the initial difference. A number of patients who have come to me, a woman, for reanalysis, after a previous analysis with a man, had made much progress with their internal and external relations with men but much less progress in their relationships with women. They seemed to require the immediacy of feelings aroused in the transference with a female analyst, which forced these fearful elements to surface, pressing for confrontation with difficult conflicts that the patient had been able to avoid in previous treatment with a man.

To illustrate the point of greater inescapability of certain gender-linked transferences, let me present the following example: The patient, a man, presenting with difficulties in establishing a satisfactory relationship with a woman, was able to work out a rather subtle sadomasochistic problem with women as it forced itself on his awareness in its manifestations in a sadomasochistic transference in a reanalysis with a female analyst. This sadomasochistic issue had not come up in his previous work with a male analyst, which had focused mainly on his competitive oedipal problem. This competitive oedipal issue, equally important in his problem with women, had been the central, affect-laden transference theme with his male analyst, but its working through had not fully resolved his problem with women. I cannot state with certainty that the sadomasochistic issue emerged only because the second analyst was a female—the variables I mentioned earlier force me to add a qualifying "may have" here. The material might well have entered the first analysis had it continued longer than it did. Or perhaps countertransference issues played their part. The first analyst, for instance, might have had his own unresolved problems with women similar to those of the patient and thus may have had a "blind spot." But I am suggesting that most probably the issue could not be avoided with a woman analyst.

In recent years, various gender-related observations about transference have been put forward. Most frequently it has been suggested that with both male and female patients, preoedipal mother transferences are apt to be established with female therapists and oedipal father transferences with male therapists. Fleming (personal communication, 1970) found specifically with male patients that separation issues seemed to predominate with female analysts, whereas more homosexual transference reactions were observed in analyses with male analysts. Karme (1979), on the other hand, postulated that preoedipal maternal transferences could be experienced with analysts of either gender, but oedipal transferences, maternal or paternal, were established according to the actual gender of the analyst. Although these observations are based on clinical material, they are not universally validated and do not have a simple explanation. Whatever the impact of therapist gender on the transference, gender-linked countertransferences are likely to be involved as well. These transference-countertransference paradigms are complex problems. For example, for the instances cited by Fleming, should we assume that closeness with a woman analyst led to regressive longing for, and fear of, the preoedipal mother of separation-individuation, while the closeness to the man analyst stirred up homosexual desires on a negative oedipal level in the male patient? Or, countertransferentially, are some female analysts more comfortable with preoedipal issues than with erotic or aggressive oedipal transference wishes from the male patient, and therefore concentrate on earlier separation-individuation issues? Do some male analysts miss the implied preoedipal maternal transference, the mother behind the father image, because of their own fears of passivity or castration? I do not know how much of the earlier mentioned findings, then, would be due to fantasies elicited in the transference as a result of the therapist's gender, how much would be due to the patient's unconscious need in selecting a particular gender therapist in the first place, and how much would be due to gender-related countertransference. Obviously, these vary with individual patients and individual therapists. Surely male therapists can be very comfortable with early issues and women comfortable with aggression and sexuality. In fact, the most common transference I have observed in my own work with male patients and supervision of male patients with female analysts is the erotic oedipal transference. I have discussed this and other specific transferences of male patients in treatment with women at some length elsewhere (Meyers, 1986).

There is another interesting phenomenon often observed when the genders of therapist and patient differ. Female analysts frequently elicit pregnancy fantasies and womb envy in their male patients, while male analysts almost universally detect penis envy in their female patients. These findings are much less so when the respective genders of patient and therapist are the same. Female therapists do not find penis envy as frequently in their female patients, and male therapists rarely observe pregnancy fantasies in their male patients. This presents another of these complex transference-countertransference combinations. I would speculate that envy of the opposite sex organ is a universal developmental issue found in everyone if one looks hard enough, but it is stirred up more in the transference in identification and competition with an analyst of the opposite sex. But another part may be based on countertransference in the analyst. A woman analyst may project pregnancy wishes while denying penis envy; a male analyst may expect penis envy and deny envy of the inner space (Kestenberg, 1968). These are intriguing questions that will need a closer look in our work.

These issues also raise concern about the impact of the analyst's theoretical orientation, that is, the therapist's understanding of female psychology. It will make a difference whether penis envy in women is viewed as "rock bottom" (Freud, 1925; Bonaparte, 1934), or as secondary or cultural (Horney, 1926; Blum, 1976) or as an organizing metaphor (Grossman & Stewart, 1976). If women are devalued or viewed by the therapist as defective in their psychological development, then not only the content of the analyst's interpretation, but the whole response to the female patient will be affected. Of course, women analysts have been just as involved in this as their male colleagues. The fact is that one's theoretical orientation will inform one's response, whether it is a classical, developmental, object relations, or self theroy approach. One reacts to what one hears, and one hears what one is able to hear. There is a thin line between knowledge and bias. Moreover, the very choice of one's theoretical orientation is itself based on inner psychological needs that may skew one's vision.

To return to our original question: The gender of the therapist does seem to affect the course of the analysis in certain cases. While the determinants of transferences are within the patient—establishing forms, content, sequence, and intensity—the gender of the analyst may also have some bearing, particularly on the sequence and intensity. Equally important to our awareness is that there are particular gender-related countertransference pitfalls that may strongly influence the transferences noted, dealt with, or permitted to develop. Such countertransference reactions may indeed have much impact on the course of the treatment, and special attention to their possible existence will be of great help in the analytic work with and by women. I discussed some of these countertransference issues earlier. Let me touch on some others. They will be elaborated on by the other authors in this section.

A SPECIFIC COUNTERTRANSFERENCE PROBLEM IN MIXED GENDER PAIRS

In the female patient-male therapist pair, the erotic countertransference—with sexual activity in response to the patient's seductiveness, often related to unresolved oedipal or self-esteem problems in the male therapist—is probably the most talked about countertransference problem related to gender. This kind of countertransference and action seems to occur considerably less frequently with female therapists and male patients. This is consistant with the relatively greater frequency and acceptance in our culture of a sexual liaison between an older, established man and a younger, inexperienced woman than between an older woman and a young man. Incest between father and daughter is considered less pathological and certainly is more frequent than mother-son incest. Vulnerability to this countertransference potential may stem, on one hand, from greater male emphasis on sexual potency for self-esteem and self-definition and, on the other, from greater inhibition on sexuality in women, including female therapists, and greater ease with the role of the preoedipal caretaker rather than the sexual oedipal mother.

In terms of transference, it has recently been suggested that what may contribute to the relatively infrequent sexual acting out of male patients with female therapists is the fear of being swallowed up again in the womb of mother, a fear that is postulated to be part of every little boy's normal oedipal complex. The oedipal complex, it is suggested, contains within it both the wish for sexual union with the oedipal mother and the earlier wish to return to the womb of the preoedipal mother. The little boy's fear, then, in oedipal gratification would be both of retaliatory castration from father and of disappearance into mother (Chasseguet-Smirgel, 1984).

Further countertransference dangers for the male analyst with a female patient lie in such other unresolved early conflictual areas as identification with the woman, touching on his own passivity and fear of castration; the therapist's own wish for, and fear of, merger with the early, powerful mother; or womb and pregnancy envy in response to a patient who is a mother or currently pregnant. In the female therapist-male patient pair, other countertransference dangers may involve penis envy and competitive castrating wishes; oedipal arousal and avoidance of oedipal issues; or the general difficulty of experiencing herself as the paternal object with all patients, as mentioned earlier. (For a discussion of transference in the male patient-female therapist pair, see Meyers, 1986).

A SPECIAL PROBLEM IN THE FEMALE-FEMALE PAIR

I would like to concentrate now on a particular transference-countertransference problem in the female-female dyad, which also touches on the issue of changing values and concepts. With a female patient and a female therapist, the obvious classical transferences—such as competition with the oedipal mother, defiance and compliance toward the preoedipal mother, dependency issues with the early mother and separation-individuation issues—abound nowadays as they did in the past and are the focus of much attention. Similarly, in the female-female pair such common countertransference issues as competition, rivalry, fear and wish for merger, rejection, envy, and overidentification frequently take center stage and are well-known danger points. Imagine, for example, a female analyst with a young child being told by her female patient about the death of her baby, or the childless analyst having to deal with her patient's problems around pregnancy. The result could easily be analytic paralysis. Often it has been.

Frequently missed, however, by both patient and therapist is the transference where the female therapist becomes the oedipal father for the female patient—leading, at times, to unexplained erotic feelings towards the therapist. I am addressing here the relatively frequent, but also often neglected, appearance of homosexual feelings in the female patient with a female therapist, without previous homosexual ideation or orientation in the patient. These are manifested in homosexual fantasies or transient homosexual acting out in adult women patients and in more prolonged homosexual activity in adolescent girls. The stories that go with this phenomenon vary a great deal: a 16-year-old girl with a narcissistic, exhibitionistic mother and a "beautiful" but remote father develops erotic feelings for her female therapist and enters into a homosexual affair with an older woman; a 15-year-old girl, whose homosexual father left the family during the patient's childhood and whose mother is overwhelmed by the parenting role, is frightened of her sexual feelings towards boys and makes brief gestures toward homosexual relations; a young mother who lost her own parents early through divorce and death develops sexual fantasies about her female therapist during a prolonged separation from the therapist; a married woman who enjoys apparently satisfactory sexual relations with her husband, but who has a background of conflict and rivalry with a possessive mother and a distant father, experiences intense erotic longings for her female therapist. The list goes on. The dominant transference meaning of the particular fantasy or acting out is, of course, different in each case. In one, it is an attempt at self-cohesion by merger with a self-object mother. In another, it represents loving attachment to a caretaking mother. The maintenance of object-relations with an ambivalent preoedipal mother is the meaning in a third case, while seduction of the competitive oedipal mother with regression to the negative oedipal object is the point in another.

What all these cases have in common is an unsatisfactory mothering experience, a father unavailable for parenting, and a female therapist and female patient. In the context of the relationship with the therapist, who for the first time in many of these situations provides a safe, empathic, consistent figure for the girl or woman, an intense, sexualized, positive, mostly preoedipal mother transference of an idealizing nature is established—while the bad mother image is split off and maintained in relation to the real mother. Simultaneously, there is an unrecognized erotic oedipal father transference that intensifies the sexual feelings towards the female therapist. The bad father image also is split off and projected onto father or other men. These erotic paternal transferences must be recognized and interpreted along with the maternal transferences so that these homosexual feelings can be dealt with; otherwise they will constitute a major resistance. It is all these intense dependency and erotic feelings together directed toward the female therapist that take the form of homosexual erotic fantasies or sexual acting out toward female objects.

CURRENT CONSIDERATIONS

Homosexual acting out phenomena appear somewhat more frequently nowadays. I suggest that this may have to do with a greater overt acceptance of homosexual alternatives in our society. What might have remained an "unacceptable" fantasy pressing to be worked on further, becomes an "acceptable" alternative gratification, which can be used defensively by the patient to avoid further therapeutic work. In today's climate of changing attitudes and self-examination, one might wonder whether such actions are indeed acting out or whether they constitute possibly viable alternatives perceived as acting out by the therapist only because of the therapist's own "old-fashioned" value system. Let me stress again the importance of these transference-countertransference problems for questions of technique. Awareness of these possibilities increases understanding, and understanding lessens the problems of avoiding areas for investigation and interpretation.

Changes in social norms have provided support and acceptance for many new alternatives for women, such as work versus home, single parenthood or abdicated parenting, legal abortions, and a dignified single life style whether divorced or never married. This provides welcome opportunity for self-expansion, liberation, and relief from previously untenable but apparently insoluble situations. At times, however, these expanded choices can also offer, instead of internal conflict resolution, less valid, "easy" alternatives, a rationalization for acting out masochistic fantasies, a resistance against further, more laborious therapeutic exploration. I am thinking of several cases where the decision not to marry or the decision to separate, consciously experienced as a step forward in relation to improved self-esteem, unconsciously also meant self-deprivation of a desired relationship. The decision reflected a need for expiatory suffering for competitive guilt towards mother—rather than a leap to freedom.

These complex considerations present a constant challenge for today's therapist, who must also struggle with her own changing values and theoretical concepts about the psychology of women. Let me demonstrate with a purposely simplified example: a masochistic woman patient complains constantly about her husband's failure to do his share of household duties—cleaning, ironing, cooking, shopping—and is making herself and him miserable. Would this be dealt with as her masochism in choosing to live with a man who does not meet today's expectations of equal participation by men? Or will a therapist who does not see this as necessarily the man's role view the complaint only as being in the service of the patient's sadomasochistic need to suffer and punish instead of enjoying the relationship? Or will classic concepts of the psychology of women lead the therapist to interpret in terms of penis envy and basic feminine masochism? Clearly, interpretation in any one case will depend on the material as it presents itself, but it is important that we be in touch with these issues which may interfere in our listening and make more complex today's therapeutic task with women.

Countertransference problems for female therapists in their work with adolescent girls has always been a special challenge, but particularly so now with changing cultural values. All the therapist's unfinished adolescent conflicts around fear and envy of sexual freedom, narcissistic gratification, and wish for or fear of action in the service of experimentation and ego growth are revived in the work with the adolescent patient and must be dealt with once again (Meyers, 1971). In light of today's sexual revolution, changing female roles and body concepts and almost limitless career choices for young women, there may be a temptation for the therapist to identify with and attempt to live once more through the young patient or, on the other hand, to place angry, envious, or frightened constraints on the youngster's freedom. These are common pitfalls that can lead to confusion and therapeutic impasse.

PREGNANCY

Finally, let me turn briefly to an area specific to women, that is, the fascinating issue of pregnancy in the patient or the therapist. On one hand, a female therapist might be uniquely qualified to empathize with her pregnant patient. On the other hand, she may compete with or envy her patient if she is conflicted or not able to become pregnant herself, and have difficulty in maintaining a neutral analytic stance. She may overidentify or use the patient's pregnancy to work out problems of her own. Curiously, I know of at least two cases where the analyst, who had previously had difficulty in conceiving, became pregnant after her patient became so.

With a male analyst and a pregnant patient, the question arises whether the male analyst can really understand the experience. Following Freud, many contributions to current literature have suggested that male therapists might have difficulty empathizing with and understanding specifically female experiences such as pregnancy and childbirth, as well as with female roles and female attitudes. One might equally ask if female therapists could properly empathize with some uniquely male experiences and attitudes, or whether one can indeed empathize with any experience that is foreign. I believe one can (Meyers, 1986). Sometimes, however, male analysts exhibit a curiously unrealistic idealization, awe, wonder, and fear of the state of pregnancy, related perhaps to early infantile idealization of mother. Some male analysts have been heard to suggest that a pregnant analyst should not see patients, because of the "complete inner absorption" of that state, which they suggest leaves no room for anyone else; a thought, I think, related to an unfinished infantile wish for complete, blissful union with a totally absorbed mother. Related to this, some male analysts have been noted to miss acting out and other resistances in their pregnant patients, going along or even encouraging leaves of absence from treatment or missed sessions in relation to the pregnancy, as if these were not subject for analytic inquiry. There are, of course, also other countertransference pitfalls for the male analyst, such as envy of the patient's pregnancy, a wish to identify with the pregnant mother, and sexual oedipal fantasies of being the father of the child.

Then there is the pregnant analyst. Pregnancy of the analyst is, of course, a very specific issue only for female analysts and their patients. Little has been written on the subject. Perhaps now, with the more frequent combination of career and traditional female roles, more young women will be pregnant while in active analytic practice, and we will have a larger literature on this. One article (Lax, 1969) did report that male patients notice pregnancy later and then drop the subject as foreign, whereas female patients notice sooner and then discuss it. The formulation offered in these cases was that men are more threatened and women more at ease with the identification with the analyst's femaleness, certainly a logical construction.

Others have had different experiences. One male patient noticed his analyst's pregnancy quite early, as evidenced by dreams, fantasies, and conscious awareness. He reacted with horror, dreaming of a dangerous tumor growing in his mother's belly for which he was responsible. Fantasizing himself as the father, he dreamt of frightful battles with dragons, revealing great guilt over his oedipal sexual and hostile wishes and expecting due punishment. However, he stayed with it and kept working on it. Finally, tender, caretaking dreams took over. The patient, who had come to treatement for severe sexual inhibitions, began to relate to women sexually and tenderly. The analyst's pregnancy apparently aided in working through his problem, stimulating his conflict but also reassuring him about his own and his mother's survival. A female patient, on the other hand, had great difficulty with her analyst's pregnancy. In her forties, the patient had no children. In her youth she had suffered much maternal deprivation as well as sibling rivalry with her younger sister. Although her dreams suggested early on that she was aware of the analyst's pregnancy, she would not acknowledge it until very late and could not handle the competition with the mother-analyst nor the sibling rivalry with the new child. Clearly, there is a wide range of reactions to the analyst's pregnancy, depending on individual meanings and conflicts. This is a subject that bears further exploration.

I have touched on many issues and left out many others, some of which are addressed by the other authors in this section. They all attest to the complexity and challenge of analytic work by and with women.

REFERENCES

Blum, H., ed. (1976). Female psychology-Supplement. *J. Amer. Psychoanal. Assn.,* 24.

Bonaparte, M. (1934). Passivity, masochism and femininity. *Internat. J. Psycho-Anal.,* 16:325–333.

Chasseguet-Smirgel, J. (1976). Freud and female sexuality: The consideration of some blind spots in the exploration of the dark continent, *Internat. J. Psycho-Anal.,* 57:275–287.

______. (1984, April). *A special case: On transference love in the male.* Paper presented at the London Weekend Conference.

Deutsch, H. (1944). *The Psychology of Women,* Vols. I & II. New York: Grune & Stratton.

Epstein, C. (1984). The politics of stress: Public visions, private realities, *The Public and the Private Woman.* Symposium conducted by Columbia University Center for Psychoanalytic Training and Research and Association for Psychoanalytic Medicine.

Freud, S. (1924). The dissolution of the Oedipus complex, *Standard Edition,* 19:173–179. London: Hogarth Press, 1961.

______. (1925). Some psychical consequences of the anatomical distinction between the sexes, *Standard Edition,* 19:248–258. London: Hogarth Press, 1961.

______. (1931). Female Sexuality, *Standard Edition,* 21:225–243. London: Hogarth Press, 1961.

______. (1933). Femininity, *Standard Edition,* 22:112–135. London: Hogarth Press, 1964.

Grossman, W., & Stewart, W. (1976). Penis envy: From childhood wish to developmental metaphor, *J. Amer. Psychoanal. Assn.* 24:193–213.

Horney, K. (1924). On the genesis of the castration complex in women, *Internat. J. Psycho-Anal.,* 5:50–65.

______. (1926). The flight from womanhood. In: *Feminine Psychology,* ed. H. Kelman, New York: Norton, 1967.

Jones, E. (1927). The early development of female sexuality. In: *Papers on Psychoanalysis,* London: Balliere, 1938, pp. 438–451.

Karme, L. (1979). The analysis of a male patient by a female analyst: The problem of the negative oedipal transference, *Internat. J. Psycho-Anal.,* 60:253–261.

Kestenberg, J. (1968). Outside and inside, male and female, *J. Amer. Psychoanal. Assn.,* 16:457–521.

Lax, R. (1969). Some considerations about transference and countertransference manifestations evoked by the analyst's pregnancy, *Internat. J. Psycho-Anal.*, 50:363–372.

Meyers, H. (1971). The therapist's response to today's adolescent, *Psychosocial Process*, 2:38–46.

——— (In press). How do women treat men? In: *Psychology of Men*, ed. J. Fogel, F. Lane, & R. Liebert. New York: Basic Books.

Schafer, R. (1974). Problems in Freud's psychology of women. *J. Amer. Psychoanal. Assn.*, 22:459–485.

Strouse, J., ed. (1974). *Women and Analysis*, New York: Grossman.

CHAPTER THIRTEEN

Reflections on Transference and Countertransference in the Treatment of Women

Harold P. Blum and Elsa J. Blum

Ideally, any competent analyst should be able to treat a female or male patient, and the particular sex of the analyst or of the patient should not be an overriding factor in treatment outcome. But this is not always the case; that the ideal is not always realized has been long recognized. Some patients in particular, for example, the Wolf Man, have deliberately been sent to a female analyst, and over the years there have been various suggestions concerning the choice of same sex or opposite sex analyst. The consideration of sex as a factor in selection of an analyst has been based mainly on the characteristics of the patient and also on the possible limitations or advantages for the analytic process. The sex of the analyst was likely to be a particular consideration in the case of a patient's special preference or prejudice initially, or in re-analysis. Questions have been raised concerning the influence of the analyst's sex on objectivity, neutrality, and empathy, all related to countertransference issues. The nature of the transference likely to be established was reciprocal, especially if certain types of transference were thought to be advantageous or threatening, facilitating or impairing the patient's capacity to establish and maintain an analytic alliance and analytic work. Although the issues in this paper are discussed in terms of psychoanalysis, they are, in the main, relevant as well for psychoanalytically oriented psychotherapy.

In scattered remarks (Tyson, 1980) Freud referred to the problem of the analyst's gender. He (1931) noted that female analysts were more likely to elicit pre-oedipal transference derivatives. His study of erotized transference love was focused exclusively on female patients with male analysts: he did not discuss homosexual transference love where the analyst was of the same gender as the patient or the male patient's transference love with a female analyst (Blum, 1973). Except for some commentary by Bibring (1936), there are no analytic reports of a male patient's erotic transference to a female analyst.

The male patient might have a more negative transference with a male analyst (Freud, 1917), or might be unable to resolve his feelings of indebtedness to a father surrogate and, therefore, refuse to accept recovery (Freud, 1937). Freud (1920) thought that his gender increased the transference resistance of his female homosexual patient.

Blum (1971) noted that real attributes of the analyst, such as age, sex, style and character traits, may color the developing transference and that, with a female analyst, a maternal transference will usually appear first. This implies that an analyst's gender may influence the sequence of transference manifestations and possibly the form and intensity of specific transferences, but not necessarily that the overall analysis of transference would be altered. Although different transferences did not always appear in the brief analyses of the pioneer days, now the analyst appears successively as father or mother, sibling or grandparent. Transference displacements and the role of objects other than the analyst as transference figures would also be evident, such as a father transference to a female analyst's husband. In a properly conducted analysis, all of the patient's key neurotic conflicts and the entire range of transferences would be explored as the transference resistance is analyzed and the transference neurosis resolved. This may not be the case, however, in psychotherapy with incomplete interpretation of the transference. Thus, the gender of the therapist might, to a greater degree, color the treatment. Tyson (1980, p. 321) noted that in child analysis the gender of the analyst may influence nontransference configurations, such as "the use of the analyst as a real object to accomplish a developmental step" and "may contribute to the evolution of transference and countertransference manifestations." In adult analysis also, although the primary goal remains the analysis of unconscious intrapsychic conflict through insight, the gender of the analyst may also influence the reaction to the analyst as new object, as well as aspects of the transference.

In addition to cases referred for re-analysis or transferred because of analytic stalemate, special problems of parent loss in childhood, homosexual panic, revival of sexual trauma, or severe regressive states and pre-oedipal disorder have sometimes led to consideration of the therapeutic implications of the sex of the analyst. There is no consensus regarding the significance of the analyst's sex, however, not even, for example, in cases of homosexuality or parent loss (cf. Greenacre, 1959; Mogul, 1982).

Although transference is blindly repetitive and distorts the reality of the therapist, transference and sequence, attenuation, intensification, regression, and resistance may be influenced by the realities of the analyst or analytic situation.

The cultural milieu influences both the prospective patient's choice of an analyst and the initial transference predispositions. Today we live and carry out our professional work in a social and cultural setting vastly different from that of the early studies of the psychology of women. There is much more concern and awareness of the cultural attitudes of women toward treatment since those early days of the first female patients—Anna O., Irma, Dora, with their particular transference-countertransference configurations. The sex of the analyst may well have colored treatment differently then than it would today. It is quite possible that the women of yesteryear tended to look toward the male doctor as a competent authority and to regard treatment by any female physician with some suspicion. The early identifications and attitudes within the family, and in the particular culture, were carried over in transferential attitudes toward treatment, the therapist, and the therapeutic establishment.

In addition to issues of education, expertise, and prestige within the medical establishment, there may have been psychological reasons why women in the past would regard father figures as providers of love and protection and would experience the mother figures as representing protracted dependency, as well as inferiority and depreciated status. The choice of analyst of either sex by a male or a female patient is influenced by a variety of conscious and unconscious reasons. The female patient may consciously seek greater understanding, an ally, and a role model in choosing a female analyst, although unconscious motives are extremely important. For example, in being a "caretaker," a woman may unconsciously seek maternal care and dependency. Actually, positive and negative transference are always present or potential, so that the analyst of either sex may be regarded sooner or later as friend or enemy, protector or punisher. Although in analysis ideally all transferences are elicited and resolved, in nonanalytic psychotherapy particular gender-linked transferences may remain fixed and unresolved with positive or negative therapeutic implications. In analysis, the patient should eventually understand the motives underlying preference for an analyst of the same or opposite sex.

With respect to contemporary psychoanalysis and psychotherapy, new questions have arisen with both theoretical and technical ramifications. The first concerns theoretical issues involving the clarity, consistency, explanatory power, and universality of concepts of female psychology; transferential issues regarding theoretical change itself will be discussed. The second question, in response especially to critiques by nonanalysts, addresses the application of psychoanalytic knowledge and theory in the treatment of women. It encompasses particular questions about male therapists treating female patients. In a more general sense, it raises the issue of clinical bias, including, but not limited to cultural bias, often internalized and unconsciously based, in the treatment of women by therapists of either sex. Similar questions of bias, lack of empathy, and impaired comprehension have been raised concerning transcultural analysis, interracial analysis, the treatment of Holocaust survivors, and also that of therapy of men by women, etc. Conversely, shared fantasies and experience may also lead to impaired comprehension. The controversial issues are by no means confined only to the sex of therapist and patient. In addition, a number of other specific transference-countertransference tendencies in the treatment of women will be discussed.

In recent years there has been re-evaluation of psychoanalytic female psychology and a major challenge to some of the "traditional tenets" of the past in this area. Although Freud made remarkable contributions to the understanding of human development of both sexes, he recognized the fragmentary nature of the knowledge of femininity that had been attained. He listened to and learned from his female patients as no one had before; he stimulated and encouraged the psychoanalytic investigations and careers of his female students. In some areas, in the light of present knowledge, Freud's tentative formulations were incomplete, and in some instances, inaccurate and inconsistent with later knowledge and models (Schafer, 1974; Blum, 1976; Moore, 1976).

Following Freud and for a long time thereafter, the basic textbooks of psychoanalytic female psychology were those of Marie Bonaparte (1953) and of Helene Deutsch (1944, 1945), two women who made very significant contributions to psychoanalysis. Their early propositions permeated much of psychoanalytic thinking about women, and with regrettable fixation, these and similar incomplete and often obsolete views remained in vogue for many years to come. It was just as often the female analyst who emphasized the women's psychobiology in terms of infantile traits and developmental deficiency. Analysts of both sexes adhered to a model of femininity derived from feelings of injury and envy, disappointment and deficiency (Blum, 1976). The emphasis on exaggerated masochism, passivity, and narcissism, and the presentation of these traits as normal or desirable further influenced subsequent psychoanalytic thinking but were never without controversy.

It must be noted that analytic training and treatment were quite different forty to fifty years ago, and analysts dealt with a different patient population. Inferences were further limited by lack of developmental knowledge; there was no monolothic point of view, and opposition and dissent from these views was always present, even if at times in a relatively silent minority. Furthermore, within psychoanalytic pratice there was independent judgment, and most analysts of forty years ago, like analysts of today, regarded a female patient's tendencies to be humiliated and victimized as an indication for treatment. Nevertheless, it is not easy for some to alter what they teach or learn, and some only relearn what they have already been taught or mold the data to fit their preconceptions.

The analyst may also have to deal with an interrelated problem of psychoanalytic education, the transference toward analytic teachings and teachers. The transference to the institute is well known as a problem, as is transference to the training analyst, supervisors, and other teachers. However, in addition to residual unresolved transference to former teachers, investments in learned theories and reliance on authority may impede the development of psychoanalytic theory and constitute fixation to the past.

Recent psychosocial investigations have explored the status of women in our society, the influence of sex stereotyping, and of attitudes of discrimination which tend to be reinforced and internalized throughout life. The psychological effects of both parental attitudes and of social, cultural, and economic inequities and disadvantages have been identified. Intense and often highly emotionally charged accusations of not only social but also scientific bias and discrimination have appeared. Within this context, female activists have charged analysts with reactionary theories and attitudes toward women, with prejudice that compromises treatment and that iatrogenically complicates psychological problems. They have also questioned whether male therapists can avoid a prejudiced view of women from a phallocentric position and whether the therapist is able to remain objective, empathic, and understanding of his female patients, or whether he will be insensitive, disparaging, or discouraging.

It is, indeed, important to retain objectivity, both in the clinical situation and in understanding the cultural pressures that impinge on both the analyst and patient. It is not necessarily easy to gain and regain distance from one's own culture and to understand the complex interplay of psychological and social forces when one looks at one's own society or tries to understand a different or changing society and culture. Our language itself may help (e.g., chairman versus chairperson; mankind versus humanity, etc.) to shape and to maintain various attitudes that remain outside of awareness, even if they are not actively denied or repressed. Can the male or female analyst, then, be free of countertransference? Are specific countertransference paradigms likely to develop in the analysis of the female patient? Is the countertransference more difficult to deal with or resolve than, for example, in the male analyst's treatment of the male patient?

The answers to these questions are not as simple as might appear and are hardly reducible to the influence of the analyst's sex. Transference and countertransference are complex concepts in themselves and refer to revived fantasy distortions about the past and not the past as it really occurred. Distinctions must be made between general attitudes toward all women, specific countertransference to a specific transference of the patient, and other subspecies of countertransference. For purposes of this discussion, we will not attempt to differentiate the different forms of countertransference, to deal with the more narrow and global definitions, or the effect of the countertransference on the transference. The countertransference refers here primarily to the analyst's irrational, unconscious reaction to the patient and, in the narrow sense, to the patient's transference. The transference will still be considered as primarily a modified repetition, a new edition of the past, in which the patient reacts to the analyst in terms of infantile object representations and revived infantile conflicts.

The establishment of an analytic process and the analysis of transference and resistance depend on the therapist's therapeutic skills, personality resources, knowledge, and what we loosely call "clinical experience and wisdom." However, what is uniquely involved in psychoanalytic therapy and intrinsic to a successful psychoanalytic process is the analyst's simultaneous capacity for self-scrutiny and analysis of the countertransference. And in recent years there has even been more emphasis than in the past on the countertransference as an additional data source for learning more about what the patient has been trying to communicate, evoke, or provoke in the analyst. The unanalyzed countertransference is an impediment to analytic understanding, analytic empathy, and insight; it may lead to lapses of analytic tact and judgment and to departures from neutrality and from correct psychoanalytic technique. We want to stress this point because we do not feel that countertransference is necessarily intensified, more tenacious, or more resistant to analysis in the treatment of a patient of one sex, or one phase of life, or one lifestyle than another. The capacity to work together effectively depends on the mix or analytic suitability of the two partners in the analytic work, influenced by style and skill and ever present transference-countertransferences. Under ordinary circumstances, analysts can treat a large range of analyzable cases of either sex, even with the great personality variations that are to be found among competent analysts and the rather widely divergent analyzable patient population.

There are, of course, variations in acuity, in awareness of subtleties and nuances, in being tuned in not only to the patients' problems but to their more mature goals and aspirations. Each male analyst brings his own perceptions and misperceptions to the treatment, and, in the treatment of women, this includes different views of women as related to his own experience, conflicts, and fantasies. Views of women as goddess or witch, idealized or inferior, phallic or castrated, comforting or castrating, nurturant or depriving, creator or destroyer; as mother, wife, daughter, as coquette or competitor—all these images and attitudes may distort the analytic attitude toward the female patient. In many respects, the same possible sources of difficulty will be operative with a female analyst treating the female patient, and interesting comparisons might be made of countertransference constellations in opposite sex or same sex treatment situations.

Given the large areas of overlapping personality characteristics between the sexes and marked differences among individuals of the same or opposite sex, there are methodological and theoretical problems about assumptions or inferences concerning the influence of the sex of the analyst on the analytic process. The capacity for analytic neutrality and analytic work depends on the analysts' awareness and integration of their own bisexuality, resolution of the positive and negative oedipus complex, and their ability to use bisexuality for empathy (female or male) and comprehension of universal bisexual conflict in people. It does make a difference whether the therapist is afraid of a woman's seductiveness, jealousy, competitiveness, dependency, and the like. Although the actual gender of the analyst and patient are treatment variables, human bisexuality introduces the complexities of dispositions and identifications of both sexes in both analytic partners. Taking into account universal bisexuality, more gross sexual and aggressive aspects of the transference and countertransference are likely eventually to be recognized and understood by the analyst, again assuming expectable stability of an analytic identity and competence. What are more likely to go unnoticed are not stormy transference or gesticulating and vociferous countertransference caricatures of analytic tact, but far more subtle, disguised, and submerged treatment issues that may nevertheless be very important. Our awareness of these issues has been enlarged with refinements in the theory of technique, with newer psychoanalytic contributions to the understanding of transference-countertransference collusion.

Erotic transference was recognized early as a particular source of difficulty for both patient and analyst; patients have behaved seductively, with acting out of the transference or flight from the treatment, because of the fear of seduction. The analyst's fear of, or even positive response to, seduction has also been noted, and seductive analysts have joined with their patients in erotic enactments, so that affairs, especially between male analyst and female patient, have been known. (Father/daughter incest seems to be far more frequent than mother/son or daughter.) Fortunately, these actual affairs have been relatively infrequent, as has been the much more complicated postanalytic marriage between analyst and former patient. Homosexual conflicts are also important and may similarly determine the choice of therapist and particular transference-countertransference problems. These problems may be more intense in phases of the treatment of a woman by a woman, but the sex of the analyst does not determine the patient's psychopathology, nor is it likely to be decisive for the conflict solutions achieved in analytic work. We have no reliable studies or statistics in these areas. Analysts' reactions to the seductive patient, or for that matter, the patient's to the seductive analyst (of either sex) are as varied as the human personality and may even take the rather defensive form of anger or apathy. Negative transference may defend against positive transference, and the same is true of the interrelated countertransference.

Attitudes toward what constitutes normal feminine behavior have undergone major cultural change, partly because of psychoanalytic influence. Analysts should be aware of their own preferences and attitudes and must examine whether they might be imposing values on their patients. Does the analyst want, as is so often misconstrued by narcissistic manipulative patients, to recreate the patient in the analyst's own image? Does the analyst regard women as having weak and unreliable superego function, or as capable of autonomous superego regulation? How does the analyst react, not only to the flirtatious or militant female, but to the very passive, inhibited female? Is passivity, not to be confused with heterosexual receptiveness, regarded as normal? Is the analyst less likely to recognize and analyze inhibited assertion and masochistic compliance or submission in a woman? This may be a particular problem if there is silent and collusive agreement by both analyst and patient that any competition with a man is always a sign of unresolved penis envy and castrating attitudes. Masochistic and submissive tendencies should be viewed as problems to be resolved through analytic work rather than as specifically feminine attributes. Women may not become aware of the unconscious conflicts that are activated by combining marriage, career, and motherhood, if the analyst is insensitive to these issues. The patient has to be free to discover her own interests and goals, priorities and options.

There is no analytic basis for bias, stereotyping, idealization, or devaluation of either sex. Masculinity and femininity are complex psychological concepts, with biological and cultural determinants, lacking in precise definition. If the analyst is threatened by that patient's choice, when it is not congruent with the analyst's own values, this may reinforce the patient's own anxiety or guilt about her own goals and her conflicts with parental or traditional values. The analyst should be attuned to conflicts and contradictions in the patient's values, standards, and goals. Both analyst and patient may be unconsciously threatened by rapid cultural change, and then the analytic work itself may be considerably impoverished.

The choice of what is to be explored and what is not to be explored may become part of a transference-countertransference bind with a conspiracy of silence about areas that may be anxiety-laden for both patient and analyst (a potential problem in any analysis). The female patient should not be a carbon copy of her mother or an echo of her analyst; successful analysis should liberate the patient for mature autonomous psychological functioning, exercise of choice, and capacities for love, work, and play, which will also mean object love and empathy combined with healthy self-esteem and self-realization.

These problems of priorities and goals tend to reverberate throughout the life cycle. They have recently and frequently been seen in what has been called "the empty nest syndrome" and "reentry" or transition from being wife and mother for many years to a career choice and work outside the home. It must also be noted that the shift from the home to the work world marks a psychologically significant transition. This must take place without an established, culturally supported *rite de passage.* It may be a relatively minor psychological challenge or a major emotional crisis in the marriage or parent-child relationship. For many women it may be a radical departure from the model of their own mother and grandmother and a major change in life with new identifications. Not only are there shifts in object ties, self-representation, and support systems, but there are new demands, requirements for functioning in new modes and relationships and in new settings, for which very often the groundwork has not been established. The analyst's unconscious reactions, like the reactions of the husband or the mother and father, will influence the patient and her ability to deal with the anxiety and guilt that are inevitably engendered by the alteration of her role, relationships, and modes of adaptation. Nor does early career choice and early combining of career, marriage, and motherhood preclude conflict; conflicting and competing inner and outer demands must still be resolved, as must unconscious conflict. Crucial object choices and object relations, as well as many other psychological dimensions and conflicts, are also involved. Conflict does not end with choice, which may resolve certain issues but may also engender new conscious and unconscious conflicts.

Particular transference-countertransference problems may be intensified and may be less susceptible to analysis if changes in life situations of the patient activate dangers or disappointments connected with the therapist's own fantasy life and real experience. The female patient may get married or divorced, have a baby or an abortion. It may make a difference if the analyst is single, married, or divorced; a parent or childless; has a relatively fulfilled personal and professional life, or feels frustrated and deprived. These problems are not necessarily inevitable, and much depends on the capacity for insight, mastery, and sublimation of conflicts. The contributions of female analysts, including those who are childless, have been of particular benefit to child analysis. It is the unresolved conflicts and the inability to sublimate unfulfilled wishes that lead to the unresolved transference and countertransference. The female analyst with a profoundly unhappy marital experience may be excessively jealous of the patient who becomes the blossoming bride, and the feminine male may wish to be made over into the protected, dependent housewife because "she's got it made." The male envy of female functioning has been described in analytic literature on the couvade and the postpartum reactions of fatherhood as well as in numerous jokes concerning not simply the fear but also the pleasures of femininity.

Can the male analyst fully identify with the female's different biology and psychobiology? Can he identify not only with the female attitudes that are in so many ways similar to his own, but also with those that are quite different and those that are unique to the female biological role? It is true that the male will never experience female structure and biological function and will not know from direct personal experience what it is like to menstruate, to be pregnant, parturient, lactating, and breast feeding an infant who has been carried in one's own body. Similar comments may be made about the female not having direct personal experience of male structure and biological function. And neither sex has had the experience of the other in parental rearing and developing into a male or female, in his or her culture.

We are in the process of redefining the innate qualities, the so-called eternal feminine, and know much more today about the influence of social and moral codes, of various labeling and rearing practices, and the crucial importance of both constitutional influences, ego development, object relations, and enduring identifications on different dimensions of the female personality.[1] In this we must be aware of the pitfalls that Freud noted in attempting arbitrary definitions of the elusive, uncertain concepts of masculinity and femininity, and, again, the importance of bisexuality in development and disorder.

A variety of significant influences have affected personality as well as environmental change. The rise of modern medicine; the availability of safe contraception, delivery, or abortion; the expectation of having healthy children who will live to adult life—all these are factors that have greatly altered women's expectations and opportunities. Analysts must be able to be in touch with their own femininity to be able to empathize as far as possible with the female patient's biological and social experience, functions, and roles, and to point out to the patient her own defended, distorted, and inhibited functioning with all of its roots. The patient's problems may be anchored both in the formative experiences of the remote past of infancy and the immediate reality of her adult life.

This discussion of the analytic treatment of women may illuminate a very significant, yet conspicuously neglected area of transference-countertransference. The analyst, as transference object, represents the patient's parent, but the analyst also represents the patient's childrens' other parent. The analyst is surrogate spouse and parent; in the case of a mother, the analyst is consciously and unconsciously asked for help in parenting and child care. This is a complementary but far different dimension of transference than the analyst as sexual partner or fantasied biological father of the patient's children. All parent patients ask for help as parents and may consciously and unconsciously look toward the analyst as the ideal parent with expertise on parent-child relationships and child development. While working out their own conflicts and identifications with both their

[1]The menstrual cycle and rhythmicity may influence female personality function and fantasy with transference manifestations during analysis. Benedek and Rubenstein (1939) reported typical fantasies in pre- and postovulatory menstrual phases, though this has not been replicated in the contemporary analytic literature.

own parents and their own children, patients may also wish to have the analyst parent them and their children; the analyst becomes the incestuous spouse but also the idealized grandparent.

The fantasy of the analyst as coparent of the patient's children is of universal import. In transference, the female patient will often be identified with her own mother, with the male analyst as father. Of course, the analyst may also represent the oedipal (or preoedipal) mother, and the patient may be identified with her father at other times. The transference paradigm will appear in various derivatives and with different developmental phase organization and quality. This transference may be particularly intense or reality reinforced, for example, in the case of the mother as the primary caretaker, with the child as her prime concern, and in the case of the single parent, particularly the parent with a young child, without the support of an extended family. A divorced mother's own needs and the desire for coparenting, as well as hostility to the husband-father, are very significant issues relevant to her child's development. The motivation for treatment may have involved the reactions to loss of the spouse and the difficulty in establishing a new or mature marriage. The pressure for gratification of the patient's transference may be very great, and the analyst, in this context, has to be aware of the invitation to and evocation of countertransference response. The hidden erotic meanings of "the lady in distress" are paralleled by the parental demands and identifications of the mother in need of help and mother-child rescue fantasy. The parent-child transference repetition is often related to, but is to be differentiated from, the current real parent-child relationship, which has so many new elements. The compelling nature of the transference fantasy should not, of course, obscure the analytic understanding of the mother's strengths and difficulties in rearing her child and that particular child's influence on the mother in the unique reality of their family situation. This is also especially important with mothers of ill, disturbed, or very difficult children, disturbed or infantile mothers, or where mother and child are mismatched. However, all mothers are conflicted and, at times, distressed about motherhood and/or their children. These issues have often motivated women to seek analytic treatment. Problems in the parent-child relationship, and in parenting surface in the analysis of every mother (really of every parent). The patient identifies with her parents and with the superego of her parents, especially in regard to the selected attitudes and values of her mother in her relationship with her own child. Having children inevitably reawakens, in the mother, childhood conflicts which attain representation and are repeated in the transference. (This is true of fathers as well, and the mother-child relationship is influenced by the relationship of each to the father, but an extended discussion of fathering is outside the scope of this chapter.)

The mother in treatment will ask the analyst's advice and counsel concerning mothering; invite the analyst's parental guidance for her child as well as herself; entreat or manipulate the analyst's participation in child-rearing decisions; and demand exoneration, absolution, or punishment, for imagined or real inadequate or inappropriate motherhood. The mother may unconsciously want to have a child with the analyst (transference baby), have the analyst take over responsibility for the child, fear the analyst's judgment of her as a mother, and expect not only realistic but magical benefits for her child from her analysis. The patient may also identify with the parent and treat the analyst as her child, who may also represent her parent or sibling.

In child analysis, the mother of the child may overtly ask for advice. The child analyst may be expected to influence decisions concerning choice of school, handling of homework or television time, sibling fighting, masturbation, sex education, drug use and abuse, hospitalization, and so forth. The child analyst is a surrogate parent for the mother and her child, an idealized supporting or dangerously competing parent. The child analyst is also the grandparent, who mediates and supervises the parents' conflicting interaction with the child. These transference and reciprocal countertransference issues are well known in child analysis. The child analyst may have countertransference reactions to the child's parents and other significant objects in the child's life.

In situations where the mother's disturbance is severely pathogenic for her child's development, the analyst's countertransference analysis and neutrality may be subject to great strain. Torn between the analysis of the mother and the protection of the child through nonanalytic educational or psychotherapeutic intervention, the adult analyst may find it difficult to maintain an analytic attitude under the circumstances. For example, the analyst may be especially conflicted about the maltreatment of her child by an alcoholic mother or about a nurse who collaborates with her physician husband to perform procedures or give enemas and sedatives to their child, etc. The countertransference to the mother includes the indirect countertransference to the child, and often the spouse tends to draw the analyst into familial conflict. The demands of the mother seeking a surrogate mothering for her child are likely to be particularly difficult for the male analyst who is uncomfortable with maternal transference. The transference may be misunderstood as a father transference.

The mother's difficulty with her child may elicit countertransference reactions as well as realistic concerns for the child's development and welfare. This concern leads to technical problems which go far beyond countertransference. The mother with alcoholic tendencies may feel guilty not only because of her fantasies, but because of actual harm to her child. The analytic working through of the maternal conflicts may take many years. Meanwhile, the analyst may feel impelled to confront, clarify, interpret, and intervene in various ways. Child analysis or guidance may be recommended, and this may enhance or complicate the mother's analysis. The analyst may be too active or too passive, and countertransference as well as reality considerations have to be taken into account. There are sometimes inevitable conflicts between the best interest of the mother and of the child, and the analyst may find himself or herself in a quandary, without a fully acceptable analytic solution.

Consider the problem of a mother with daughters in their pre- and early teens, daughters with their own social and school problems. This mother, it develops in the analysis, has many transference, erotic-exhibitionistic conflicts, which are reactively defended against by excessive modesty, prudery, and inhibition of curiosity. Analytic clarification gradually uncovers a disguised, vicarious enactment of her forbidden fantasies through passive collusion with her husband and daughter. (One is reminded of the collusion of Dora's parents (Freud, 1905) in the seductive relationships with the Ks.) This mother was seemingly indifferent to her husband's nearly nude appearance before his daughters, his intrusion into his daughters' room when they were undressed, and her acquiescence to his requesting that their parental bedroom should always be left partially open, even during sexual relations. At the same time, her husband railed against the sexual abuse of patients by doctors and dentists, castigated his daughter for exposing herself to the winter cold without a coat, and worried about the exposure of children to pornography and vulgarity. His projection of blame for his own incestuous exhibitionism could be readily inferred.

What does the analyst do, if anything, other than analyze the unfolding clinical picture and the patient's living-out of her fantasies without accepting responsibility for feeling conscious guilt. The analysis of her own primal scene experience and childhood conflicts would take years, during which time she would have complicity and guilt in the familial incestuous behavior with her daughters. Would she not feel more hurtful, guilty, resentful, remorseful if her contribution to these problems went on unchecked and unchanged during years of treatment? Fortunately, in this case, her superficial behavior was rather rapidly modified long before there was inner conflict resolution and structural change. She recognized in the analyst's inquiry, albeit with denial and silent collusion, elucidation of the pattern, and linkage to the transference fantasies, an area of her own maternal conflict. She gradually saw the elements of familial perverse tendencies and the punitive provocations of unconscious guilt. It seems likely that she may have sensed in the analyst's silent disapproval both a countertransference departure from neutrality and a realistic concern for the patient's long-range analytic treatment and life goals. Here, what seemed ego syntonic pathological behavior gave way to clarification and to possibly suggestive containment as well as working through within the analytic process. All the technical problems of dealing with pathological acting-out may be pertinent here, and we want to stress the undesirable effects of coercive prohibition without empathy and understanding, and the undesirable effects of unanalyzed chronic countertransference as distinguished from transient countertransference reactions (which the analyst may use analytically for expanded insight).

Perhaps the adage, "When in doubt, analyze," should be invoked here, but the limitations of both adult and child analysis have to be recognized realistically. It should be noted that similar issues may arise in regard to disturbed fathers in analysis.

In summary, although in the analytic treatment of women specific transference-countertransference issues emerge, any competent analyst should be able to treat a patient of either sex. The sex of the therapist may influence the sequence in which transferences emerge and may be of greater significance in psychotherapy than in analysis, since ideally in the latter all transferences would be analyzed. The analyst's awareness of and integration of his/her own bisexuality, resolution of the positive and negative oedipus complex and empathy for and comprehension of universal bisexual conflicts are essential for analytic work. In addition, however, transference issues in regard to analytic teachings must be understood in order to evaluate theory, specifically aspects of older psychoanalytic theory regarding the development of women that may be obsolete in the light of newer knowledge.

In the treatment of women who are mothers, a specific transference fantasy generally emerges. In addition to the fantasy of analyst as parent, the analyst becomes in fantasy the patient's child's parent as well as the child, with both fantasied and real requests for guidance in parenting. Not identified elsewhere in the literature, these issues and their transference-countertransference ramifications were elaborated.

REFERENCES

Benedek, T. & Rubenstein, B. (1939). The correlations between ovarian activity and psychodynamic process. In: *Psychoanalytic Investigations,* ed. New York: Quadrangle.

Bibring, G. (1936). A contribution to the subject of transference resistance. *Internat. J. Psycho-Anal.* 17:2, 181–189.

Blum, H. (1971). On the conception and development of the transference neurosis. *J. Amer. Psychoanal. Assn.,* 19:41–53.

______. (1973). The concept of erotized transference. *J. Amer. Psychoanal. Assn.,* 21:61–76.

______. (1976). Masochism, the ego ideal, and the psychology of women. *J. Amer. Psychoanal. Assn.* (Suppl.), 24:157–192.

Bonaparte, M. (1953). *Female Sexuality.* New York: International Universities Press.

Deutsch, H. (1944, 1945). *The Psychology of Women.* Vols. I & II. New York: Grune & Stratton.

Freud, S. (1905). Fragments of an analysis of a case of hysteria. *Standard Edition* 7:1–122. London: Hogarth Press, 1953.

______. (1917). Introductory lectures on psychoanalysis. *Standard Edition* 15:1–463. London: Hogarth Press, 1963.

______. (1920). Beyond the Pleasure Principle. *Standard Edition,* 18:1–64. London, Hogarth Press, 1955.

______. (1931). Female sexuality. *Standard Edition,* 21: 221–243. London: Hogarth Press, 1961.

______. (1937). Analysis terminable and interminable. *Standard Edition,* 23:209–253. London: Hogarth Press, 1964.

Greenacre, P. (1959). Certain technical problems in the transference relationship. *J. Amer. Psychoanal. Assn.,* 7: 484–502.

Mogul, K. M. (1982). Overview: the sex of the therapist. *Amer. J. Psychiat.* 139:1–11.

Moore, B. (1976). Freud and female sexuality: A current view. *Internat. J. Psycho-Anal.,* 57:287–300.

Schafer, R. (1974). Problems in Freud's psychology of women. *J. Amer. Psychoanal. Assn.,* 22:459–485.

Tyson, P. (1980). The gender of the analyst: in relation to transference and countertransference manifestations in pre-latency children. *The Psychoanalytic Study of the Child,* 35:321–340. New Haven: Yale University Press.

CHAPTER FOURTEEN

Women in Therapy: Therapist Gender as a Variable*

Ethel Spector Person

Psychoanalysts favor the proposition that an analyst of either sex can treat a patient of either sex and that transference, by definition, bears little relation to the reality of therapist attributes. In direct contrast, many patients regard the sex of the therapist as the critical variable. In truth, we have no systematic evidence to support either belief or to suggest those instances in which gender may be paramount. Our suspicions, one way or the other, are largely anecdotal.[1]

Over the past ten years, the choice of therapist by gender has assumed a central role for women patients. Whereas at one time women sought male therapists as the embodiment of professional authority, today more women preferentially seek women therapists. Many insist on it. The vociferous preference for a woman is in marked contrast to patterns of referral ten and fifteen years ago. At that time, the referring physician sometimes reassured a women therapist that he had discussed her sex with the patient, and the patient didn't mind! Black therapists often suffered analogous discrimination.

This shift in preference is seen in New York City and in other urban centers, where the women's movement has had a significant impact, where women therapists are available, and where there is a high concentration of professional and professionally aspiring women. The shift in New York City has been reported by Symonds (1976) and Turkel (1976) and has been privately noted by virtually every woman therapist I know. I am talking about a shift, not about percentages. We don't yet know the numbers. Because most therapists are male and most patients female, more women are probably still in treatment with men. What is most indicative of the new female preference is the increasing difficulty finding a well-trained woman ther-

*This paper first appeared in *Internat. Rev. Psycho-Anal.,* 10:193–204. Reprinted by permission of the publisher.

[1]For an excellent review of the literature, see Mogul (1982).

apist with open therapy time. No comparable problem exists when placing a patient in therapy with a man.

This is not to say that women were never previously sought out. Greenacre, writing in 1959, addressed the implications of the sex of the analyst in a discussion about reality factors that might influence an analysis. She had noticed that over the preceding decade (the 1950s) her consultation patients asked more frequently whether the sex of the analyst was critical to the analysis. She didn't speculate as to the cause of that increasing preoccupation. It almost certainly related to the widespread clinical tradition, not dwelt upon or ever substantiated in the literature, that preoedipal problems were best dealt with by women, who were believed more intuitive and empathic.

In addition, therapist gender was considered an issue in failed cases. Reassignment of therapist was often made on the basis of gender. Both Bibring (1936) and Greenson (1967) reported that in a stalled analysis, or one in which a transference neurosis never occurred, or in one that was abruptly terminated by the patient, switching from a male to female analyst (or vice versa) might have a beneficial effect. Most often such transfers have been from male to female therapist. In some few, the initial reaction to a therapist (often mediated through gender) is so intensely negative as to preclude therapy and necessitate a new referral. But there is reason to doubt that gender is actually the controlling factor in the majority of failed cases. Sometimes transfer is rationalized as a recommendation about therapist gender, while in reality it is the therapist's face-saving way of avoiding responsibility for a failure, a way of avoiding acknowledgment of the extent of the patient's psychopathology or one way to effect transfer of someone perceived as a chronic patient. Consequently women are often referred difficult patients. As a by-product of this practice, a relatively large number of women have considerable experience with second analyses.

Initial recommendations for one sex over the other may derive from specific concerns of either referring therapist or patient. Greenacre noted that in patients with unrecognized latent homosexuality, with the propensity for homosexual panic, the sex of the analyst was a factor for concern. Certain men preferentially request women therapists, for example, some entrepreneurs too competitive to form an initial therapeutic alliance with another man.[2]

However, the current impetus to study therapist gender systematically as a variable grows out of the increasing self-referral of women to women.

---

[2]See also specific therapist gender issues discussed by Ottenheimer (1979) and Zetzel (1966).

Goz (1973) suggests that the underlying reason for selecting a female therapist is almost always the wish to rework the relationship with the mother. She argues that this wish is frequently disguised behind the socially sanctioned terms of women's liberation. Her observations undoubtedly obtain in a number of instances. But if we take Goz's statement at face value, we have no conceptual framework to answer the question of why women patients seek women therapists *now*. The mother problem has always existed. Even if we agreed that this problem was the singular motive in all such requests, we would still have to acknowledge that it appears to have become more urgent. We are forced to recognize that changes in values and perceptions dictate dramatically different adaptations, choices, and conflict resolutions.

The explanations that women give for their preference for a female therapist are various but fall largely under four headings; first, a fear that men will hold to sexist values; second, a belief that it is too easy and tempting to fool a male therapist and thereby avoid problem areas; third, the wish to avoid an erotic transference or countertransference; and fourth, the explicit desire to have a strong competent woman with whom to make a positive identification.

Obviously, this list is composed of the conscious reasons women give. Although surface phenomena have not always been of premium concern to analysts, it is a grave error to treat these arguments as irrelevant or superficial rationalizations. They are crucial to both practical and theoretical issues. From the practical side, we must decide whether such requests are in the best interests of the patient and if they should be honored. From the theoretical side, the requests themselves are revelatory of certain aspects of female psychology.

It is my purpose in this paper to examine the arguments raised by women in favor of female therapists, their validity, their relevance to understanding female psychology, and their relation to different transference and countertransference issues that emerge depending on therapist gender. To some extent, the opening phases of treatment may be eased in therapies of women by women; but there are characteristic transference-countertransference problems that arise later on. In general, the question of therapist gender is a special case of the effect of the real object on analytic process.

In what follows, I present observations based on my own practice, including analyses, dynamically oriented psychotherapies, and consultations. My observations on interactions between female patients and male therapists come from four sources; re-analyses of women formerly in treatment with men, supervision of male therapists, analyses of male therapists, and the literature. Because women I see in consultation and treatment are largely self-referred and tend to place a high priority on the sex of the therapist, I am presenting a necessarily skewed sample. There are women, probably fewer in number, who say to male therapists that they could never reveal themselves to another woman. The questions raised in this paper will be fully addressed only by pooling information from therapists of both sexes, from different geographical locations, dealing with a wide variety of socioeconomic backgrounds.

In choosing to deal with material from both psychodynamically oriented therapies and analyses, I am taking the position that analyses are not entirely gender blind as theory might have us believe. Psychotherapies rely more on transference cures and utilization of the real relationship and are less committed to full exploration of transference-countertransference issues. To this extent, they are more likely to show the greatest impact from all reality aspects about the therapist, including gender. In her thoughtful review, Mogul (1982) argues that

> It appears to follow that therapist sex matters least in traditional psychoanalysis with neurotic patients; however, this is not as true for face-to-face psychotherapies, which are less intensive, involve more partial transference reactions, and are more oriented to symptom alleviation, and for patients with developmental defects involving impaired ego functions or object relations [p.5].

I would argue, instead, that the effects are more subtle in analyses than in other psychotherapies, but may well be just as pervasive. I will present some clinical evidence that supports this later proposition. To the degree that any therapy can be gender blind, one might examine the biologic therapies in which the active ingredient is predominantly a drug or electro-shock, not the relationship.

A FEAR OF SEXISM

There is evidence that therapies of women, whatever the sex of the therapist, have suffered contamination by pervasive cultural and intellectual biases about female psychology and nature. I need cite only a few instances: the frequent misinterpretation of professional aspirations as either derivative from penis envy or as a flight from femininity (Person, 1982) or the assertion, in the older literature, that true femininity depends on the achievement of vaginal orgasms. Such errors are easiest to demonstrate in psychotherapies, in which the therapist often takes an active and vocal stance, though they occur in analyses as well.

Clinical Vignette

> Mrs. B, a 30-year-old mother of two, had reached an impasse four years into psychotherapy. She was withdrawn, felt isolated, and was unable to form intimate ties with her children despite loving feelings and ability to provide good physical care. Her marriage was deteriorating. She decided to return to work, at which she had been successful, in the hope of restoring self-esteem that would allow her to be more functional at home.
>
> She had previously had good rapport with her therapist, but fell into a silent rage when he interpreted her intent to return to work as acting out, as a defense against closeness with her children, and as the wish to abandon them.
>
> I was asked by the therapist to consult with the patient and evaluate the possibility of breaking through the therapeutic impasse of several months' duration. The patient appeared to be in the throes of a negative identification with her own mother, precipitated by staying at home, like her mother. The decision to return to work was a symbolic attempt to break that identification. The therapist's incorrect (or inexact) interpretation and interdiction derailed attention from the actual conflict. It confirmed the patient's conviction that she was no good and unable to give, just as her mother had been, and led to more depression, guilt, and withdrawal. It intensified her masochistic stance, itself a defensive posture. She was unable to express her rage and was obsessed about whether the therapist was correct; but she withdrew from the therapy. The therapist began to perceive the patient as schizoid.
>
> Surprisingly, this treatment was salvaged, largely because the therapist was able to see that he had made a serious countertransference mistake stemming from his own values. The treatment was also salvageable because so much good collaborative therapy had preceded his judgmental interpretation and the therapeutic impasse.

This vignette illustrates a common form that value biases, sexism included, take. Both the therapist and I saw Mrs. B's problem in virtually the same way. By virtue of her own childhood experiences, motherhood and the care of small children threatened Mrs. B with a loss of autonomy and symbiotic regression viewed as threatening to her integrity, her children's, or both.[3] Our difference was in the way we perceived the decision to return to work: Mrs. B's therapist viewed it as symptomatic and I viewed it as an adaptive maneuver.

---

[3]Fear of loss of autonomy is a very common problem among women with infants. As it turns out, mothers who do best with infants may have a more difficult time with older children and vice versa, because different skills and personality attributes are required. Baby nurses have different personalities from governesses.

This vignette reveals how systematic cultural biases can hold sway for so long. Analysts and therapists of different persuasions encounter the same underlying data: symbols, dream content, fantasies, and so forth. When a bias occurs, it does not usually or necessarily take the form of a misperception of the symbols or conflicts; it is not based on thin air. Most commonly, the bias is reflected in the misinterpretation of the data in one of two ways. First, as in the vignette just cited, the therapist views attempted conflict resolution as symptomatic rather than adaptive. Second, and perhaps more common, certain symbols are interpreted as causal, irradicable, or intrinsic rather than as secondary mental products, themselves maladaptive attempts at conflict resolution.

Grossman and Stewart (1976) illustrate the second point in "Penis envy: From childhood wish to developmental metaphor." They present two clinical examples of analyses in which the interpretation of penis envy, apparently grounded in clinical data, "*had an organizing effect, but not a therapeutic one*" (their italics). In both cases the interpretation of penis envy was close enough to the data of the analyses for the women accept the interpretation and use it to rationalize and consolidate their real pathological constellations.

Sexist interpretations are just one subclass of value biases that inform therapies, including analyses, as the paper under discussion reveals. Grossman and Stewart, discussing Mrs. A, report a sexist and class bias on the part of her first analyst though they don't label it as such. Mrs. A's first analysis had been terminated at a time she was presumably improving, the improvement gauged by her ability to date a man her parents found acceptable. According to the authors, "the analyst later mentioned to one of us that he felt pleased that the analysis had led the patient to give up her Bohemian ways and to marry a respectable man of her own class" (p. 195–196). Despite the apparent relief both the patient's parents and the analyst felt, the marriage itself proved empty and she became depressed. Mrs. A sought treatment with her original analyst and was referred to a new analyst only because the original one had no time. I make the last point to underscore the fact that the patient herself did not realize the shortcomings of her original treatment. In her subsequent analysis, she discovered that "in her mind the marriage was meant to make her more acceptable to the analyst; that he would continue to see her, protect her, and recognize her true but hidden values" (p. 196).

Cultural biases are easiest to observe at times of cultural change; they fall under the rubric of countertransference only in its broadest definition. They are hard to eliminate. It is useful to acknowledge the goal of value-free therapy as an ideal, rather than a reality, and to maintain vigilance about possible value contaminants. Sexist biases have been widely examined in the feminist and psychoanalytic literature, rightly so and with discernible results. Sexist interpretations and values are not restricted to male therapists. Some of the most reactionary theories about female psychology were written by women.

Viederman (1976) has suggested, "the psychoanalytic encounter can only occur if discrepancies between analyst and analysand are not too great in the area of values." (p. 233) Consequently the concerns of women patients about the biases and values of a prospective therapist can be realistically based even when they patently mask other conerns.

'FAKING IT'

Women frequently fear they will be able to delude a male therapist. Either they will beguile him with feminine wiles and thus avoid root problems or they will be too ashamed to reveal themselves and will keep secrets. Consequently, they request a female therapist.

The tendency toward deception is potentially present in both sexes, implicit in early object relations, particularly in the child's perception or fantasy that he or she has to be mother's all gratifying narcissistic perfect object to be lovable. However, this tendency is reinforced in women by their cultural experience.

Ingratiation

The fear of hiding behind a façade of femininity can be understood only in the context of the culturally sanctioned, or prescribed, relationship of woman to man. It is widely acknowledged that the 'feminine' woman should please and placate man. She is charming, engaging, compliant, ingratiating, admiring, nonaggressive, nonassertive. This mode of behavior is so well rewarded in the social world, so often adaptive, that it is hard to abandon at will. Women fear they will be tempted to revert to such a façade of stereotypic femininity if confronted with difficult material, unpleasant truths, and so forth. Many do not believe that any male, even a well-trained therapist, will be able to tolerate anger, confrontation, or equality.

Until recently, the ideology (or cult) of femininity just described was widely culturally disseminated. It found expression and was in fact prescribed in the scientific and psychoanalytic literature. A now famous quote from Helene Deutsch describing "the ideal-life-companion," is widely cited in the literature as an example of the psychoanalytic confusion between nature and culture (see Symonds, 1976; Dowling, 1981):

> they are ideal collaborators who often inspire their men, and are themselves happiest in this role. They seem to be easily influenceable and adapt themselves to their companions and understand them. They are the loveliest and most unaggressive of helpmates and they want to remain in that role; they do not insist on their own rights—quite the contrary. They are easy to handle in every way—if one only loves them.
>
> If gifted in any direction they preserve the capacity for being original and productive, but without entering into competitive struggles. They are always willing to renounce their own achievements without feeling that they are sacrificing anything, and they rejoice in the achievements of their companions, which they often inspired. They have an extra-ordinary need of support when engaged in any *activity directed outward* . . . [Deutsch, 1944, p. 192].

Reformulations of female psychology reveal that an ingratiating stance is not intrinsic to female development, but rather that ingratiation is one of the distinguishing features in the attitude of any powerless group vis-à-vis the dominant one. The dialectic of femininity and masculinity is not so much a dialectic of sex as it is one of power.

Yet cultural ideals change slowly, as do actual power relations. The old posture of defenselessness remains prominent among women; in it, the power of the weak emerges as the ability to manipulate the strong. This secret strength of women is not unknown to those who wield it. Take, for example, the stock literary type: the deliberately manipulative Southern woman encased in femininity, the iron hand in the velvet glove. It is a reversion to this well-honed and 'successful' position that many women fear. They trust other women to know about female 'deviousness' and to challenge them when they use the mask of femininity as an avoidance and defense.

Another Form of Dissembling: Secrets and Disguises

Certain bits of behavior are not consciously witheld but habitually 'overlooked.' They are 'overlooked' in therapy, as in life, largely out of shame. The girl who hid her blood-stained panties at menarche does not discuss menstruation in therapy; it seems irrelevant. Menstruation is widely regarded as a 'curse,' not openly discussed, out of shame. It is treasured only when one fears its untimely disappearance, for example when a delay suggests an unwanted pregnancy or is the harbinger of the dreaded menopause. One menopausal woman, fearing the effect of her aging on her husband, stained the bed with blood from an accidental cut, to suggest she was still in the prime of life. In general, women have been less open about physicality than men have been. It is more often the woman who lights a match after her bowel movement to counteract any lingering smell.

Women are also habitually and culturally silent about behaviors and practices enacted to further self-beautification and decoration, Hair-dye, make-up, facial surgery, shaving and tweezing, the artifice of dress are all second nature to women, but not nature. Again, this material is not withheld; it tends not to come up in therapy. Its centrality to fantasy preoccupations and life goals goes unremarked.

The important issue is not the concerte bit of behavior; it is the trend toward unconsciously dissembling and pleasing men. Simone de Beauvoir (1953) summarizes both aspects of women just described:

> Confronting man, woman is always playacting; she lies when she makes believe that she accepts her status as the inessential other, she lies when she presents to him an imaginary personage through mimicry, costumeing, studied phrases. These histrionics require a constant tension; when with her husband, or with her lover, every woman is more or less conscious of the thought: 'I am not being myself,' the male world is harsh, sharp-edged, its voices are too resounding, the lights too crude, the contacts rough. With other women, a woman is behind the scenes: she is polishing her equipment, but not in battle; she is getting her costume together, preparing her make-up, laying out her tactics; she is lingering in dressing-gown and slippers in the wings before making her entrance on the stage: she likes this warm, easy, relaxed atmosphere . . . [p. 605].

Faking It: A Paradigm for a Transference Dilemma

The tendencies toward ingratiation and dissembling, wearing disguises and keeping secrets, come together in the widespread practice of faking orgasm.

It is important to many women to appear adequately sexual to men, in male terms. Faking is based on deference to the male, need for his approval, and shame at presumed sexual inadequacy. Sometimes it is motivated by fear of loss of the male sexual partner. Despite the contemporary enlightenment about female sexuality, many sophisticated women continue to fake. Brunswick (1943) was one of the few analysts to address this practice. She observed that women did not question the legitimacy of the 'accepted lie' regarding orgasmic gratification. She attributed the practice to the woman's intuitive sense that it reassured men (and women) that women possessed the same kind of phallic sexuality as men. In other words, it served to reassure men that women were not "castrated," a fear left over from their early boyhood. Thus, faking denies the sexual difference.

Some women systematically distort or disguise their sexual behavior to male therapists, sometimes to females, but to a lesser degree. Once a patient tells her analyst that she has vaginal orgasms, as well she might in an initial interview, she will have difficulty changing the story. Distortion in the therapy situation is equivalent to faking orgasms in sexual life. Such a deception or avoidance, conscious or unconscious, is paralleled by other transferential behavior.

> *Clinical vignette:* Mrs. C is a 32-year-old married housewife who reentered treatment after an unsuccessful analysis with a man. She had avoided discussing her sexual life in her previous analysis out of shame that she was unable to achieve orgasm in any way whatsoever. She learned to achieve orgasm through self-stimulation, but she didn't modify her sexual behavior in the interpersonal situation and continued to fake. Gradually she began to complain that treatment was empty despite her seeming ability to make associations, utilize interpretation, and so forth. The transferential attitude was ultimately related to her need to appear to be a good patient and perform according to the therapist's expectations. This was analogous to her continuing pretenses in the sexual situation ("faking orgasms") and her generalized belief that she must comply in order to achieve acceptance. Her complaint about treatment paralleled her sense that sex was empty for her; she did treatment for her therapist, sex for her husband.

Faking orgasm has received little attention in the psychoanalytic literature aside from the paper by Brunswick (1943). Yet is is a paradigmatic behavior for many women. It is emblematic of the general urge to dissemble to gain approval and is thus related to the overriding need for love. But the constant pressure toward ingratiation leads to a subjective sense of inauthenticity, lack of autonomy, denial of the inner self. This subjective sense emerges in very different areas, for example, in the fears of successful women that they are fraudulent, about to be found out and exposed. I am not suggesting that faking orgasm is the source of these other fears and behavior; I am suggesting they are symbolically linked.

Clinical vignette: Mrs. D, 45 years old, an extremely successful executive, is dreading the imminent retirement of her immediate superior. While she has opportunity to move laterally in her corporation, neither of two possible openings suits her particular talents or long-term interests. Yet she is panic stricken at the thought of making inquiries in other companies. Thus far, her success has been predicated on performing brilliantly within the framework defined by her mentor. Despite her autonomous accomplishments, she is frozen with terror and perceives herself as passive, a designation her mentor, associates, husband, and children would find ludicrous. She ultimately believes she has no special talents, is fraudulent and fears exposure. Unconsciously she believes femininity is incompatible with professional mastery. She protects her "femininity" by denying the authenticity of her success. She hides the extent of her ambition behind an ingratiating mask. The sense of fraudulence is displaced from her imposture about her intent to a subjective sense of inadequacy, and she constantly refers to 'faking it,' particularly when she has to make a presentation, or write a report. In fact, she is scrupulously honest. As regards her sexual life, she is orgasmic and never fakes orgasm, but 'faking it' retains its symbolic significance and imaginative centrality.

In therapy, as in life, once a woman has committed herself to faking, she has difficulty owning up to the deception. This, too, leads to a subjective sense of inauthenticity. Furthermore, dissembling and ingratiation in the transference engenders unconscious rage, which can express itself as contempt for the therapist whom the patient has successfully deceived.

Men, too, and not just women may rely on dissembling and ingratiating as deceptive manuevers. In both sexes, when these maneuvers are predominant, personality is akin to what Winnicott (1965) has described as the "false self." These particular personality trends are more widespread among women but not restricted to them. Men, too, may feel they are "faking it," but the symbolic elaborations are different in the two sexes. "Faking it" in men may reflect more serious consequences in terms of ego integration, precisely because it is not so pervasively sanctioned by the culture. The sexual paradigm that has cultural relevance for men is not "faking" but "cheating." While "cheating" may be accompanied by guilt, it is also intimately related to pride.

This tendency toward "faking" should not be understood to confirm Freud's assessment that women have defective superegos relative to men (Freud, 1924, 1925, 1933). On the contrary, the trend toward withholding dissembling and ingratiation, originating in childhood fantasies (in both sexes) is reinforced in women by cultural institutions. The trend is implicit in gendered power relations, not just individual development. Furthermore, it is erroneous to infer that dissembling in women is derived primarily from shame, itself generated from penis envy or a sense of organ inferiority. Dissembling is reinforced by a social tradition in which woman is the "other," whose worth is validated by her status as an erotic object and who must consequently please man in order to chosen.

EROTIC TRANSFERENCE AND COUNTERTRANSFERENCE

Some women fear not just their ability to fool male therapists through ingratiation and submissiveness, but also through their power to draw them seductively into an erotically tinged relationship. Others feel they are themselves too prone to "crushes" or erotic fantasies to enter treatment with a man, fearing they will be sidetracked, wasting too much time on romantic fantasies. Both groups hope to get to their basic problem, frequently conceptualized as an unresolved conflict with their mothers or a flawed feminine identification, by entering treatment with a woman. Thus, it is suggested by these prospective patients that erotic transference and countertransference evoked in treatment with a male is, at best, a waste of time and, at worst, an insuperable impediment to therapy. Moreover, they continue, the most workable transference is facilitated by a "maternal" or female therapist.

These propositions find an able and most eloquent proponent in Sigmund Freud. In his paper "Female sexuality" (1931), discussing the preoedipal phase in girls, he suggests it "comes to us as a surprise, like the discovery, in another field, of the Minoan-Mycenean civilization behind the civilization of Greece." Freud believed that stage almost impossible to revivify, at least in analysis with him, because the patient clung to the "very attachment to the father in which they had taken refuge from the early phase that was in question. It does appear that women analysts—as, for instance, Jeanne Lampl-de Groot and Helene Deutsch—have been able to perceive these facts more clearly because they were helped in dealing with those under their treatment by the transference to a suitable mother-substitute" (pp. 226–7).

Many women have had successful treatments with male therapists, yet some therapies have floundered around erotic transference or countertransference. This ought not to surprise us if we recall that the very paradigm for transference was the female patient falling in love with her male therapist (Freud, 1914). The talking cure itself was developed in the course of Breuer's therapy with Anna O, a therapy finally disrupted by eroticism. Breuer, preoccupied with Anna O's treatment, evoked his wife's jealousy. Belatedly recognizing her jealousy, he terminated Anna O's treatment. He was called back to find his patient in the throes of an hysterical childbirth. He calmed her down and the next day took his wife on a second honeymoon. Freud recounted the story in a letter to Martha. According to Jones (1953), Martha "identified herself with Breuer's wife, and hoped the same thing would not ever happen to her, whereupon Freud reproved her vanity in supposing that other women would fall in love with *her* husband: 'for that to happen one has to be a Breuer' " (p. 225). Freud, then, denied even the possibility that such an event might happen to him, while Martha seemed intuitively to understand the universality of the problem. Only later was Freud able to perceive Anna O's reaction as the rule rather than the exception. Szasz (1963) believes Freud first understood transference in the context of Breuer's experience and that by its nature it was perhaps necessary that the theoretical observations of transference were made by someone other than the therapist involved first hand in the experience. In other words, the transference and countertransference experienced belonged to Anna O and Breuer, the theoretical explanations to Freud. As Szasz put it, "because Anna O was not Freud's patient it was easier for him to assume an observing role toward her sexual communication than if they had been directed towards himself" (p. 441). Here Szasz raises a critical question as to the inherent difficulty for a male therapist in recognizing an erotic transference directed at himself.

While Freud suggested the stickiness of the father transference as the potential limitation in therapies of women conducted by men, the major limitation is better described as ongoing, sexually toned transference-countertransference interaction, not usually acted upon but not fully analysed, in which the patient maintains a sexualized overidealization of the therapist, reciprocated in some way by the therapist.

The erotic transference expresses many different motivations integrated at different levels. It may simply reflect oedipal dynamics and libidinal strivings. As suggested by Freud, the erotic transference may reveal a father transference as a screen for the preoedipal attachment to mother. The stickier the erotic transference the more it is powered by other than simple oedipal dynamics. Most often eroticism then masks dependency needs. However, eroticism may be used manipulatively in the same way as ingratiation. It is frequently distorted by aggression, by the need to discredit and trivialize the therapy, and as the vehicle to control the male (therapist).

The acted-out erotic transference-countertransference demonstrates in bold relief some of the dynamics more subtly expressed in a great number of therapy dyads. I have seen nine such women, either in treatment or consultation. Prognosis was positively correlated with how much responsibility the women took. Insofar as a woman saw herself only as passive and victimized she tended to do less well in subsequent therapy.[4] This observation is not meant to condone the male therapist's behavior, but to stress female motive and complicity. Seductive intent on the part of the patient was invariably intermixed with the need for control and hostility. Sexuality was used as an equalizer, a resistance, and a hostile maneuver to discredit the male therapist. Voth (1972) makes a similar point. Reanalysing a woman who had a love affair with her previous therapist, he reports on the meanings that emerged in treatment. Originally skeptical about her own participation, she came to see "No man ever seduced me, I seduced them." Voth comments that she recognized "she resented being helped, equating, as it were, cure with submission and seduction" (p. 396). In the therapy situation, as in life, not all sexuality is purely erotic. What initially appears as a masochistic stance is a sadomasochistic one. The sadism, aggression, and negativity, joined to eroticism, are often embedded in an intense preoedipal maternal transference played out with a series of males, including the male therapist.

The limitation to the analysis of an erotic transference does not usually reside in the patient, but, too often, in the susceptible therapist. Tower (1956) points out, "Virtually every writer on the subject of countertransference, for example, states unequivocally that no form of erotic reaction to a patient is to be tolerated. This would indicate that temptations in this area are great, and perhaps 'ubiquitous'" (p. 230). It is sometimes a puzzle that the therapist has trouble recognizing and responding appropriately to the patient's erotic transference. The multiple meanings of the erotic transference, like the meanings of dissembling and ingratiation, are easy to miss because the transference is blurred by socially conditioned expectations about male–female interactions. Individual meaning is buried in stereotypic expectations of gender relations, the typical

---

[4]I am not speaking of those situations in which a therapist is moved to sleep with his female patients. In those cases, a woman may submit out of intimidation or passivity without the more complex motivations I am describing.

responses older men (therapists) expect from younger women (patients). When the therapist's vision is clouded not just by cultural stereotypes of appropriate behavior but also by personal need, the outcome is dismal.

To some degree, stereotyping is corrected by experience. The first-year male resident seldom sees serious pathology in pretty, hysterical women and, given a choice, picks such women for long-term supervised therapy, oblivious to levels of ego integration. The more experienced male therapist can distinguish hysteroid from hysteric, irrespective of manner, charm, and beauty. Yet some degree of stereotyping remains, even among experienced therapists of both sexes.

I have seen in treatment male therapists intensely erotically tempted by female patients, including two who succumbed to that temptation and who entered treatment for that reason. Two important factors emerged in their propensity to act out. First, an impulse toward self-destruction was part of the motivation. Experienced therapists know that a woman patient, whether regarded as seducer or seduced, will ultimately seek help elsewhere and thereby 'betray' their secret. In other words, they know their behavior will be revealed, even though such revelations made on the couch will not probably become public information. Second, both male therapists had formerly been in treatment with analysts who had 'betrayed' them in a very specific way. Each had discovered himself described in a paper published by his former analyst, although in a disguised way, without permission ever having been asked or granted. Although neither had reacted negatively at the time of the discovery, in re-analysis each expressed the feeling that he had been "raped." Therapists who act out with patients are often reenacting problems in their own analyses, much as the parents who abuse their children were themselves abused as children. This observation is made with the express consent of the individuals involved.

The extent of the contamination of therapies by unanalysed erotic transference and countertransference reactions is suggested by actual affairs between female patients and male therapists, more frequent than one imagines. Surveying 460 physicians, Kardener, Fuller, and Mensh (1973) found that between five and thirteen percent had engaged in erotic behavior with patients, although the psychiatrist was the least likely to do so. Speaking of such relationships between women and their analysts, Greenacre (1954) remarks, "That this is not so infrequent as one would wish to think becomes apparent to anyone who does many re-analyses. That its occurrence is often denied and the situation rather quickly explained by involved analysts as due to a hysterical fantasy on the part of the patient . . . is an indication of how great is the temptation" (p. 683). It may be that more women analysts see women who have had sexual relations with their previous therapists, and for a particular reason. Women who have had affairs with their therapists are subsequently sent to women as a reassurance to the patient that the event will not be repeated.

However, women analysts should not be misled into the false idea, suggested by some patients, that problematic erotic transference can be avoided. To the extent that sexuality would be problematic in treatment with a man, that is the precise extent to which it is a crucial issue. Sexuality as a significant issue in its own right or used defensively and hostilely is not invented in therapy, only reenacted there. In treatment with the (female) therapist, it cannot be avoided; it must be analyzed vis à vis extratherapeutic experiences, if not directly experienced. Most frequently it emerges in terms of sexual competitive themes in the analyses of women working with women analysts, both in transference and countertransference reactions. I know of two instances in which women therapists acted out erotic competition with female patients by becoming erotically involved with the patient's male relatives. There is a special case in which erotic transference is unusually intense: the analyses of homosexual women by women. This is a difficult transference to interpret or manage and it often leads to the disruption of treatment.

Sexual acting out has not been reported in the therapies of men by women. This is not because of any special virtue on the part of women analysts. The relative subordination of the patient and authority of the analyst is not congruent with the most predominant type of female sexual fantasies. Yet women do have sexual fantasies about male patients. Because of cultural prohibitions, women therapists are less likely to dwell upon or openly acknowledge such fantasies.

THE WISH FOR A ROLE MODEL

The three reasons just discussed that lead women to request a female therapist have one theme in common. They express the wish to avoid a therapeutic contact with a male, either because he is viewed as biased or because of fear that the relationship is intrinsically subject to distortion. The minor theme in these requests is the belief that a woman will cut through distortions and habitual, culturally sanctioned defenses. The fourth reason given for the preference is substantively different.

This wish for a role model, the explicit desire to have a strong, competent woman with whom to make a positive identification, addresses directly the issue of female-female relations. The presumed beneficial results of therapy with an appropriate same sex role model seem to be borne out in certain short-term therapies. In these, the patient develops a positive transference, seems to form a positive identification, performs better, and achieves greater self-esteem (Zetzel, 1966). Zetzel regards such changes as transference cures and therefore as valid psychotherapeutic, not psychoanalytic, goals.

While the reasons behind a wish for a role model seem at first glance to be intuitively obvious, further examination suggests the motives may be more complex. We know that changes in female identification can take place in the context of treatment with a male. Viederman (1976) reports a case "in which the patient presented herself with a markedly defective feminine self concept or self-representative." She showed great improvement, because in part, "a structural modification and revision of this self-concept occurred on the basis of the development of a transference fantasy of my wife with which she, the patient, identified and made part of her ideal self and self-concept, at first in an effort to win my love" (p. 233–234). The question arises why the role model has to be the patient's therapist. Even if a female role model is required, why can't it be some admired woman known to the patient either professionally or personally?

Closer scrutiny of female-female therapy dyads reveals that the active ingredient in improvement is not just identification, but the permission the patient gets from the therapist to compete, succeed, enjoy. Such permission may be explicit or implicit. One does not necessarily need to know one's role model, but an impersonal role model cannot grant permission to achieve and 'promise' not to exact retribution.

This contention, that women benefit by *permission* in short-term therapies, not by identification alone, is borne out by evidence from psychoanalytic therapies. In analyses, we see the complexities that lie behind the apparently simple wish for a role model. A woman's wish for a role model may be a component of an idealizing transference which, in part, defends against competition and homosexual themes. These are not usually analyzed effectively until late in the analytic process. Late in the analysis, one may elicit maternal and self depreciation, irrespective of political ideology (Kernberg, 1975). In the later stages of female-female psychoanalysis, one sees the emergence of rivalrous oedipal material; envy, rivalry, and fear are intensely expressed. Fears are often cast in oral, sometimes cannibalistic terms. The woman fears loss of love, starvation, and annihilation. Competitive fears take these forms because the object of competition is also the source of nurturant and dependent gratification.

This is not to argue that women alone are subject to the fears just enumerated. Many men, particularly those with narcissistic personality disorders, also fear loss of love, starvation and annihilation. But, for most men, the equivalent fear is that of castration. These gender differences in fearful unconscious fantasy are related to discrepant object relations in childhood; the feared consequences of female-female competition are different from those of male-male competition.

In sum, then, the female therapist is sought not just as a role model. More important, she is sought as a stand-in for the mother. In this role, it is her permission to compete and to achieve that is required. In short-term therapies, such permission may lead to a transference "cure." In long-term therapy, an intense rejecting mother transference is frequent. Current cultural attitudes may sometimes engender countertransference attitudes in female analysts that encourage idealizing transference and derivative defensive identifications and thereby short-circuit the working through of underlying conflicts.

CONCLUSION

It is impossible at this time to judge the impact of therapist gender on therapy outcome. Yet preliminary reports suggest that therapist gender facilitates or hinders in special circumstances (Zetzel, 1966; Goz, 1973). Because initial resistance can thwart effective therapy, I generally honor the patient's request if a well-trained analyst is available. This is the policy advocated by Greenacre (1959) "if a little discussion indicates that this is a definitely established attitude of the patient's, I myself always treat it with the utmost respect and compliance, since I recognize that such a patient really *would* find it difficult, if not impossible, to work with an analyst of the undesired sex" (p. 494).

This is a time of social change. Women's liberation, itself a product of that change, has focused our attention on cultural value biases and on some institutionalized interactions between women and men. Recognizing sexist values and their own proclivities to stereotypic defenses, women have sought to circumvent these problems by seeking women therapists. While therapist requests based on gender are not predictive of outcome, they underscore certain aspects of female psychology. I have discussed the defensive and manipulative functions of ingratiation, dissembling, and eroticism, those attitudes women fear will contaminate therapy with a male. I have suggested a further motive in the request for a female therapist, the wish for a maternal blessing for permission to compete and achieve in order to avoid unconscious conflicts centring around mother-daughter competition.

REFERENCES

Beauvoir, S. De (1953). *The Second Sex.* New York: Knopf.

Bibring, R. M. (1936). A contribution to the subject of transference-resistance. *Internat. J. Psycho-Anal.,* 17:181–189.

Brunswick, R. M. (1943). The accepted lie. *Psychoanal. Quart.* 12:458–464.

______ (1948). A supplement to Freud's "History of an infantile neurosis." In: *The Psychoanalytic Reader,* R. Fliess, ed. New York: International Universities Press, 1972, pp. 65–103.

Deutsch, H. (1944). *The Psychology of Women, Volume I.* New York: Grune & Stratton.

Dowling, S. (1981). *The Cinderella Complex: Women's Hidden Fear of Independence.* New York: Summit Books.

Freud, S. (1914). Observations on transference love (further recommendations on the technique of psycho-analysis). *Standard Edition,* 12:157–168. London: Hogarth Press, 1958.

______ (1924). The dissolution of the Oedipus complex. *Standard Edition,* 19:171–179. London: Hogarth Press, 1961.

______ (1925). Some psychical consequences of the anatomical distinction between the sexes. *Standard Edition,* 19:248–258. London: Hogarth Press, 1961.

______ (1931). Female sexuality. *Standard Edition,* 21:225–243. London: Hogarth Press, 1961.

______ (1933). Femininity. *Standard Edition,* 22:112–133. London: Hogarth Press, 1964.

Goz, R. (1973). Women patients and women therapists: Some issues that come up in psychotherapy. *Internat. J. Psychoanal. Psychother.,* 2:298–319.

Greenacre, P. (1954). The role of transference: Practical considerations in relation to psychoanalytic therapy. *J. Amer. Psychoanal. Assn.,* 2:671–684.

______ (1959). Certain technical problems in the transference relationship. *J. Amer. Psychoanal. Assn.,* 7:484–502.

Greenson, R. R. (1967). *The Technique and Practice of Psychoanalysis.* New York: International Universities Press.

Grossman, W. I., & Stewart, W. A. (1976). "Penis envy" from childhood

wish to developmental metaphor. *J. Amer. Psychoanal. Assn.*, 24 (Supplement): 193–212.
Jones, E. (1953). *The Life and Work of Sigmund Freud, Vol. I.* London: Hogarth Press.
Kardener, S. R., Fuller, M., & Mensh, I. N. (1973). A survey of physician's attitudes and practices regarding erotic and nonerotic contact with patients. *Amer. J. Psychiat.*, 130:1077–1081.
Kernberg, O. (1975). Cultural impact and intrapsychic change. In: *Adolescent Psychiatry, Vol. 4,* S. C. Feinstein & P. L. Giovacchini, ed. New York: Aronson, pp. 37–45.
Mogul, K. M. (1982). Overview: The sex of the therapist. *Amer. J. Psychiat.*, 139:1–11.
Ottenheimer, L. (1979). Some psychodynamics in the choice of an analyst. *J. Amer. Acad. Psychoanal.*, 7:339–345.
Person, E. S. (1982). Women working: Fears of failure, deviance and success. *J. Amer. Acad. Psychoanal.*, 10:67–84.
Symonds, A. (1976). Neurotic dependency in successful women. *J. Amer. Acad. Psychoanal.*, 4:95–103.
Szasz, T. (1963). The concept of transference. *Internat. J. Psycho-Anal.*, 44:432–443.
Tower, L. (1956). Countertransference. *J. Amer. Psychoanal. Assn.*, 4:224–255.
Turkel, A. R. (1976). The impact of feminism on the practice of a woman analyst. *Amer. J. Psychoanal.*, 36:119–126.
Viederman, M. (1976). The influence of the person of the analyst on structural change: a case report. *Psychoanal. Quart.*, 45:231–249.
Voth, H. M. (1972). Love affair between doctor and patient. *Amer. J. Psychother.*, 26:394–400.
Winnicott, D. W. (1965). *The Maturational Processes and the Facilitating Environment.* New York: International Universities Press.
Zetzel, E. R. (1966). The doctor-patient relationship in psychiatry. In: *The Capacity for Emotional Growth.* New York: International Universities Press, pp. 139–155, 1970.

CHAPTER FIFTEEN

Eve's Reflection: On the Homosexual Components of Female Sexuality

Joyce McDougall

INTRODUCTION: FREUD'S CONCEPTS

Freud's revolutionary discoveries concerning the psychology and the dynamic importance of human sexuality in child and adult life are now almost a century old. They are so much an established part of western thought today that we take them for granted and are highly critical of Freud's conceptual limitations, above all his theories on female sexuality. This is, in fact, an area of research in which Freud is particularly vulnerable. However, it is interesting to recall that Freud owed to women the initial insights that led him to the concept of the Unconscious. Anna O, Lucy R, Irma, Emmy von N, Dora and Katarina, and many others were the fountainhead of his inspiration. It is equally remarkable that he actually *listened* to them and found everything they had to tell significant and important. In Freud's dominantly phallocratic day, this in itself was revolutionary. He was the first of all explorers into the functioning of the human mind to take a serious and scientific interest in women's sexuality. Obviously he was fascinated by the mystery of femininity and by the female sex itself (a characteristic, as he claimed, that he shared with men of all centuries). But Freud was also a little afraid of the objects of his fascination. His metaphors constantly reveal a representation of the female genital as a void, a lack, a dark and disquieting continent where no one can see what is going on. There be lions, perhaps? He also insisted that in this line of research he was obliged to proceed from his knowledge of male sexuality. With this refracting telescope in hand, he was clearly going to be bemused by the absence of a penis and suppose the little girl's envy of the boy's visible and interesting organ and her desire to possess a penis of her own. But it was also Freud himself who first avowed deep feelings of dissatisfaction and uncertainty with regard to his theories about women and the nature of their sexual desires. In fact he waited until 1931 to publish "Female Sexuality," his first paper on the subject. He was then 75 years old!

In his second celebrated and much criticized paper, "Femininity," (Freud 1933) published two years later, he writes: ". . . psychology . . . is unable to solve the riddle of femininity" (p. 116) and further on ". . . the development of a little girl into a normal woman is more difficult and more complicated, since it includes two extra tasks, to which there is nothing corresponding in the development of a man" (Freud, 1933, p. 117). The "tasks" in question refer to Freud's two major conceptions of the difficulties in becoming a woman: First, she must come to terms with her anatomical configuration and effect a change of organ—from clitoris to vagina; second, she must effect a change of object—when and why does she give up her fixation to her mother in favour of her father?

Here I discuss these two concepts; the anatomical hypothesis, or "Anatomy as destiny"; and the change of object hypothesis, or "How to eat your mother and have her too." It will be seen that while I agree with Freud that these two dimensions do present genuine difficulties in the attainment of adult femininity and sexual functioning, I express points of view that differ considerably from those of the founder of psychoanalysis.

"ANATOMY AS DESTINY"

I think most analysts would agree today that envy of her father's penis is but a partial explanation of the difficulties encountered by the little girl on her path to mature sexuality, and indeed is not specific to the young female. Boys too suffer from their own characteristic form of penis envy—they invariably find their penises too small in comparison with their fathers'. If the belief persists into adult life that one's penis is smaller than it should be, based on the unconscious fantasy that the only adequate sex is the paternal one, this precipitates neurotic symptoms and anxieties that occur as frequently as those arising in the sexual life of the girl who still clings in unconscious fantasy to the fear that she is a castrated man. Clinical experience also confirms that the boy's envy and admiration of his mother's body and sexuality is similar to the girl's envy and admiration of her father's penis: the mother embodies the magical power to attract the father's penis and make the babies that both parents desire. Thus, the *phallus,* the erect penis—symbol of fertility, narcissistic completion and sexual desire—becomes the fundamental signifier of human desire for children of both sexes. Each possesses half of what is required to complete the symbol.[1]

In point of fact, every child wants to possess the mysterious sexual organs and fantasized power of *both* parents. And indeed why not? Whether we are male or female, one of the greatest narcissistic wounds of childhood is inflicted by the obligation to come to terms with our ineluctable monosexuality—its scar of course, the problem of what to do with our psychic bisexuality. But I shall return to that question later. Suffice it to say now that the discovery of the sexual difference is matched in traumatic quality only by the earlier discovery of Otherness and the later revelation of the inevitability of death. Some people never accept any of these universal traumas, and all of us deny them in the deeper recesses of our mind. In the world of dreams we are all magical, bisexual, and immortal!

While many would concede that the little girl's anatomical configuration presents her with particular problems in her psychosexual development, envy of the boy's penis is but one part of her sexual preoccupations. Psychoanalytic research had to wait for the work of women analysts, in particular, the seminal research of Melanie Klein (1945) to highlight additional complications for the young female. Klein was the first to formulate that the possession of a penis is narcissistically reassuring to the little boy because it is visible and mentally representable, whereas the little girl tends to see her sex as something missing and must wait till puberty to gain equivalent narcissistic confirmation, through the appearance of her breasts and periods, of her own unique sexual identity and the assurance that she will one day be able to make babies. Another landmark in psychoanalytic research concerning female sexuality is Kestenberg's (1968) paper on sexual differences.

But further difficulties inherent in the girl-child's development of gender identity also have their roots in her anatomical destiny. Since the interiority of her sex is a door into her body, the vagina is destined to be equated in the unconscious with anus, mouth, and urethra, and therefore is liable to be invested with both the masochistic and sadistic libidinal fantasies that these other zones carry. The little girl, and later the woman, are more likely to fear that their bodies are regarded in some way as dirty or dangerous because of these zonal confusions and, again, because there is no visible organ that can be controlled and verified. For woman, too, her body often rep-

---

[1]As we know, the word *symbol* comes from the Greek *symbolon* which originally meant an object cut in two that serves as a sign of recognition when two persons, each carrying a part of the whole, meet.

resents a dark continent in which anal and oral monsters lurk. Much of her unconscious representation of her body and her genitals will depend, of course, on the way in which her own mother invested with libidinal meaning her daughter's physical and psychological self, and the extent to which she may have transmitted to her girl-child unconscious fears concerning her own body and sexuality. Early bodily, and later verbal, communications between mother and daughter determine, in large part, whether oral erotism triumphs over oral aggression and whether anal-erotic impulses become more important than anal-sadistic ones.

This brings me to a third aspect of feminine anatomical destiny. Since the little girl cannot visually verify her genitals nor create other than a vague or zonally condensed psychic representation of them, she has difficulty in locating the sexual sensations of which she has been aware since early infancy. Clitoral, vaginal, urethral, and other internal sensations tend to be confused. This has important repercussions, for example, on her fantasies concerning masturbation. Although masturbation is the normal sexual expression of small children, it will eventually be interfered with by the parents. All children learn that it is not permissible to defecate, urinate, or masturbate in public. Even when these restrictions are imposed with kindness and understanding, they leave an imprint on unconscious fantasy life. When they are dealt with harshly because of the parents' own internal anxieties and a subsequent attempt to control these through their children's bodies, the risk of later neurotic problems is notably increased.

The little boy told to give up masturbating publicly is apt to imagine that his father will attack his penis because of his sexual feelings towards his mother and his ambivalent feelings to his father. The little girl, in the same phase of oedipal reorganization, is more likely to fear that her mother will attack and destroy the whole inside of her body as a fantasized punishment for the child's wish to take her mother's place, to play erotic games with her father, and make a baby with him. Thus, for the boy, the feared punishment for sexual wishes and masturbation is castration, whereas for the girl-child masturbation and sexual desire are frequently equated with death.

Much more could be said on this aspect of female sexuality, but I shall limit myself to a brief and typical clinical example. A young woman psychiatrist, highly intelligent and intellectually informed on psychoanalytic theory, claimed that she had never masturbated as a child nor in adult life. It was two years before she could even pronounce the word masturbation, finding the idea of autoerotic activity dirty and expressing doubts that it is truly an inevitable part of infantile experience. Although she had no apparent sexual difficulties, she suffered from a large array of psychosomatic manifestations that seemed to me often to be linked to tense states of sexual anxiety. This patient was in no way alexithymic or operational in her ways of thought. On the contrary, her associations were full of affect. A delicately built and pretty woman, she experienced her body as shapeless, large, and dirty. When she had her periods she would cry, saying she feared I would find her presence distasteful. In the fourth year of her analysis, she brought the following dream: "I was picking flowers in the garden outside the house where I lived as a child. I was dancing with delight, when suddenly my cousin Pierre appeared in the doorway and I woke up with a scream." Since this was the first time Cousin Pierre had ever appeared on the psychoanalytic stage, I asked her to tell me more about him. She sighed and said, "I suppose I've never wanted to think of him. He was much older than me and he once touched me sexually when I was little. Then, when he was twenty and I was about twelve, he was electrocuted in his bath. At least that's what we were told." Because she seemed to question this version of the facts, I asked, "What did you think about it?" With great difficulty, she admitted that she believed it had happened because he was playing with his penis in the bath. After all, she had known since childhood that he was a bad "sexual" boy. She then began to cry. I asked her to tell me what she was feeling at that moment and she said, "As you know my husband's been away for three weeks, and I'm so afraid you might think I've been masturbating. But I swear it isn't so . . . I'm sure you don't believe me!" I replied, "Of course, I believe you—otherwise you'd be dead!"

For the first time she was able to laugh over her sexual fears and fantasies, but we still needed many months to reconstruct, beyond significant elements such as "electricity," "picking flowers" and "dancing," all the long repressed memories of a little girl's spontaneous sexual sensations and masturbation fantasies. As was to be expected, this patient's erotic life with her husband then became fuller and considerably more satisfying to her. However, another interesting fact for which I can offer no conclusive theoretical explanation is that the majority of her psychosomatic symptoms also disappeared. For many years she had suffered from recurring digestive pain associated with gastric ulcer, arthritic pain, bronchial asthma and rhinitis, a constant septic throat condition, and an allergy to seafoods. These all cleared up and, with the exception of one mild asthmatic attack (associated by my analysand with cat fur), none of these symptoms returned in the remaining three years of her analysis with me.

HOW TO EAT YOUR MOTHER AND HAVE HER TOO

I come now to the second area of difficulty specific to female sexuality, that is, the integration of the profound homoerotic tie to one's mother. From birth, babies of both sexes begin to weave strong libidinal and sensuous ties to both parents—provided both are tender, sensual, and loving with them. In its mother's arms every infant is experiencing the earliest blueprint, or perhaps an imprint, of sexual and love relationships to come. The father's attitude is equally vital in this transmission of early libidinal investments, for a father who is absent or uninterested in his tiny offspring, or who is treated by the mother as a nonentity and accepts this exclusion, runs the risk of leaving his children to fulfill a role arising from the mother's unconscious problems. A mother who regards her baby as a narcissistic extension of herself, or who takes as her love objects her children instead of their father, may be laying the cornerstone for future pathological relationships. It should be noted that a mother who brings her children up singlehandedly does not necessarily incur these risks if she does not regard her relationship with them as a substitute for an adult love relationship. From infancy on, if children see their parents as a loving couple, who sexually desire and respect each other, and if children observe also that even fierce quarrelling does no lasting harm (that is, they learn that aggression is not dangerous when love is stronger than hate) children will tend to repeat these attitudes in adult life, following the parental model. The little girl will then identify with her mother not only as a mother but also as a sexual woman and will daydream about the man (modeled after the image of her own father) who will one day be her lover, her husband and the father of her children.

In its primordial beginnings, libidinal seeking is deeply intertwined with the desire to live, and it is the mother's task to "seduce" her child to want to live. This privileged relationship, which every infant shares with its mother in the first months of life, provides the baby girl with a double identification. The somatopsychic images that will become mental representations of her feminine body and its erogenous zones are already being formed. It is at this early stage of the construction of the sexual body image that mouth and vagina become linked and other internal sensations of an erogenous kind are experienced. To these we must add the clitoral sensations stimulated by the mother's physical handling and cleaning of her baby. The latter were the only early erogenous links to which Freud gave emphasis in his theory on the development of feminine erotism.

This early psychosexual structure provides the primitive foundation of the little girl's future love life. Upon it will be grafted the elements of the heterosexual model mentioned earlier, namely, a relationship with each parent that is physically and psychically loving and sensual, in addition to the model of a parental couple who love each other, who enjoy their sexual relationship, and who do not seek to give the child the impression that she is their chosen object for erotic or narcissistic completion. Furthermore, the little girl needs to hear that the mother herself values and respects the father and men in general and that she values her sexual and social life as a woman. A girl who is told that men are selfish pigs, out to profit from women, to seduce or dominate them, and the like will certainly have difficulty both in being prepared to like people of the opposite sex and in being able to separate from her mother.

So much for the factors that prepare the way for heterosexual identifications. These do not entirely liquidate the strong libidinal tie to the mother. Freud's question remains real: how does the little girl detach herself from her mother and integrate the profound erotic tie to her? Where is this vital homosexual component invested in her adult life? Freud's theory may be summarized as follows: the little girl's first desire is for her mother; she then replaces this with the desire for a penis, then for a child from her father, finally for a male child of her own. Included in the apparently implacable logic of this chain of signifiers is the implication that the girl's desire for a baby is merely a substitute for the penis she does not possess, and her love for her father a mere consequence of penis envy. These fantasies and desires are certainly frequent in women patients, but they are far from being the only factors or even the dominant ones among the complexities that contribute to each woman's image of femininity or motherhood. In addition, Freud's concept of the object-substitutions implies that homosexual ties are eliminated through penis envy.

What is meant by "homosexual" libido? The term is inexact. As we know, libido was the name given by Freud to include all aspects of instinctual sexual energy in human beings. The homosexual component, therefore, designates, in the first instance, that part of the libidinal impulses directed to the same-sex parent. Homosexual desires in children of both sexes always have a double aim. One is the desire to *possess,* in the most concrete fashion, the parent of the same sex, and the second is the desire to *be* the opposite sex and to possess all the privileges and prerogatives with which the opposite-sex parent is felt to be endowed. Although it is important to differentiate between these two complementary homosexual desires, they coexist in every small child—and in the unconscious of every adult! Thus the little girl not only wants to possess her mother sexually, create children with her, and be uniquely loved by her in a world from which all men are excluded; she also desires just as ardently to be a man like her father, to have his genitals as well as the power and other qualities she attributes to him. Since these various homosexual components are destined to remain totally unfulfilled, they frequently become associated with strong feelings of jealousy and aggression. Thus, to the deep attachment to both parents are added fierce and envious wishes; that is to say, the homosexual components are both tender and aggressive at the same time.

The little girl's problem is manifestly more difficult that that of her brothers. How does the small female extricate herself from this doubly complex situation with the mother? In face of the incitement and, indeed, strong erotic attraction to the father, girl-children must introject, very early on, all aspects of the mother's image. These will, in turn, coalesce to form a fundamental figure of identification affecting all future feminine development.

But at this point there are a number of different "internal mothers" in our psychic world. One of these maternal introjects is adored, another desired, another resented, another deeply feared. The small girl needs to wrest from her mother the right to *be* her through identifying with her as an internal object, but she also needs her mother externally as a guide, comforter, and helper for some years to come. After the turmoil of adolescence, when she usually rejects her mother in almost every way, she will often turn to her with renewed attachment when she herself becomes a mother. It is perhaps at this point that many girls finally forgive their mothers for all the infantile resentments they harbour against her, and they become close adult friends. Just as every child she bears represents, in woman's unconscious fantasy, a baby she has made with her father, so too her babies are often felt to be a gift to the mother. These factors may cause psychic pain and conflict, or they may add to the immense joy of each new birth.

Others may identify with the mother as a sexual woman but do not themselves desire children. They frequently produce what we might call symbolic children in their professional, intellectual, or artistic activities. Here again specific feminine problems arise. Many women in analysis reveal the fear that they are obliged to choose between being lovers or mothers, between both of these and being professionally competent people. The articulation of these three distinct feminine desires—the sexual, the maternal, and the professional—requires a delicate balance, and women frequently feel impelled to sacrifice their own narcissistic and libidinal needs in any one of these areas.

These considerations concerning woman's love life, social life, work life, and motherhood bring me back to the question of feminine homosexual libido in adult life. How and where is it invested? My reflections upon myself, as well as upon all that my women patients have taught me during 25 years' analytic work, have led me to the following conclusions:[2]

1. Our homosexual libido serves first of all to enrich and stabilise our narcissistic self-image. In other words, every little girl needs to be able to give to herself some of that early love and appreciation of the mother and her body, in order to have affection and esteem for her feminine self and sex organs. She is then free to offer to the other sex what she herself does not possess, for this is the fundamental factor that leads each sex to become the object of the other's desire. In other words, the young girl gives up wanting to *have* the woman in order to *be* the woman. Through the same psychic movement, her envy of the penis is transmuted into desire for it.

2. The profound wish to be the other sex, if and when it is relinquished, finds an important investment in woman's love life, particularly in the sexual relationship itself, in which identification with her partner's pleasure and desire adds to her own erotic pleasure. For it is in love making that we can best recreate the illusion of being both sexes and losing, even if momentarily, the narcissistic limits that monosexuality imposes upon us all.

3. I believe that our relationship to our children offers a treasure trove of homosexual riches. I can still remember my overwhelming pleasure in having given birth to a son and the feeling that his penis was also mine. I well remember too my narcissistic wish two years later, after my daughter was born, that she would achieve all I had failed in, as well as the complex relationship I had with her throughout her adolescence. All these memories leave me with little doubt today as to the importance of the homosexual dimension to my maternal feelings in both their pleasurable and their conflictual aspects.

4. It has always seemed to me that the pleasure experienced in intellectual and artistic achievements is pregnant with considerable narcissistic and homosexual fantasy since in such production, every one is both man and woman at the same time. Our intellectual and artistic creations are, in a sense, parthenogenetically created children. Furthermore, clinical experience has taught me that conflicts over either of the two poles of feminine homosexual wishes—that is,

---

[2]Despite the important differences between male and female sexuality, it should be noted that the following paths of integration of homosexual wishes apply equally to male sexuality.

taking over the mother's creative power as well as the father's penis—may create serious inhibition or even total sterility in the capacity to "put forth" symbolic children.

5. Finally, the homosexual investment, usually divested of its conscious sexual aim, gives warmth and richness to the affectionate and essential friendships we maintain with other women.

All of the foregoing is, of course, something of an ideal description of the way in which narcissistic and homosexual wishes may be invested in sexual life, family life, and social and professional activities. Leaving aside the question of manifest homosexuality, with which I have dealt extensively elsewhere (McDougall, 1964, 1978), we find in analytic work innumerable signs of profoundly unconscious homosexual conflict that may express itself in any of the fields of investment already mentioned. Endless domestic scenes, sexual problems, difficulties with children, with colleagues, with friends or with creative pursuits, are all liable to reveal, in analysis, their homosexual counterpart.

And what of the therapeutic relationship itself? How often are homosexual fears, wishes, and projections overlooked? And whose unconscious homosexuality is causing an obstruction to the analytic process? The unrecognized homosexuality of the analysand? Or of the analyst? I would like to explore this question further by means of a clinical illustration.

THE FEMALE ANALYST AND THE FEMALE ANALYSAND: A CLINICAL VIGNETTE

Madame T was 35 when she first came to see me because of a number of crippling phobias that had caused her intense suffering since childhood. She was claustrophobic as well as agoraphobic; her fear of flying was so great that after the sale of the luxury liner "France," she could no longer visit the United States and thus effectively renounced both personal and professional interests; an impending appointment with a stranger filled her with anticipatory panic; staying alone at night brought her a thousand tortures. I was the same age as Madame T when she came to see me and was delighted at the prospect of having such an interesting and "classically neurotic" patient on my couch. A rare event! Our analytic adventure began within a matter of weeks, and in these auspicious circumstances.

For the purpose of this illustration I shall refer only to Madame T's phobia of being alone at night. Her nocturnal anguish recurred with unfailing regularity each time her husband left her alone because of business, which frequently took him overseas. An overwhelming affect of terror and a sense of impending danger drove Madame T at these times either to taking strong doses of medication or else to telephoning her parents to announce that she was coming home for a few days. As time went on, we learned that her anxiety became uncontrollable only at the moment Madame T got into bed. In her lighted kitchen, she was uneasy but able to cope. With my encouragement she tried to find a scenario that would fit her panic: "Someone" was planning to force an entry through the window—a man, of course. What was he after? Well, she was not going to allow herself to be raped, so naturally he would kill her.

It required many months of analytic work by both of us before Madame T could accept that the anxiety-arousing script had been written by herself and that the character of the rapist-killer was also a personal creation. She proceeded to search for proof that my interpretations were erroneous and supported her contention by meticulous gleaning of the daily news for evidence that women were constantly in danger of sexual attack by unknown men. Her insistence impelled me to tell her the well-known story of the woman who dreamed that a tall black man with a strange light in his eyes was approaching her bed. The woman cries, "What are you going to do to me?" and the handsome black man replies, "I don't know yet. It's *your* dream!" In spite of the uncertain outcome of such interventions, Madame T's terror of nocturnal solitude eventually disappeared. It was replaced, interestingly enough, by masturbation. This now became the condition that allowed Madame T to sleep peacefully at night without medication. She complained, however, that there was a compulsive dimension to her autoerotism. It had become somewhat addictive, replacing the once indispensable sleeping tablets, and she also felt compelled to masturbate whether she wanted to or not.

Another equally important part of her discourse at this point in her analysis centered on the overwhelming maternal solicitude by which she claimed to be persecuted. According to my analysand, Madame X, her mother, would seize any slim pretext to get her daughter home, as though she were constantly replaiting the umbilical cord in a symbolic attempt to draw her phobic child back into her womb. Invitations to dine, to stay for the weekend, or to accompany the parents to the theater were rained upon Madame T. "A real cannibal mother," I thought to myself, "and perverse as well! Not only does she complain that her daughter has been neurotically crippled for the past 30 years, but she also does everything in her power to keep her in this state!" Although I kept telling myself that this was purely an internal object that Madame T needed to maintain in a persecutory role, I found myself violently disliking this mother as a threatening external object who was preventing her daughter—my patient—from getting well.

The session from which I wish to quote came at the end of our second year of analytic work. Madame T announced proudly that she was sure her nocturnal phobias were over but complained that her daytime terrors were as strong as ever and she felt increasingly ashamed of them. The day before the session in question, she had gone to meet an elderly friend to whom she was very attached. To her dismay, she was unable to park her car near to her friend's house, which meant that she would have to cross the empty boulevard, a situation that always aroused panic-reactions in her. However, she found a brilliant solution to the phobic problem: she backed into a one-way street in the wrong direction and landed close to the place assigned for the rendezvous. Her friend remarked that she was "rather late" for their appointment and that she had worried about whether Madame T was coming or not.

Madame T then proceeded in our session to give numerous associations to her panic, drawing on everything we had discovered together during the past two years. Her transference feelings, as well as most of her personal relationships, had led us to conclude that she was spending her life trying to escape any situation, or any relationship, that was apt to represent an archaic image of her mother as an omnipresent figure about to devour her. In particular, she seemed to be avoiding situations where it might be suspected that she was still awaiting the amorous approach of her father, disguised as the rapist-killer of her phobic fantasy-construction. Madame T herself proposed that her own unconscious desires had once again pushed her to agoraphobic terror; that she alone was the script writer and director of this infernal play; and that she apparently continued to endow her mother with environmental omnipotence, which she experienced as her mother's wish to possess her body and soul.

I was not particularly pleased with this session. It seemed to me that we were treading yet again on familiar ground and had had many sessions of a similar kind. I completely overlooked the fact that I had paid no attention to certain of Madame T's associations and, in particular, to her predicament, in which she was anxious to reach an older womanfriend but could only do so by taking a forbidden, one-way street. These, then, were the daytime residues I used to make a dream that surprised me by its manifest theme. The dream left me with an uncanny and vivid impression that I have never forgotten. A further significant detail is that due to a dispute with the most important man in my life, I too was sleeping alone in my bed that night.

Here is the dream: I am to meet someone in a little-known quarter of Paris. As I approach the house, I am filled with what might correspond to that familiar feeling Freud designated as "uncanny." Nevertheless, I hurry on, pushing aside several people who get in my way. I then find myself in the presence of a very attractive Oriental woman, dressed in a provocative, sexy style. She says to me in a stern voice, "You're rather late you know!" I stammer out some sort of excuse and reach forward to caress the silken material of her dress, as though to be forgiven or to be seductive to her. It becomes evident that I am to have an erotic relationship with this lady, and I feel embarassed, not only because I am late but also because I am afraid of looking foolish, since I am not sure what is expected of me. Am I to take the first steps, or should I leave myself entirely in her hands? I am then convinced that I must renounce all willpower and passively submit to whatever this beautiful woman wants. The anxiety, no doubt mixed with excitement, that was aroused by this disquietingly erotic situation woke me suddenly with the feeling that my life was in danger. In the dead of night I had plenty of time to ponder the hidden significance of this manifestly homosexual dream. I thought to myself that my two analysts, both men, had hardly ever interpreted any genuinely homosexual material (no doubt because I had failed to furnish the necessary associations!) and here I was, left to fathom it alone.

Madam T's session came immediately to mind—through the verbal link of *being late* for an appointment. But why the langorous Oriental? Slowly there came back the memory of an Oriental patient who had once come to consult me. I must have seen her only five or six times. The nature of her therapeutic demand had completely disappeared from my mind. All I remembered was that her father had had three legal wives, of which her mother was the third and was described as "more of a big sister than a mother." I vaguely recalled understanding this patient's disappointment at having a "mother-sister" rather than the "real" one, that is, the first wife, who ruled over the household. Why had it not occurred to me (I ask myself today) that it could be very agreeable to have a "mother-sister," in complicity with her daughter and always there to play games with you? Without knowing why, I felt it was important to recall the name of this patient. After groping around in my memory, I recalled her first name in a flash: she was called "Lili." I could no longer refuse the evidence that was staring me in the face. My mother, who in no way resembles a beautiful Oriental, is called Lillian. I began to explore and to understand the more obscure references in my dream, factors that went beyond its manifest content and had to do with the links between sexual excitement, feelings of love and hatred, and the fear of death.

I began to wonder what my dream had to do with Madame T's analysis. I realised for the first time that my own mother was, in every possible way, the opposite of the mother described by Madame T. My mother had many personal activities and seldom made demands on her daughters. In fact I considered myself lucky in comparison with some of my schoolmates, who had envied my liberty. Of course, I had spent several years on the analytic couch, lamenting my mother's failings on almost every conceivable plane and complaining of my father's blind devotion to her in spite of her obvious faults. Were some of my feelings about Madame T's mother due to an unacknowledged wish to have a "mother-sister"?

Following on my attempt to understand the link between my patient's session and my dream, I came to the astonishing conclusion that I was *envious* of her and her possessive mother. Why did I not have a mother like that? I had analyzed so carefully—in both myself and Madame T—all the hostile feelings attached to the internal mother-image; but had I not, at the same time, overlooked the supreme importance of Madame T's positive feelings and her homosexual attachment to her mother, because of my need to keep in repression my own childlike wish to be the chosen subject of *my* mother's erotic desire? To have waited so many years to find dream-fulfillment of my homosexual wishes confirmed that I was, effectively, "rather late." Even more disquieting was the fact that up until then I had not been listening to Madame T's wish to have a homosexually desirous mother. I had failed to realise that she never tired of showing me this aspect of the daughter-mother relationship. I had taken her complaints at face-value!

At a later session, I found the occasion to ask Madame T if she had ever thought that behind all her dissatisfaction with her demanding mother, there was also a wish to prove to me and to herself just how much her mother desired her company. My remark was received with a tense silence followed by an embarassed confession. Perhaps the demanding one was really herself, she said. Quite recently her mother had remarked, rather tersely, that she and her father were tired of holding her hand every time her husband went abroad; they dreaded her continual phone calls and dearly wished to go on a holiday alone without having to worry about her! Madame T began to cry, while I was struck silent. Although I had few doubts about the complicity of Madame T's mother in this dependent relationship, it was above all *my own unconscious complicity* that had prevented Madame T's becoming conscious of her positive desire to be the exclusive object of her mother's love and to put her mother in the place of her husband.

As a consequence of my personal elaboration of the situation, I was now able to turn to another "late" area in my understanding, namely, why I had shown so little interest in Madame T's masturbation fantasies, especially since her nightly autoerotic activity had, by her own description, become the prime condition for falling asleep; it had taken the place of her old phobia and her fantasy of the rapist-killer. My newly acquired receptivity bore immediate fruit. One day Madame T complained that she had difficulty talking to me about her masturbation. I had pointed out that her phobic scenario used to take as its theme the violent aspect of sexual desire and that this in turn had become associated in her mind with certain images of her father as a violent intruder. Consequently, she might have difficulty in telling me her present autoerotic fantasies if they were in any way linked to the old fantasies and perhaps to her mother as well as her father. To this she replied: "Not at all! I would have no difficulty in telling you what I imagine, nor that there are both men and women in my daydream. But what is painful for me to say is that I masturbate with an electric, water-jet toothbrush given to me by my mother." I shall not dwell here on the multiple unconscious meanings linked to the little electric apparatus with its erotic jet of water, nor on the links between the autoerotic and the phobic scenarios. It is sufficient to say that the window-intruder was of a thoroughly *bisexual* nature. My countertransference deafness had been an opaque screen, hiding not only the analytic exploration of Madame T's erotic fantasies but also further insight into their underlying significance, especially in their homosexual dimension.

The latter, once they could be uncovered and verbalized, allowed us to go beyond Madame T's hitherto unacknowledged attitude of envy of her mother and her mother's sex, and her childhood longing to be her mother's sexual partner. This, in turn, gave access to Madame T's radical rejection, up to this point in her analysis, of her own body, which she experienced as an unclean, dangerous, and death-dealing organ. Through the medium of the electric toothbrush, she was able to maintain a certain distance from her sex, yet at the same time to absorb, in fantasy, some of the idealized qualities she attributed to her mother. But much analytic work lay ahead before this erotic "transitional object" gave way to a genuine identification within her to a genital mother. On the contrary, her fantasies, at least in their homosexual orientation, were already conscious to her and, as a halfway step to fuller identification with the genital mother, had been integrated into her autoerotic scenario. It was an aspect of my own homosexual wishes that had remained in abeyance and hence was "rather late" in submitting itself to analysis!

CONCLUSION

In this presentation I hope to have shown that the path from infancy to adult femininity is infinitely more complex than Freud envisaged in his "change of zone" and "change of object" concepts. Not only are the roots of feminine erotism laid down in early infancy, giving rise to a multiplicity of zonal confusions, but the identification to the genital mother, even when the object-change to heterosexuality has been adequately achieved, still leaves in its wake many problems regarding the integration of feminine homosexual libido.

REFERENCES

Freud, S. (1931). Female Sexuality. *Standard Edition,* 21:225–243. London: Hogarth Press, 1961.

———. (1933). Femininity. *Standard Edition,* 22:112–135. London: Hogarth Press, 1964.

Klein, M. (1945). The Oedipus complex in the light of early anxieties. *Internat. J. Psycho-Anal.,* 26:11–142.

Kestenberg, J. (1968). Outside and inside, male and female. *J. Amer. Psychoanal. Assn.,* 16:457–520.

McDougall, J. (1964). Homosexuality in women. In: *Female Sexuality,* (ed.) J. Chasseguet. Ann Arbor: University of Michigan Press, 1970.

CHAPTER SIXTEEN

Transference and Countertransference Issues in the Treatment of Women by a Male Analyst

Robert S. Liebert

Helene Deutsch (1969) hailed the young God Dionysus for his revolutionary emancipation of the women of Thebes through Dionysian rituals. She went so far as to suggest that a statue of Dionysus be placed at the entrace to all girls' dormitories. Ancient myth informs us that only two men ever attended the orgiastic rites at Mount Cytheron—Dionysus himself, and the young Theban king Pentheus. Dionysus, the liberator of women, always had a perfectly splendid time, but Pentheus ended up with his flesh torn to pieces by the throng of women, enraged by his presence, who were led by Pentheus's own mother, Queen Agave.

The myth of Dionysus informs us of two essential aspects of the patriarchal view of women: First, the belief that the power to liberate women resides with a man; and, second, the male fear that full liberation of women will result in the unleashing of their latent primordial destructive force. The psychoanalytic vision of women and central elements in the conduct of therapy, along with all social institutions and ideologies, have shared in this belief system. The myth touches on the inner experience of everyone ever born into and reared within the nuclear family structure.

It is not my intention here to pursue a critique of the psychoanalytic psychology of women. The arguments are familiar, and others can do it far more effectively than I. Nor will I plead on behalf of the community of male psychoanalysts that women should trust us—now that we have acquired liberated views in tandem with those of enlightened women. Quite simply, that is not regularly the case. And I will not contend that with an analyzable patient—female or male—in treatment with a highly competent male or female analyst, the sequence of the process will be different, but the outcome will be the same. I do not believe the outcome will be the same.

What follows is rooted largely in common clinical experience, gathered primarily from my own practice and my supervision of men and women conducting both psychoanalysis and dynamic, nonanalytic therapy. The material is shaped by the fact that I am very much a child of this culture, and my perceptions, reasoning, and abstractions are further shaped by what is unique to me in my character, personal experiences and choices, and sustaining fantasies.

To begin, we should inquire why many prospective female patients prefer not to be in treatment with women. My phrasing of a negative choice is, as will become clearer, deliberate. Perhaps the constellations of conscious and unconscious factors that determine the choice of a therapist or passive acceptance in the referral vary considerably. I will address only a few themes.

It is no longer politically correct for a woman to say apologetically at the end of a consultation, "I know it's crazy, but I just don't feel that women are as good as men"—a statement, incidentally, that I heard with some regularity from women medical students when I was the Psychiatric Consultant to the medical students at the College of Physicians and Surgeons during the years from 1964 through 1971. But a decade or more of postchildhood consciousness-raising has not obliterated the devaluing and derogatory attitudes of some women toward women, attitudes firmly imprinted early in life at home and by the institutions of the culture. Thus, as a means of avoiding an anxiety-laden confrontation with a female therapist over this inner representation of her mother, her sisters, and herself, entering treatment with a man offers a sanctuary. In this connection, I draw on what Dr. Person has so persuasively argued: that many women have cultivated the defensive and manipulative functions of ingratiation, dissembling, and eroticism in their encounters with men—strategies of the relatively powerless. Whereas many prospective patients are drawn to the female-female therapeutic dyad *because* of the possibility for dispensing with this facade and having a more authentic encounter, others are too frightened at the prospect of unfolding the maternal transference with a woman. For the authentic encounter can carry with it the rageful reproaches, contempt, and dread of retaliatory attitudes from the female therapist. Many of the patients who can thus be characterized have, paradoxically, a warm, mutually supportive circle of women friends. One of the unspoken, binding forces in many of these friendships is a parity in the sense of being neurotically damaged and in the problems of trying to negotiate a viable relationship with just one of the men out there who seem to form an endless sea of narcissistic creeps and clingy, obsessional puppy dogs. These friendships are intense and authentic. They also are composed of positive elements of a split inner representation of the mother of early childhood and, sometimes, of sisters. The result of this structural split is that the woman is left with an inner representation of mother as unduly primitive, harsh, and unnurturing, a negatively skewed version of the actual experience of her.

The group of women I have been schematically describing often begin therapy with a male. Their reasoning is at the same time both true and a defense against the pain of experiencing a full and unbuffered maternal transference: "It is too easy and comfortable relating to a woman; but I'm anxious with, and have problems with, strong men." This initial statement often sounds strange to the male therapist because the woman speaking it appears quite composed, is articulate, and appropriately charming and ironic about herself. This initial presentation tempts a collusion at the outset in a shared fantasy; if the male therapist conducts himself with kindness, decency, and a bit of wit of his own, while letting the analytic process naturally unfold within the context of a "positive working alliance," the patient will feel much better about herself and resolve the difficulties that stood in the way of fulfilling marriage and family. And she will in future years look back warmly on what is commonly coded as her "positive experience with Dr. X." He will be the liberating Dionysus. And the collusion will circumvent the expression of the rage towards him that would accompany the unearthing and working through of the crippling internal representations of the "bad" mother.

The male therapist will be spared the premonitory rumblings of his own "Pentheus" fantasy with respect to the destructive power of angry women. Women with this therapeutic experience often come back for a second analysis as the achievements from the first begin to unaccountably erode into depression and a relatively contentless restlessness, as if trapped by life itself. In psychoanalytic terms, the unmodified inner representation of the mother continues to exact her toll. Although manifestly functioning more effectively, the former patient labors on with her unconscious sense of herself as inadequate remaining intact. Her inchoate anger is expressed in the low grade, chronic depression.

The situation I have just outlined suggests comment on another frequently encountered problem in the female patient-male therapist dyad. It is when a woman enters therapy dissatisfied with her marriage or is unmarried and neurotically inhibited from sustaining an intimate relationship. If an eroticized and idealized transference to the therapist develops and is not vigorously analyzed, the effects on the patient's life can be pernicious. Rather than address her neurotic contributions to the marital difficulty, the woman will split spouse and analyst into the denigrated, oppressor husband and the idealized, empathic, and compassionate analyst. This situation then leads to a disintegration of the marriage, which was not necessarily destined and in which a successful resolution would otherwise have been possible. The comparable dynamics prevail with the single woman in this transference paradigm, and each new male suitor can too easily be dismissed as inadequate when measured against the therapist as the standard for manhood.

I mentioned in passing my conviction that an analysis is not the same in the female patient-male therapist dyad as in the female-female dyad. I shall elaborate. Upon meeting her male analyst, a woman has, of course, the accurate perception of his gender and, with that, a specific set of socialized as well as uniquely private psychological responses. I am referring to constellations of organized fantasies, associated affects, and styles of behavior that are remarkably constant and recurrent in encounters with men who are of potential importance to them.

Thus, the opening phase of the analysis involves the woman insistently conveying to the male analyst that, for better or worse, she regards and responds to him as male. The analytic process will be compromised, however, if this initial response to the analyst as a male suits him *too* well. The issue has to do with an aspect of psychological development that remains conflicted in all men.

If I may take a brief excursus and speak again in highly schematic terms, one may view "becoming a man" as a protracted uphill struggle to transcend the early identification with mother—or her surrogates—the female models in constant caring attendence during the first years. Although the mothering and nurturing aspects of doing psychotherapy are among the central unconscious attractions in the vocational choice of psychoanalysis by men, it is another matter for the male psychoanalyst to comfortably acknowledge that he is perceived and reacted to *as if* he were a woman. I will not belabor the conventional storehouse of fears that can be aroused—passive homosexual yearnings, concerns of genital intactness, memories perhaps of being teased as a sissy, and so on. In short, the easy recognition of, sustained focus on, and working through of the maternal transference tempts a regression in male analysts that they tend to resist experiencing. There is, however, *no* necessary reason why these impediments cannot be surmounted.

I should interject that if in the course of forthrightly addressing problems inherent in the female patient-male therapist dyad, it appears that I am implicitly arguing that women patients are better off with women therapists—that is not so. It has been my observation that women therapists have the mirror image of many of the same problems besetting men as well as others that are specific to their being female. But the discussion of these issues is beyond the province of my present undertaking. Suffice it to say that neither women nor men have an intrinsic advantage as therapist for the female patient. We should firmly bear in mind that the adaptive triad of ingratiation, dissembling, and eroticism that Dr. Person has described, and which has allowed many women to get through an analysis with a male by "faking it," are an integrated defensive characterologic system. As such, they are no less amenable to the principles of character analysis and analysis of resistance than any other integrated defensive characterologic system. In this instance, the problem in the analytic situation largely resides in this defensive system being more difficult to see as defensive because it approaches a cultural norm.

Returning to the female patient in therapy with a male, many analyses unfold with her efforts to win, and sometimes despair at winning, the respect and affection of the analyst. This phase is commonly a reenactment of an aspect of what has been the experience of a significantly high percentage of daughters—at least in the past. Whereas fathers tend to be enchanted by sons from birth on—at first as narcissistic extensions, vehicles for reliving elements of their unfulfilled past—daughters, more often than not, do not elicit a comparably intense involvement from their father until about their fourth year. And, if the girl is first-born, she is not infrequently an initial disappointment to him. It is with the onset of what we strangely call the oedipal phase for girls—strange since Oedipus was male—that the little girl's cognitive apparatus and social skills enable her to melt away father's distance and draw him into the passionate romance that can follow over the next several years.

One psychological legacy of this particular developmental history is that a man's love is experienced as conditional—to be earned and maintained through an amalgam of charm and eroticism—a legacy about which enlightened women now feel no small amount of bitterness. If the woman's early history is complicated by her mother's envy of this daughter-father romance, and particularly if it is coupled with her resentment over the barrenness of her own marriage to father, the initial phase of the analysis will often be marked by symptomatic and masochistic masking of the emerging positive feelings. Whatever the balance of sorting out what the patient is doing in her current life—learning about her past, while also studying the emerging transference—what is taking place is more easily comprehended as a triadic process involving the woman patient, male analyst, and her father. That the patient will frequently talk with great feeling about her past and present relationship with her mother can be highly misleading. Although about mother, it is usually a narrative told to the analyst in the form of a daughter soliciting father's sympathy and creating a bond with him over this less than adequate history of mothering. It should be underscored that because the patient talks about her mother in a feeling and articulate way does not per se mean that she is reexperiencing with the analyst what she is describing. That is, she is not experiencing him as she did her mother.

I will now try to bring together threads of some of the themes I have touched on with a clinical illustration.

Margaret entered psychoanalysis in her mid-twenties. Born in Europe and given an early bilingual education, she was artistically gifted but unable to feel a personal fit with any of several plausible career directions. She had been intimately involved for several years with a charismatic and influential, middle-aged political figure who was also, in important ways, a kindly mentor. But he made it clear that their relationship, one, had to be completely secret and, two, would never become anything more than it was. As she sensed her life foundering she sank into increasing depression.

With respect to some significant features in her background, father, a former researcher and now a university administrator, was a tyrranical and frightening figure. The condition for his love seemed to Margaret to be total submission to his control of her life—choosing schools, or jobs, approving or disapproving of friends, supporting her financially, etc. Mother, on the other hand, was a fearful and emotionally shallow woman, whose life seemed to have lost what uncertain purpose it had when her children moved out of their teens. She was both dependent on and continuously undermining of the patient and her one sibling, a younger sister, feeling displaced here and separated from her family roots in Europe. Margaret's sister was quite emotionally crippled and her conscious feelings toward this sister were largely those of guilt of the survivor.

Oedipal issues were insistently present early in the analysis. They were particularly marked by secret relations with older married men that allowed Margaret to preserve a primary tie to her father. Her view of me was quite fluid, but often during the first year of treatment she was anxious that if she relaxed her vigilance I might attempt to sexually exploit her.

Over the following several years of an often stormy analysis, continuous gains were achieved—depressive periods were short lived and much less debilitating; a career appropriate to her talents took form; and relationships with "unavailable" men yielded to others that were potentially more satisfying. Moreover, she felt increasingly free of the demands and claims of her family. Life was certainly much better, but a relaxed sense of pleasure seemed to take place only in the company of a few close women friends. As you might imagine, there was a continuous process of working through the pathological ties to her father by means of the analysis of the transference. In contrast, although she spoke frequently about her mother—often with bitter complaints and disdain—she seemed to keep this material apart from thoughts and feelings about me. Some exceptions to this pattern were her sense of being "pushed around" to make room for other patients if I rescheduled appointments, and her anxious thoughts about "falling apart" when I was on vacation. By and large, however, attempts to understand Margaret's earlier relationship with her mother *within the context of the transference neurosis* were met with assent which remained, however, intellectual. One effect of this was that I gravitated towards a greater focus on the paternal transference, since progress yielded by that emphasis seemed more immediate and apparent.

Progress came to a halt abruptly after the following events: My wife, who shared the same office suite, but uses a different professional name, was pregnant. During the pregnancy, Margaret spoke in an increasingly idealized way about her, consciously unaware that she was my wife. She talked of her admiration for this pregnant, married woman, who looked so content and had everything she herself ultimately wanted. She even fantasized that I was envious of this woman's apparent good fortune. Then, after the birth, when Margaret did not see my wife in the office, she gradually became more and more depressed. I confronted her denial of the several clues that strongly suggested that this woman was my wife. Concluding that this was, of course, the case, Margaret became increasingly critical of me. She blamed me for failure and wasted years of analysis and for my insensitivity, male arrogance, and more. After a month or so of this turn of events, she announced that she was terminating treatment. My interpretations during this difficult period were addressed at the oedipal level—to variants of the theme surrounding her humiliation and sense of betrayal in learning that it was with this other woman that I was sharing my life and having a baby. These, and related interpretations, seemed to have little effect on the downward course of the analysis. I was confused and quite upset. In what seemed like a desperate last effort, I suggested to Margaret that she have a consultation with a woman colleague before terminating the analysis.

The consultation was invaluable in making clear to me that the recent unfolding of events in the analysis most traumatically resonated with her childhood abandonment, after the birth of her sister, by her, at best, not very adequate mother. Margaret was now convinced that I would withdraw from her in a comparable way. I had, incidentally, at times suggested the terror of abandonment and sadistic responses that she must have experienced at her sister's birth, when she spoke of her later guilt over having fared so much better in life than her sister. She agreed that, indeed, my interpretation must have been so, but the affect and actual memory remained out of her grasp. At this time, when the conflict was fully energized and when both as an older sibling myself and as a male valiantly trying to stabilize my newly activated role as "father," I was less than open to either seeing myself as the "bad" mother in the analytic narrative or re-experiencing, by identification with Margaret, affects better left repressed as far as I was concerned.

With my shifting the analysis to the aggressive aspects of the maternal theme that were revealed by the consultation, our work again became a productive, collaborate effort. This episode I have recounted allowed for the working through of significant impounded elements of Margaret's early trauma with mother.

The subsequent course of the analysis and Margaret's life need not concern us here.

In sum, women will continue to be in analysis with both female and male therapists. It has been my purpose in this paper to illuminate some of the motivational patterns that contribute to a woman's choice in the gender of her therapist, when the possibility of choice is present. Further, I have examined some of the ways in which this choice is related to the specific nature of her internal object world and characterologic defensive organization. I have focused particularly on issues surrounding the unfolding of the maternal aspect of the transference neurosis that takes place in analysis with a male therapist. It seems to me intuitively correct that what transpires in the female-female therapeutic dyad has qualitative differences from what takes place in the female-male dyad. The possibility for collusion between patient and therapist for avoiding the working through of fundamental problems inheres in either dyad. It is my conviction, however, that either arrangement offers the possibility for successful resolution of the same conflicted material.

REFERENCES

1. Deutsch, H. (1969). *A Psychoanalytic Study of the Myths of Dionysus and Apollo.* New York: International Universities Press.

CHAPTER SEVENTEEN

Transference and Countertransference: Definitions of Terms

Frederick M. Lane

TRANSFERENCE

It is not only useful but essential in a study of the concepts of transference and countertransference to establish definitions of the basic vocabulary used in these considerations. These terms refer to concepts that span several levels of abstraction, from observed clinical data through clinical theory and the theory of technique to the level of metapsychological discourse. The same term, therefore, has come to be used in several different senses. The concept of transference is one of Freud's central discoveries, the one that facilitated the transition from psychotherapy by means of "catharsis" to psychoanalysis as we currently know it. It is a term which, because it is ubiquitous in clinical discourse, has accrued to it multiple shades of meaning with consequent blurring of focus.

Let us begin with Freud's (1905) definition. In referring to ". . . a special class of mental structures, for the most part unconscious, to which the name of 'transference' may be given," he stated.

> They are new editions or facsimiles of the impulse and fantasies which are aroused and made conscious during the progress of the analysis; but they have this peculiarity, which is characteristic for their species, that they replace some earlier person by the person of the physician. To put it another way; a whole series of psychological experiences are revived, not as belonging to the past, but as applying to the person of the physician at the present moment. Some of these transferences have a content which differs from that of their model in no respect whatever except for the substitution. These then—to keep the same metaphor—are merely new impressions or reprints. Others are more ingeniously constructed; their content has been subjected to a moderating influence—to sublimation, as I call it. . . . These then, will no longer be new impressions, but revised editions. [p. 116]

Though this definition is limited to phenomena occurring during the progress of analysis, Freud (1915) made it clear that he felt transference occurred in all significant relationships, especially in romantic love, which he felt contained important infantile elements.

Let us redefine transference in a much less succinct manner for purposes of outlining the various aspects of the concept.

Transference—General Definition

Transference may be defined as an unconscious repetition in a current relationship of patterns of thought, feeling, and behavior that originated in an important object relationship of infancy and are displaced onto the current person. Many, along with Freud, view this as occurring in all relationships (Brenner 1976). Others (Macalpine, 1950) view this more specifically as a phenomenon of psychoanalysis alone. In this way it is seen as being actively induced in a "transference ready" person by the special setting of analysis, which leads to a regressive adaptation that produces the transference.

These patterns are anachronistic; they belong to an earlier time frame, which implies regression, and therefore they are largely inappropriate to the contemporary person with whom they are being lived out. Elements such as drive and defense patterns, wishes, fears, demands, guilts, self and object representations, all of which remained or became repressed in the early object tie, seek repeated expression and realization throughout life. They are unconsciously displaced onto the new object relationship. The direct link between the new object and the earlier infantile object remains unconscious as well. Only derivative thoughts, attitudes, feelings, and fantasies come to awareness and expression. This definition contains the notions of displacement from one object to another, of repetition of the past, and of regression as intrinsic to a definition of transference. This inappropriate application of the infantile tie as a model and template for the experience in the new relationship results in distortions in the subject's appraisal of the new person and in inaccurate responses in their interactions. This implies a disturbance in reality testing within the bounds of the relationship. Though such transference reactions may be short lived, they tend to become repetitive and stereotyped in the new dyad.

Transference Defined by "Signs and Symptoms"

No definition of a clinical phenomenon is complete without a description of observable data that determine the conclusion that transference is occurring in a given relationship. Transference will emerge in bolder relief in an analysis or an analytic psychotherapy in response to the technical neutrality of the analyst, who establishes the environment of safety, therapeutic abstinence, relative anonymity. The following observable phenomena indicate the probable presence of transference.

1. Distortion of appraisal and representation of the analyst by the patient. Using the framework of earlier object representations, the image of the contemporary object is distorted and reshaped to fit the mold of the object of infancy. As Freud mentioned, this new representation is either an identical "reprint" or, in altered form, a "revised edition."

2. Affective reactions or emotional postures and attitudes that have an inappropriate or an unexpected quality. These to not seem to fit with the real person of the analyst or his behavior. For example, the patient may be filled with fear of attack by the analyst, who may in fact be to all witnesses a mild and gentle soul. Emotional responses of unusual and unexpected intensity or, the reverse, those of a surprisingly muted nature may indicate the presence of transference.

3. Repetitive and stereotyped behavior or responses to the analyst appearing in all varieties of interchange in the treatment may signal intensifying transference. Related to this stereotypy is the tenacious nature of these emerging reactions, which repeat themselves in the face of interpretive effort and only slowly give way in the process of working through (Greenson 1967). These behaviors may appear as manipulations designed to evoke responses from the analyst which repeat early life interactions (see Countertransference later) (Sandler, Dare, & Holder, 1973).

4. Widening of the polar distances in ambivalent attitudes toward the therapist. This increase in love-hate disparities implies a regressive trend in the therapeutic relationship and may in certain pathological entities (i.e. borderline states) imply the revival of archaic split object and self representations. (Kernberg, 1975).

5. In contrast to the repetitive and tenacious attitudes toward the analyst, unexpected and frequent shifts of attitude in a seemingly random or capricious way may reflect the overdetermined nature of the burgeoning transference. Glover (1955) termed these "floating transferences."

6. Schafer (1983) points out that data indicating transference may vary ". . . from bodily fantasies and enactments, such as constipation, masturbation, and archaic ideas of retribution and damage, to sober attempts to remember, reconstruct, and organize just how events, long remembered in a neurotic way, had actually transpired" (p. 118).

To be defined as transference, these phenomena must appear in the matrix of the relationship to the analyst though they may be expressed in a displaced manner. Lacking this relationship to the analytic situation, they must be considered aspects of character behavior with which the patient greets all personal interactions. They are part of the neurotic distortions of the patient's daily life. This issue was discussed by Fenichel (1941), who considers all such early attitudes toward the analyst transference only if defined in the broadest sense of any attitude toward the therapist, but not in the narrower sense of attitudes fixed in the object relationship to the analyst. Gill (1982) differs with this more narrow view of transference and includes attitudes early on in the analysis expressed not only toward the analyst, but about figures external to the analytic relationship.

Transference Defined in Terms of Conflict Resolution with Specific Early Objects

In this definition, transference is depicted as a relived repetition of drive and defense conflict resolutions along with characteristic ego states and accompanying affects. In addition, there is the revival of early representations of self and object, and finally infantile solutions and adaptations in the form of compromise formations. These represent elements of all psychic structures—ego, id, superego—according to the principle of multiple function. These conflict resolutions are achieved in the matrix of the object tie and are repeated in the contemporary therapeutic experience. The transferences, akin in formation to the presenting neurosis itself and presumably reasonably similar to the evolution of the infantile neurosis, are identified by the major object relationship in which they originally formed. Hence we have the father transference, the mother transference, a sibling transference. Occasionally other early nurturing figures are the objects of conflict and resolution in infantile life, and these may become discernible during an analysis with revival of early memories. Such may be grandparents, nursemaids, and the like. These would generally be considered equivalents of maternal or paternal transferences. This definition of transference resembles the compromise value of symptoms, character traits, and dreams as well.

Transference Defined as Revival of Arrested Developmental Processes

Transference may be defined in terms of regressive revival of developmental processes of infancy, originally centering on an important nurturing figure. It refers to the arrests and distortions in development repeated and revived in the current relationship. This definition turns attention away from earlier modes of conflict resolution and focuses on developmental arrests, distortions and deformities in ego function and development. These matters include the development of the representations of self (fragmented or cohesive), distortions of object representations (split or part objects, self-objects), and disturbances in the separations-individuation processes. It is these revived developmental movements with their attendant affective and behavioral accompaniments that produce the transference phenomena within the analytic setting.

Kohut (1971), in tracing the development of the self, sees two separate developmental lines, each leading to the mature endpoint—the narcissistic line of development leading to healthy self-esteem and mature esteem for others (normal narcissism), and the object libidinal line, leading to normal object love. In the narcissistic personality disorders, there is arrest in the developmental line of narcissism, leading to persistent forms of object ties that distort the sense of self and the regulation of self-esteem. In the analysis of narcissistic character disorders, these forms of object relations are regressively revived as self-objects, and the transferences evoked are termed self-object transferences. This implies in libido terms that the object is cathected with narcissistic libido; the objects are experienced in intimate connection with the archaic self-representation. People therefore are not experienced as separate and independent from the self. They are experienced narcissistically and are the self-objects. In analysis with these character disorders, the analyst is experienced as a self-object, and the transferences that occur in these analysis Kohut classifies as self-object transferences. The consequent blurring between patient and analyst in these transferences is described by Kohut (1971) as follows: "The expected control over such (self-object) others is then closer to the concept of the control which a grownup expects to have over his own body and mind than to the concept of control which he expects to have over others" (p. 27).

He describes various kinds of self-object transferences:

(a) The idealizing transference results from a regressive revival of idealized parental imagoes that are projected onto the person of the analyst, who then becomes an idealized self-object; (b) The mirror transference results from a mobilization of the infantile grandiose-self image. This then leads to demands for approval and confirmation from parental objects—displaced onto the person of the analyst—a demand for mirroring, like the beaming mother responding to the grandiose infant's exhibitionism; (c) More regressed forms of mirror transference are seen in alter-ego and twinship transferences, which repeat forms of merger fantasies with the parent.

Transferences Defined by Ego-Libidinal Phase

Oedipal transferences are characterized by the triadic family constellation in which libidinal and aggressive drive derivatives are invested in parental object representations (and transfered consequently to the analyst) in the following patterns:

The Positive Oedipal transference exists when incestuous libidinal strivings appear toward the parent of the opposite sex (when the analyst represents this gender), accompanied by rivalrous aggressive wishes toward the parent of the same sex as the patient (when the analyst represents this parent). This is accompanied by castration anxiety and fantasies of retaliation by the rival parent, which can of course become a transferential dread of the analyst.

The Negative Oedipal transference exists where there are erotic strivings toward the parent of the same gender as the patient (homoerotic wishes) and hostile wishes toward the parent of the opposite sex with accompanying fears of relatiation and castration.

Thus, an erotic transference toward the analyst may represent either a positive or negative Oedipal transference depending on the transferred parental imago. The gender of the analyst is not of key importance in the evolution of these transferences, as the patient will experience both maternal and paternal transferences to the same analyst. It is often true, however, that the negative oedipal transference (homoerotic in nature) usually emerges in more sharply recognizable form in patient and analyst of the same sex, and the positive oedipal transference more clearly in cross sex analyses.

Preoedipal transferences are characterized by more infantile regressive trends, increased oral and anal fantasy content, more primitive defensive operations such as projection, denial, splitting, and projective identification (Kernberg 1975). A predominance of oral and anal sadistic aggression often suffuses these transferences.

Transference Defined by the Degree of Ego Function-Dysfunction

These transferences are categorized according to the degree of differentiation between self and the object world (Greenson, 1967) and by the degree of impairment of reality testing the transference invokes.

Neurotic transference is one in which the revived object tie demonstrates the patient's ability to distinguish self from object and in which there is relative object constancy. The affective attitudes toward the therapist, though inappropriate, are basically reality bound through the retained ability to split the ego into a self-observing as well as an experiencing portion. Structural differentiation is preserved and superego is regressively transformed in the transference into parental introjects that are readily projected onto the person of the analyst.

Borderline-transference involves fragmentation of self and object imagoes, though self-object boundaries usually remain stable, even though blurred by projective processes. Transferences tend to represent "all good" or "all bad" parental imagoes, or, via projective identification, the therapist may come to represent various aspects of the patient's own split self representations (Kernberg, 1975). Intense fear and distrust of the therapist often characterize these transferences as the therapist begins to appear omnipotent, demanding, and sadistically punitive. Primitive superego elements are transferred to the therapist along with an intense need to control the therapist.

"Transference paradigm," a term used by Kernberg (1975), is particularly apt in discussing borderline transferences characterized by split object representations and ego states dissociated from one another. Kernberg states: "lt is as if each of these ego states represents a full-fledged transference paradigm, a highly developed, regressive transference reaction within which a specific internalized object relationship is activated in the transference" (p. 77).

Narcissistic transference in this sense is characterized by a basic denial of the the analyst as a separate and independent person. This does not imply a blurring of self-object boundaries, but rather a mode of relating to the analyst as ancillary to the patient, assigning to him a "satellite existance" (Kernberg, 1975). Grandiosity leads to marked denial of any dependence on the analyst and represents a defense against severe narcissistic aggression. Longings to be loved conflict with disparaging attitudes toward the analyst, and idealizations are followed by disappointments in the analyst. (See also earlier reference to Kohut's (1971) work in this area).

Psychotic transference does appear to form, although Freud believed that no transference was possible in states of psychosis (termed by him "narcissistic neuroses"). In addition transferences may form in therapies that begin to assume a psychotic character. These transferences are characterized by severe blurring of self and object boundaries and severe regressive impairment of ego functions, with the transference taking on a delusional quality. This is often accompanied by marked dysfunction in affect and impulse control. It may be marked by a general regressive trend and decompensation beyond the transference and the appearance of a full-fledged psychotic state. When these phenomena are restricted to the analysis or therapy relationship and are not part of a psychotic decompensation, they may be defined as a *transference psychosis* (Sandler et al., 1973).

Transference Defined by Valence

Freud (1912) felt that to understand how transference functions as resistance, it is helpful to distinguish two types:

> We must make up our minds to distinguish a "positive" transference from a "negative" one, the transference of affectionate feelings from that of hostile ones, and to treat the two sorts of transference to the doctor separately. Positive transference is then further divisible into transference of friendly or affectionate feelings which are admissible to consciousness and transference of prolongations of those feelings into the unconscious. As regards the latter, analysis shows that they invariably go back to erotic sources [p. 105].

Though *positive transference* describes the derivatives of the transference that dispose the patient kindly toward the analyst and strengthen the alliance in the therapeutic effort, they do not always imply a tie free from aggressive wishes. Indeed, a positive transference may at times be a defensive layer against threatening aggressive impulses in the transference. Still, the general idea is that the transference situation being described as positive consists largely of libidinal ties of an erotic and bonding nature.

Negative transference refers to transference accompanied by dysphoric affects and hostile feelings toward the therapist and towards treatment. What may be consciously experienced are hatreds, distrust, fear, repugnance, disdain. Negative aspects of the transference may remain hidden long into the analysis, or may never surface to be analyzed unless actively sought for by the analyst. They may emerge early as resistance, defending against positive libidinal wishes toward the analyst. The negative transference may be so intense that it may endanger the continuity of the analysis or therapy.

Transference Defined by Major Drive Content

This definition of transference refers to the major instinctual trends in the patient's reactions to the analyst and is more dynamically revealing than the terms positive or negative transference, as the "sign" valences may conceal instinctual content, which is opposite from the overt affective phenomena.

The *erotic transference* relates to the regressively revived object tie in which the object is libidinally cathected. This, of course implies a love bond where the accompanying fantasies (conscious and unconscious) and the affects reflect the phase of ego development and libidinal aims of the given era of infancy. Thus oral, anal, and phallic erotic strivings will differ from one another in their clinical manifestations and accompanying fantasies. Often the term erotic transference is used to refer more specifically to the phallic-oedipal level of transference in which fantasies of sexual union more clearly resemble adult sexual desires. Voyeuristic, exhibitionistic, or genital sexual fantasies may be manifest at the phallic level. If these libidinal aims are highly conflicted, the erotic transference may be accompanied by aversive feelings and unpleasant affects and will therefore be difficult to recognize as an erotic transferential state.

The *aggressive transference* implies the object tie is suffused with aggressive wishes and drives. The wish basically is to destroy the object. Once again, this may manifest all phase levels, from oral sadistic wishes to destroy with the teeth (an element in the oral incorporative fantasy), to anal sadistic wishes to control, dirty, and torment, to oedipal patricidal or matricidal wishes. Through reaction formation and sublimation these drives in the transference may be so altered or reversed as to make it difficult to discern them as having an aggressive base. Such transferences are almost always present and exist along with erotic transference. Dealing with these transference derivatives is seen as the "hardest part of analysis" (Bird, 1972).

The *erotized transference* (as opposed to the erotic transference) is a special and unusual form of transference in which there is marked pressure by the patient to form a real life relationship with the analyst. It is most often manifested by blatant erotic wishes toward the analyst, feelings of romantic love, and overt sexual intentions toward the analyst. Another variety, of a more regressed kind, would have the analyst become an actual substitute parent for the patient. This is generally considered a major and serious resistance not necessarily reflecting an erotic transference (it may be in the service of aggressive impulses), though it may be an extreme form of erotic transference as well. These transferences threaten to disrupt the analysis and should be interpreted vigorously in terms of its resistive function (Blum, 1973; Sandler et al., 1973).

Transference Defined According to Dynamic Function in the Analytic Process

Split transference (displaced transference) refers to transference that develops in the treatment situation and is then defensively displaced partially or wholely to a person or persons outside the therapy situation. The transference is often split along lines of "good" and "bad" parental imagoes, so that the analyst may be represented as the all-good parent and the spouse or supervisor as the all-bad parent (or vice versa). Again, the analyst may represent the desired oedipal object and the spouse the rival parent. Splitting the transference this way often helps defend against the negative elements.

The *defense transference* is the entering into the transference of an infantile defensive operation against some instinctual wish or object representation (A. Freud, 1936). These defensive operations often serve to ward off other aspects of transference. Gill (1982) carefully separates and defines three entities in this regard. The defense transference implies that the transference has a defensive quality; the transference of defense implies the appearance of a specific defensive operation that manifests itself as part of the transference; and defense against transference implies that the transference itself is being massively resisted.

Transference resistance refers to attitudes and behavior deriving from the transference which tend to interfere with the evolution of the analytic process. Seductive behavior, compliant attitudes, defiance, and the like, rooted in transference and aimed at preserving or actualizing the transference distortions, may be used in the service of opposing a genetic understanding of their origins and their analysis and consequent resolution. Other resistances may be manifest only by their omission from the analytic discourse. (Stone, 1961, 1967, 1973).

Gill (1982) anchors and restricts the definition of transference resistance firmly to the interactive transactions between analyst and patient. He sees transference not as the source of resistance but rather the means of resistance.

Transference Defined in the Treatment Alliance

The *working alliance* (Greenson, 1965) refers to the rational and relatively non-neurotic rapport the patient has with the analyst. This alliance allows the patient to continue the reflective work despite the vicissitudes of an intense transference. It is seen as a cooperative enterprise between the reasonable ego of the patient and the analyst's analyzing ego. Other terms related to this concept are the rational transference (Fenichel, 1941), and the mature transference (Stone, 1961, 1967).

The *therapeutic alliance* (Zetzel, 1958) relates to the nuclear aspect of transference, which promotes continued analytic work and which derives from early dyadic (often preverbal) aspects of the infantile object tie. It is supported by various ego capacities from the conflict free ego sphere.

The Transference Neurosis

This phenomenon is usually distinguished from transference per se and is considered a clinical entity limited to and a distinct product of psychoanalysis. (Blum, 1971; Loewald, 1971). It is felt to be present when the analyst and the analysis become the central concern in the patient's life. (Greenson, 1965). Freud (1917) states that in this development,

> . . . what happens is that the whole of his illness's new production is concentrated on a single point—his relation to the doctor. . . . All the patient's symptoms have abandoned their original meaning and have taken on a new sense which lies in relation to the transference. . . [p. 445].

This amounts to a revival of the infantile neurosis in toto but in altered form in the analytic situation. (Weinshel, 1971). It is seen as the gradual unfolding in the here and now analysis of a new edition of the infantile neurosis in its entirety. It is lived out in the relationship with the analyst and may include the reappearance in the patient of old symptoms or the appearance of new ones. It may appear in the analysis as a total integrated pattern, or in fragments, or, as Greenacre (1959) describes it, as a series of transference pictures, analogous to a film strip.

Though many see the transference neurosis as forming passively because of the regressive form of the analytic situation, Schafer (1977) for example, believes the transference neurosis forms from the revived infantile experience actively redescribed in the analysis by the analyst's transference interpretations and is thus truly a "new edition" of the infantile neurosis synthesized in the psychoanalytic process.

The object of transference may be defined as the target upon whom the transferred infantile conflict and object representation are displaced. In the broadest view, transference may be defined as a universal phenomenon occurring spontaneously in all human relationships to varying degrees (Brenner, 1976). It may be directed to groups or institutions that are derivative of human relationships, such as nations, hospitals, schools, ethnic or racial groups. It is more likely to occur in situations of greater intimacy, such as in marriage or between siblings, or with important persons in one's life such as employer or supervisor. Freud (1895) observed that the person of the physician is a likely object of transference, as are others who are in a helping position. Transference of course is most clearly observed in the therapy or psychoanalytic situation, to the person of the analyst, especially when such treatment is conducted in the manner of technical neutrality and with a minimum of personal intrusion by the therapist.

Transference and Time—The Past and The Present

Two major contributions to psychoanalytic theory deal with transference and attempt to define and clarify the interdigitation of the past infantile life with the present contemporary experience in the analytic situation itself.

Schafer (1983) sees transference as a product of the interaction of analysand and analyst engaged in the cooperative formation of the "analytic narrative." The analysand develops attitudes, feelings, and behaviors toward the analyst that result from an interaction among the analysand's past relationships, his reactions to the person of the analyst, his redescriptions of the past, and the interpretive interventions of the analyst, who has in the analysis established and preserved an atmosphere of safety and neutrality. The analyst's interpretations and even his countertransferential reactions all effect the creative evolution of transference. As analysis proceeds, the analysis itself and the analytic relationship act more and more like the single lens through which the past and present are viewed. If neutrality on the therapist's part has been preserved, the analyst's interpretations and the patient's recollection result in new understandings, new creative metaphors, and a new experience of the patient's past. The analysand realizes (with interpretive aid) that many of his attitudes toward the analyst are of his own devising. It is the interpretive function of the analyst that brings these attitudes forth (transference) and integrates them into a recognizeable pattern.

Schafer (1983) presents a hermeneutic view of analysis, suggesting that the entire analytic narrative, the transference, are products of the mutually creative efforts of patient and therapist. Meanings are discerned and organized in the analytic process, and the past is created anew. Schafer presents his view of the then-and-now elements in the transference in the following way:

> The transference phenomena that finally constitute the transference neurosis are to be taken as regressive in only some of their aspects. This is so because, viewed as achievements of the analysis, they have never existed before as such. Rather, they constitute a creation achieved through a novel relationship into which one has entered by conscious and rational design (in part) [p. 132].

Gill (1982) sees transference, though rooted in early object relationships, as a product of the current life experience within the analytic situation. All transference is experienced in relation to the actual situation in the analysis, although determinants of transference relate to the past. Intrinsic to his technical suggestions regarding the analysis and interpretation of transference are his clarifying definitions regarding transference resistance. He defines two major types of resistance relating to transference: (a) resistance to the awareness of transference and (b) resistance to the resolution of the transference.

Interpretation is aimed initially at revealing allusions to the analyst—that is the patient's unintentioanl allusions to the transference enlarge an understanding of the transference when interpreted as referring to the analyst rather than to the person external to the analytic situation. These interpretations, which deal with resistance to recognizing the transference, Gill terms the analysis of the transference. In contrast to this form of interpretation (which brings remote allusion into the here-and-now relationship to the therapist), *interpreting* the transference (as opposed to *analyzing* transference) involves demonstrating to the patient that his or her attitudes toward the analyst may be determined by influences outside of the "here and now"—that is, the past relationships of the patient and by the immediacy of the analysis. In summary, the analysis of transference is an interpretation of an allusion to the transference and deals with resistance to recognizing transference; interpreting transference tells the patient that an attitude is determined by factors apart from the analyst as well as the person of the analyst and deals with resistance to resolution of the transference. In Gill's words: "Rather than regard transference as primarily a distortion of the present by the past, I see transference as always an amalgam of past and present" (p. 177).

COUNTERTRANSFERENCE

The narrow definition holds that countertransference is an unconscious reaction in the therapist or analyst of a regressive nature, in which elements of the therapist's neurosis, with accompanying distortions toward the patient, arise in response to the needs and pressures exerted on the therapist by the patient and the patient's transference. It is a transference to the patient and parallels exactly the definitions of transference. It is regressive and displaced, and has its roots in the infantile neurosis, which is repeated by the therapist toward his patient. In this definition, countertransference is seen largely as an unwelcome interference with the therapeutic process, producing in the therapist a distorted view of his patient and inappropriate reactions to him. Sources of countertransference (Reich, 1952, 1960) are paradoxically those empathic trial identifications which are necessary in the analytic process. Not only, then, is countertransference the analyst's reaction to the patient's instinctual strivings, but it may be an identification with the patient in these wishes (counteridentification).

Countertransference in the broader definition is described by Kernberg (1965) as the "totalistic" definition. This includes the entirety of the therapist's reactions to aspects of the patient's personality, to material rising in treatment, and to the patient's here-and-now behavior in the treatment situation. It includes not only revivals of the therapist's infantile conflicts, but his total response to the patient. These reactions, viewed as undesirable and detrimental to the treatment (which indeed they can be), may also furnish the therapist with valuable clues from within himself to origins of the patient's pathology, to the shape of his unconscious representations of self and early objects.

In this totalistic view might be included aspects of the therapist's attitudes and background as potential sources of countertransference. In addition to his neurosis and character, we would include his world view, attitudes related to his generation, socioeconomic background, racial and ethnic attitudes, gender attitudes, political, religious and moral views. These may be especially important sources for countertransference distortions, if these views interlock with and serve particular unconscious motives and needs, including narcissistic gratification even from particular theoretical points of view. All of these aspects of the therapist or analyst may interfere with clinical neutrality and foster distorted reactions to his patient.

Countertransference Mechanisms Defined

Aside from direct reactions to instinctual pressures of the transference, identification mechanisms play a major part in the evolution of countertransference (Racker, 1957).

Concordant Identification is related to empathy and may be defined as the identification of the analyst with the structural part of the patient's mind in question, ego with ego, superego with superego, and so forth. This results directly in the analyst's sharing the patient's feelings and attitudes or directly reflecting them. (Hate for hate, love for love returned.)

Complementary Identification occurs when the analyst identifies with the parental object or other transferred object. For example, the fearful patient may see the analyst as the critical, sadistic father, and the analyst may in response feel harshly critical and contemptuous of his patient. Kernberg (1965) feels that this is most likely to occur when the therapist regresses to a level at which projective identification takes place.

Countertransference Defined by "Signs and Symptoms"

Those manifestations previously defined, which reflect the probable presence of transference in the patient, apply equally well to probable countertransference in the therapist. Inappropriate reactions to the patient, peculiar affective responses, and inaccurate appraisals of the patient reflect countertransference distortions. So likewise do fixed and stereotyped feelings toward the patient, fear, guilt, or romantic love feelings, sexual desire, which do not shift from one session to another, but become a fixed response. The inappropriateness and intensity of these feelings signal these distortions. Examples (Kernberg, 1965) may be masochistic submission to the patient's aggression, marked self-doubt about dealing with the patient, marked detachment from the patient, or unreasonable certainty about being able to help the patient. A common striking sign is marked opacity to the patient's communications and cessation of empathic function.

Countertransference Neurosis

This concept, little used, refers to a state in which the infantile neurosis is revived in the analyst and is focused on the relationship with the patient (Tower, 1956). This may imply a serious disorder in the therapeutic relationship leading to disruption. Tower believes, however, that the countertransference neurosis is ubiquitous in all well-engaged analyses and must be analyzed by the analyst. This process then becomes part of the interpretive process, which promotes a successful analytic resolution as she sees it.

Countertransference Defined as a Specific Entity

Just as there is a problem of definition and mutual convention in distinguishing transient transference reactions to the analyst from the transference as a distinct and organized entity in the analysis (or the transference neurosis), the same confusion presents itself when discussing countertransference. Whether the term is used in the narrow or broader sense, there still remains the problem of distinguishing transient reactions to the patient on the part of the analyst from a more distinctly organized set of responses. In either case, we view the analyst's response to the patient as an amalgam of contemporary reactions to the patient's person with the analyst's character and other defenses, with his affect and drive pressures, with his own past infantile life and object relations. Countertransference, like all responses, is a product of both infantile and contemporary conflict resolutions with conscious and unconscious elements serving multiple functions, and it represent compromise formations. Though all of this is true with reference to fleeting transient reactions to the patient, it becomes more useful and meaningful to distinguish countertransference from the welter of transient thoughts, feelings, affects, and fantasies evoked during an hour the analyst spends with his patient. To this end, the following considerations are suggested:

1. Countertransference is a distinct phenomenon consisting of thoughts, feelings, actions, fantasies, and dreams (conscious and unconscious) that occur in the analyst in response to his patient and, though they may be transient, begin to form a pattern that then tends to become stereotyped, repetitious, and in extreme instances, fixed.
2. Countertransference becomes a notable entity in an analysis when it results in interference with the analyst's neutrality or his empathic response, and when it creates disturbances in his interpretive function. It does so often outside the analyst's conscious awareness, and its unconscious components are by far the most important.
3. Whatever elements of countertransference do become conscious may reveal some new understanding of the patient that has either been blocked from recognition by the therapist's unconscious resistance or is revealed as the transference counterpart to the analyst's countertransferential feeling. For example, a sadistic attitude on the analyst's part may reveal, when it is self-analyzed, that it is in response to the patient's masochistic submission to the analyst in covert and overt ways.

To understand and study countertransference, whether in supervising another therapist or oneself, and in attempting self analysis, one must try to distinguish countertransference from the general flow of the analyst's psyche. One looks for repetitiousness and fixity of attitude or feeling and disturbances in the therapist's neutrality, empathic response, understanding and interpretation. One should recognize the potential for revelation of new data via these reactions on the patient's part.

Countertransference Defined as a Data Source and Therapeutic Tool

There is much debate about the utility of countertransference in learning more about one's patient. Those who deny its usefulness as a data source see the analyst's countertransference as the result of the reawakening of the analyst's own early object ties (in a manner identical with the formation of transference), which is then transferred to his patient. These attitudes, defensive postures, and so forth are derived from the analyst's infantile life and therefore are inappropriate to the real person of his patient. A transference by itself is useful mainly in the analyst's own analysis. As a source of data, it is highly unreliable and is seen mainly as a potential interference to the analytic process. It is not seen as revelatory about the patient in any special way different from other data sources. Proponents of this viewpoint feel that the patient cannot put something into the analyst's head that is not derivative basically of the analyst's own persona.

On the other hand, proponents of the view that countertransference is a unique source of data feel that by projective and identificatory mechanisms, especially projective identification, coupled with the therapist's empathic receptivity, images, affects, fantasies, and attitudes can be generated in the analyst by the patient. These, in turn, are experienced by the reflective analyst, who will use his own inner life to form conclusions about the patient's archaic self and object representations. The analyst concludes (after searching via self-analysis for his own infantile sources) that what he is experiencing with a patient is a revival in the transference-countertransference interlock of an early self and object experience on the patient's part. In this view, the analyst, functioning as empath, becomes the clarifying lens that discerns early and often the split, or part, object and self-representations of his patient.

Although there are strong arguments on both sides of the issue and probably most therapists share elements of both viewpoints, one should take into account the vagaries of self-analysis, the difficulties in recognizing projective identifications, and the defensive operations of the analyst. Utmost caution must be taken before an analyst can conclude that what he is experiencing with his patient is indeed a reflection of the patient's transference and inner world, and that the therapist is mentally actualizing a projected transference role. Though there is no doubt that this is possible and does occur via projective identifications on the patient's part and empathic identifications on the analyst's part, one would need corroboration from sources other than the analyst's subjective feeling and behavior. To interpret on the basis only of the analyst's sadistic feelings or fantasies toward his patient that a patient may unconsciously wish for the analyst's sadism because this represents to the patient the longed for sadistic mother who demands masochistic submission from her child may be no more than an acting out of the analyst's own sadism. There may be no masochistic wish on the patient's part. Such an hypothesis must be supported by evidence from the patient's past history, his dreams, his fantasies, his acting out behavior within and outside the analysis, before such a pattern is to be interpreted. A countertransference feeling is not sufficient data by itself.

REFERENCES

Bird, B. (1972). Notes on transference: Universal phenomenon and hardest part of analysis. *J. Amer. Psychoanal. Assn.,* 20:267–301.

Blum, H. P. (1971). On the conception and development of the transference neurosis. *J. Amer. Psychoanal. Assn.,* 19:41–53.

———. (1973). The concept of erotized transference. *J. Amer. Psychoanal. Assn.,* 21:61–75.

Brenner, C. (1976). *Psychoanalytic Technique and Psychic Conflict.* New York. International Universities Press.

Breuer, J., & Freud, S. (1895). *Studies on hysteria.* Standard Edition, 2:London: Hogarth Press, 1955.

Fenichel, O. (1941). *Problems of Psychoanalytic Technique.* New York: The Psychoanalytic Quarterly (Publ.)

Freud, A. (1936). *The Ego and the Mechanisms of Defense.* New York: International Universities Press, 1966.

———. (1905). A Case of hysteria. *Standard Edition,* 7:7–122. London: Hogarth Press, 1953.

———. (1912). The dynamics of transference. *Standard Edition,* 12:97–108. London: Hogarth Press, 1958.

———. (1915). Observations on transference-love. *Standard Edition,* 12:157–171. London: Hogarth Press, 1958.

———. (1917). *Introductory lectures on psychoanalysis.* Standard Edition, 16 (Part III). London: Hogarth Press, 1961.

Gill, M. M. (1982). Analysis of transference, Vol. 1, Theory and technique. *Psychological Issues,* Monogr. 53. New York: International Universities Press.

Glover, E. (1955). *The Technique of Psychoanalysis.* New York: International Universities Press.

Greenacre, P. (1959). Certain technical problems in the transference relationship. *J. Amer. Psychoanal. Assn.,* 7:484–502.

Greenson, R. R. (1965). The working alliance and the transference neurosis. *Psychoanal. Quart.,* 34:155–181.

———. (1967). *The Technique and Practice of Psychoanalysis I.* New York: International Universities Press.

Kernberg, O. F. (1965). Notes on countertransference. *J. Amer. Psychoanal. Assn.,* 13:38–54.

———. (1975). *Borderline Conditions and Pathological Narcissism.* New York: Jason Aronson.

Kohut, H. (1971). *The Analysis of the Self.* New York: International Universities Press.

Loewald, H. W. (1971). The transference neurosis: Comments on the concept and the phenomenon. *J. Amer. Psychoanal. Assn.,* 19:54–66.

Macalpine, I. (1950). The development of the transference. *Psychoanal. Quart.,* 19:501–539.

Racker, H. (1957). The meaning and uses of countertransference. *Psychoanal. Quart.,* 26:303–357.

Reich, A. (1952). On countertransference. *Internat. J. Psycho-Anal.,* 32:25–32.

———. (1960). Further remarks on countertransference. *Internat. J. Psycho-Anal.,* 41:407–412.

Sandler, J., Dare, C., Holder, A. (1973). *The Patient and the Analyst.* New York: International Universities Press.

Schafer, R. (1977). The interpretation of transference and the conditions for loving. *J. Amer. Psychoanal. Assn.,* 25:335–362.

———. (1983). *The Analytic Attitude.* New York: International Universities Press.

Stone, L. (1961). *The Psychoanalytic Situation.* New York: International Universities Press.

———. (1967). The psychoanalytic situation and the transference: Postscript to an earlier communication. *J. Amer. Psychoanal. Assn.,* 15:3–58.

———. (1973). On resistance to the psychoanalytic process: Some thoughts on its nature and motivations. *Psychoanalysis and Contemporary Science,* Vol. 2. New York. Macmillan.

Tower, L. (1956). Countertransference. *J. Amer. Psychoanal. Assn.* 4:224–256.

Weinshel, E. M. (1971). The Transference Neurosis: A Survey of the Literature. *J. Amer. Psychoanal. Assn.* 19:67–88.

Zetzel, E. (1958). Therapeutic alliance in the analysis of hysteria. In: *The Capacity for Emotional Growth.* New York. International Universities Press 1970.

Author Index

Numbers in *italics* denote pages with bibliographic information.

Subject Index

E

F